SOUL

at the

WHITE HEAT

Nonfiction by Joyce Carol Oates

SOUL

at the

WHITE HEAT

*Inspiration, Obsession,
and the Writing Life*

JOYCE CAROL OATES

An Imprint of HarperCollinsPublishers

HarperCollins books may be purchased for educational, business, or sales promotional use. For information, please email the Special Markets Department at SPsales@harpercollins.com.

FIRST EDITION

Designed by Suet Yee Chong

Library of Congress Cataloging-in-Publication Data has been applied for.

ISBN 978-0-06-256450-4

16 17 18 19 20   PC/RRD   10 9 8 7 6 5 4 3 2 1

For Eric Karl Anderson,
A lover of literature

Dare you see a Soul *at the White Heat?*
  Then crouch within the door—
  Red—is the Fire's common tint—
  But when the vivid Ore
  Has vanquish'd Flame's conditions,
  It quivers from the Forge
  Without a color, but the light
  Of unanointed Blaze.
  Least Village has its Blacksmith
  Whose Anvil's even ring
  Stands symbol for the finer Forge
  That soundless tugs—within—
  Refining these impatient Ores
  With Hammer, and with Blaze
  Until the Designated Light
  Repudiate the Forge—

EMILY DICKINSON, 1862 (365)

Contents

I. THE WRITING LIFE

II. CLASSICS

III. CONTEMPORARIES

IV. REAL LIFE

I

THE WRITING LIFE

IS THE UNINSPIRED LIFE WORTH LIVING?

Thoughts on Inspiration and Obsession

This is not a traditional lecture so much as the quest for a lecture in the singular—a quest constructed around a sequence of questions— *Why do we write? What is the motive for metaphor? "Where do you get your ideas?" Do we choose our subjects, or do our subjects choose us? Do we choose our "voices"? Is inspiration a singular phenomenon, or does it take taxonomical forms? Indeed, is the uninspired life worth living?*

Why did I write? What sin to me unknown Dipt me in Ink, my Parents' or my own?

Alexander Pope's great "Epistle to Dr. Abuthnot" (1734) asks this question both playfully and seriously. *Why* did the child Pope take to verse at so young an age, telling us, as many a poet might tell us, with the kind of modesty that enormous self-confidence can generate—

I lisp'd in numbers and the numbers came.

—by which the poet means an intuitive, instinctive, "inborn" sense of scansion and rhyme for which some individuals have the equivalent of "perfect pitch" in music: you are born with it, or you are not. For sheer virtuosity in verse, Pope is one of the great masters of the language; his brilliantly orchestrated couplets lend themselves ideally to the expression of "wit" (usually caustic, in the service of the poet's satiric mission). The predilection to "lisp in numbers" suggests a kind of entrapment, though Pope doesn't suggest this; the perfectly executed couplet with its locked-together rimes is a tic-like mannerism not unlike punning, to which some individuals succumb involuntarily ("pathological punning" is a symptom of frontal lobe syndrome, a neurological deficit caused by injury or illness) even as others react with revulsion and alarm. Pope's predilection for "lisping in numbers" seems to us closely bound up with his era, and his talent a talent of the era, that revered the tight-knit grimace of satire and the very sort of expository and didactic poetry from which, half a century later, Wordsworth and Coleridge would seek to free the poet. Pope never suggests, however, that the content of poetry is in any way inherited, like the genetic propensity for scansion and rhyme; he would not have concurred—(who, among the poets, and among most of us, would so concur?)—with Plato's churlish view of poetry as inspired not from within the individual poet's imagination but from an essentially supra-natural, daimonic source.

To Plato, poetry had to be under the authority of the State, in the service of the (mythical, generic) Good; that it might be "imitative" of any specific object was to its discredit. "No ideas but in things"—the rallying cry of William Carlos Williams in the twentieth century— would have been anathema to the essentialist Plato, like emotion itself, or worse yet, "passion"—"the passions." Thus, all "imitative" poetry, especially the "tragic poetry" of Homer, should be banished from the Republic, as it is "deceptive"—"magical"—

and "insincere." With the plodding quasi-logic of a right-wing politi-
cian Plato's Socrates dares to say

> In fact all the good poets who make epic poems [like Homer]
> use no art at all, but they are inspired and possessed when
> they utter all those beautiful poems, and so are the good lyric
> poets; they are not in their *right mind* [italics mine] when they
> make their beautiful songs. . . . As soon as they mount on their
> harmony and rhythm, they become frantic and possessed. . . .
> For the poet is an airy thing, a winged and a holy thing; he
> cannot make poetry until he becomes inspired and goes out of
> his senses and no mind is left in him. . . . Not by art, then, they
> make their poetry . . . but by divine dispensation; therefore,
> the only poetry that each one can make is what the Muse has
> pushed him to make. . . . These beautiful poems are not hu-
> man, not made by man, but divine and made by God: and the
> poets are nothing but the gods' interpreters.
>
> *Ion, Great Dialogues of Plato,* trans. W. H. D. Rouse

The poets whom Plato disdained (and feared) were analogous to
our rock star performers, before large and enthusiastic audiences;
we can assume that it wasn't the fact that these poets were popular, as Homer was popular, to which Plato objected, but the fact
that his particular heavily theologized philosophy didn't form the
content of their utterances. The poet's *right mind* should be under
the authority of the State—indeed each citizen's *right mind* should
be a part of the hive-mind of the Republic. That the free-thinking,
rebellious, and unpredictable poet-type must be banished from the
claustrophobic Republic is self-evident. (In one of the great ironies
of history, it was to be Plato's Socrates who was banished from the
State.)

The work-sheets of poets as diverse as Dylan Thomas, William

Butler Yeats, Elizabeth Bishop and Philip Larkin suggest how deliberate is the poet's art, and how far from being inspired by a (mere) daimon; though it is often the poet's wish to appear spontaneous, unstudied—see William Butler Yeats's "Adam's Curse":

> We sat together at one summer's end,
> That beautiful mild woman, your close friend,
> And you and I, and talked of poetry.
> I said, 'A line will take us hours maybe;
> Yet if it does not seem a moment's thought,
> Our stitching and unstitching has been naught.
> Better go down upon your marrow-bones
> And scrub a kitchen pavement, or break stones
> Like an old pauper, in all kinds of weather;
> For to articulate sweet sounds together
> Is to work harder than all these, and yet
> Be thought an idler by the noisy set
> Of bankers, schoolmasters, and clergymen
> The martyrs call the world.'
>   And thereupon
> That beautiful mild woman for whose sake
> There's many a one shall find out all heartache
> On finding that her voice is sweet and low
> Replied, 'To be born woman is to know—
> Although they do not talk of it at school—
> That we must labour to be beautiful.'
> I said, 'It's certain there is no fine thing
> Since Adam's fall but needs much labouring.'

Very different from the Beats' admonition—"First thought, best thought."

To appear spontaneous and unresolved, even as one is highly

calculated and conscious—this is the ideal. As Virginia Woolf remarked in her *Diary* in an aside that seems almost to prefigure her suicide in 1941, at the age of fifty-nine:

> I do not any longer feel inclined to doff the cap to death. I like to go out of the room talking, with an unfinished casual sentence on my lips . . . no leavetakings, no submission, but someone stepping out into the darkness.
> *Virginia Woolf, A Writer's Diary, April 8, 1925*

———

"Inspiration" is an elusive term. We all want to be "inspired" if the consequence is something original and worthwhile; we would even consent to be "haunted"—"obsessed"—if the consequence were significant. For all writers dread what Emily Dickinson calls "Zero at the Bone"—the dead zone from which inspiration has fled.

What does it mean to be *captivated* by an image, a phrase, a mood, an emotion—

> A *picture* held us captive. And we could not get outside it, for it lay in our language and language seemed to repeat it to us inexorably.
> *Ludwig Wittgenstein, Philosophical Investigations*

Most serious and productive artists are "haunted" by their material—this is the galvanizing force of their creativity, their motivation. It is not and cannot be a fully conscious or volitional "haunting"—it is something that seems to *happen to us,* as if from without, no matter what craft is brought to bear upon it, what myriad worksheets and note cards. Here is Emily Dickinson's *cri de coeur*—

To Whom the Mornings stand for Nights,
What must the Midnights—be!

Most of the Dickinson poems we revere, and have lodged deeply
into us, are beautifully articulated, delicately calibrated cries from
the heart—formulations of unspeakable things, at the point at which
"poetic inspiration" has become something terror-filled:

The first Day's Night had come—
And grateful that a thing
So terrible—had been endured—
I told my Soul to sing—

She said her Strings were snapt—
Her bow—to Atoms blown—
And so to mend her—gave me work
Until another Morn—

And then—a Day as huge
As Yesterdays in pairs,
Unrolled its horror in my face—
Until it blocked my eyes—

My Brain—begun to laugh—
I mumbled—like a fool—
And tho' 'tis Years ago—that Day—
My Brain keeps giggling—still.

And Something's odd—within—
That Person that I was—
And this One—do not feel the same—
Could it be Madness—this?

This is the very voice of inwardness, compulsiveness, the "soul at the *White Heat*" of which Dickinson speaks in the remarkable poem that seems almost to deconstruct the Platonic charge of "god"-inspiration:

> Dare you see a Soul *at the White Heat?*
> Then crouch within the door—
> Red—is the Fire's common tint—
> But when the vivid Ore
> Has vanquish'd Flame's conditions,
> It quivers from the Forge
> Without a color, but the light
> Of unanointed Blaze.

(DICKINSON, 365)

There is another Dickinson whose inspiration is clearly more benign, drawn from the small pleasures and vexations of daily life, a shared and domestic life in her father's house in Amherst, Massachusetts:

> A Rat surrendered here
> A brief career of Cheer
> And Fraud and Fear.
>
> Of Ignominy's due
> Let all addicted to
> Beware.
>
> The most obliging Trap
> Its tendency to snap
> Cannot resist—

Temptation is the Friend
Repugnantly resigned
At last.

(DICKINSON, 1340)

(This is surely the most brilliantly crafted poem ever written on the subject of a rat found dead in a rat trap—in the cellar perhaps.) And, behind the house—

A narrow Fellow in the Grass
Occasionally rides—
You may have met Him—did you not
His notice sudden is—

The Grass divides as with a Comb—
A spotted shaft is seen—
And then it closes at your feet
And opens further on—

Several of Nature's People
I know, and they know me—
I feel for them a transport
Of cordiality—

But never met this Fellow
Attended, or alone
Without a tighter breathing
And Zero at the Bone—

(DICKINSON, 986)

In the tersely titled "Pig" by the contemporary poet Henri Cole, the (trapped, doomed) animal that is the poem's subject fuses with the poet-observer in the way of a vivid and revelatory dream:

Poor patient pig—trying to keep his balance,
that's all, upright on a flatbed ahead of me,
somewhere between Pennsylvania and Ohio,
enjoying the wind, maybe, against the tufts of hair
on the tops of his ears, like a Stoic at the foot
of the gallows, or, with my eyes heavy and glazed
from caffeine and driving, like a soul disembarking,
its flesh probably bacon now tipping into split
pea soup, or, more painful to me, like a man
in his middle years struggling to remain
vital and honest while we're all just floating
around accidental-like on a breeze.
What funny thoughts slide into the head,
alone on the interstate with no place to be.

HENRY COLE, "PIG," IN *TOUCH*

(Parenthetically, I should mention that when I taught several writing workshops at San Quentin in 2011, on my first meeting with the inmate-writers I read this poem; in fact, I had to read it twice. The students were riveted and moved by this poem in which they saw themselves all too clearly.)

In these striking poems by Dickinson and Cole the poet appropriates a "natural" sighting of "one of Nature's People."

These are not "found" poems except in their suggestion that the poet's sighting has an element of accident, one within the range of all of us—the rat in the trap, the snake in the grass, the pig on the flatbed being borne along a highway to slaughter. The poet is the seer, the poem is the act of appropriation. We might wonder: Would the poem have been written without the sighting? Would another poem have been written in its place, at just that hour? Is it likely that the poet's vision is inchoate inside the imagination and is tapped by a sighting in the world, that triggers an emotional rapport out of which the poem is crafted? If we consider in such cases what the poet has made out of the sighted object that is, but is not, contained within the subject, we catch a glimpse of the imagination akin to a flammable substance, into which a lighted match is dropped.

Dickinson's poems, and her letters as well, which seem so airy and fluent, give the impression of being dashed off; in fact, Dickinson composed very carefully, sometimes keeping her characteristically enigmatic lines and images for years before using them in a poem or in a letter. It is a fact that the human brain processes only a small selection of what the eye "sees"—so too, the poet is one who "sees" the significant image, to be put to powerful use in a structure of words, while discarding all else.

> This is to be fairly short; to have father's character done complete in it; and mother's; and St. Ives; and childhood; and all the usual things I try to put in—life, death, etc. But the central figure is father's character, sitting in a boat, reciting We perished, each alone, while he crushes a dying mackerel.

Here is Virginia Woolf musing in her diary for May 14, 1925, on *To the Lighthouse*, about which she will say, months later, that she is being "blown like an old flag by my novel. . . . I live entirely in it, and come to the surface rather obscurely and am often unable to think." (Woolf, *A Writer's Diary*)

A different sort of inspiration is the sheerly autobiographical—the work created out of intimacy with one's own life and experience. Yet here also the appropriative strategy is highly selective, as in memoir; the writer must dismiss all but a small fraction of the overwhelming bounty of available material. What is required, beyond memory, is a perspective on one's own past that is both a child's and an adult's, constituting an entirely new perspective. So the writer of autobiographical fiction is a time traveler in his or her life and the writing is often, as Virginia Woolf noted, "fertile" and "fluent"—

I am now writing as fast and freely as I have written in the whole of my life; more so—20 times more so—than any novel yet. I think that this is the proof that I was on the right path; and what hangs in my soul is to be reached there. . . . The truth is, one can't write directly about the soul. Looked at, it vanishes; but look (elsewhere), and the soul slips in.

Virginia Woolf, *A Writer's Diary, February 6–7, 1926*

John Updike's first novel, *The Poorhouse Fair* (1959), published when the author was twenty-six, is a purposefully modest work composed in a minor key, unlike Norman Mailer's first novel, *The Naked and the Dead* (1948), also published when the author was twenty-six. Where Mailer trod onto the literary scene like an invading army, with an ambitious military plan, Updike seems almost to have wished to enter by a rear door, claiming a very small turf in rural eastern Pennsylvania and concentrating upon the near-at-hand, with the meticulous eye of a poet. *The Poorhouse Fair* is in its way a bold avoidance of the quasi-autobiographical novel so common to young writers; the *Bildungsroman* of which the author's coming-of-age is the primary subject. Perversely, given the age of the author, *The Poorhouse Fair* is about the elderly, set in a future only twenty years distant and lacking the dramatic features of the typical future, dystopian work; its concerns are intrapersonal, and theological. By 1959 Updike had already published many of the short stories that would be gathered into *Olinger Stories* one day, which constituted in effect a *Bildungsroman*, freeing him to imagine an entirely other, original debut work.

The Poorhouse Fair, as Updike was to explain in an introduction to the 1977 edition of the novel, was suggested by a visit, in 1957, to his hometown Shillington, which included a visit to the ruins of a poorhouse near his home. The young author then decided to write a novel in celebration of the fairs held at the poorhouse during his childhood, with the intention of paying tribute to his recently deceased maternal grandfather, John Hoyer, given the name "John Hook" in the novel. In this way *The Poorhouse Fair* both is not, and is, an autobiographical work, as its theological concerns, described elsewhere in Updike's work, were those of the young writer at the time.

Appropriately, Updike wrote another future-set novel near the end of his life, *Toward the End of Time* (1997), in which the elderly protagonist and his wife appear to be thinly, even ironically disguised portraits, or caricatures, of Updike and his wife in a vaguely post-apocalyptic world bearing a close resemblance to the Updikes' suburban milieu in Beverly Farms, Massachusetts. Is it coincidental, that Updike's first novel and his (near-to-last) so mirror each other? Both have theological concerns, and both are executed with the beautifully wrought, precise prose for which Updike is acclaimed; but no one could mistake *Toward the End of Time,* with its bitter self-chiding humor, and tragically diminished perspectives, with a work of fiction by a reverent and hopeful young writer.

———

Love at first sight. In literary inspiration, as in life, such a blow to one's self-sufficiency and self-composure can have profound, ambiguous consequences. For here is another sort of inspiration which we might call the encounter with the Other.

He had been a highly successful young writer with his first two novels, quickly written in his early twenties following his seafaring adventures in the South Seas—*Typee: A Peep at Polynesian Life* (1846) and *Omoo: A Narrative of Adventures in the South Seas* (1847). Now he was working energetically on a third seafaring novel narrated in a similar storytelling voice, this time set on a New England whaling ship called the *Pequod.* (As a young man, he'd sailed with a New Bedford whaler into the South Pacific where, after eighteen months, he'd jumped ship in a South Seas port; go-

ing to sea, for Herman Melville, was "the beginning of my life.")
And now he was working industriously on this new novel when a
book of short stories came into his house—Nathaniel Hawthorne's
Mosses from an Old Manse, which had been published a few years
before, in 1846.

Melville, at thirty-one younger than Hawthorne by fifteen years,
read this collection of anecdotal and allegorical tales with mounting astonishment. There was the affable, sunny Hawthorne, as he
seems to have been generally known to contemporary readers, and
there was the other, darker and deeper Hawthorne: "it is that blackness in Hawthorne . . . that so fixes and fascinates me." ("Hawthorne and His Mosses") Soon, Melville was moved to write the
first thoughtful appreciation of Hawthorne, "Hawthorne and His
Mosses" (1850), in which Melville speculates that "this great power
of blackness in Hawthorne derives its force from its appeal to that
Calvinistic sense of Innate Depravity and Original Sin, from whose
visitations no deeply thinking mind is always and wholly free."

Hawthorne's influence upon Melville was immediate and profound. What would have been another seafaring adventure tale,
very likely another best seller, was transformed by the enchanted
Melville into the intricately plotted, highly symbolic and poetic
Moby-Dick, the greatest of nineteenth-century American novels, as
it is one of the strangest of all American novels; Hawthorne seems
to have entered Melville's life at about chapter twenty-three of the
new novel, transforming its tone and ambition. Again, one is moved
to think of a flammable material into which a struck match has
been cast, with extraordinary, incendiary results. For Melville was
consumed by Hawthorne's prose style as well as Hawthorne's tragic
vision, which he was to align with the Shakespeare of the great
tragedies, and their great soliloquies, as well as with the magisterial
poetry of John Milton's *Paradise Lost;* the result is a novel that is unwieldy, extravagant, and unique, unsurprisingly dedicated to Hawthorne "in token of my admiration for his genius." (*Moby-Dick* was

published in 1851, the year of Hawthorne's *The House of the Seven Gables,* and a year after Hawthorne's *The Scarlet Letter.)* For Melville, this homage to the older Hawthorne seems to have constituted the great passion of his life. From a letter to Hawthorne in 1851:

> I felt pantheist then—your heart beat in my ribs and mine in yours, and both in God's. A sense of unspeakable security is in me this moment, on account of your having understood the book. . . . Whence come you, Hawthorne? By what right do you drink from my flagon of life? And when I put it to my lips—lo, they are yours and not mine. I feel that the Godhead is broken up like the bread at the Supper, and that we are the pieces. Hence this infinite fraternity of feeling. . . . [T]he very fingers that now guide this pen are not precisely the same that just took it up and put it on this paper. Lord, when shall we be done changing? Ah! It's a long stage, and no inn in sight, and night coming, and the body cold. But with you for a passenger, I am content and can be happy. I shall leave the world, I feel, with more satisfaction for having come to know you. Knowing you persuades me more than the Bible of our immortality.
>
> *(See David Kesterson, "Hawthorne and Melville," online essay)*

It's a bitter irony, and must have been a considerable shock to the ecstatic young Melville, that *Moby-Dick,* in which he had poured his soul, was, to most readers of the era, including even educated reviewers, unreadable—a great classic, we are accustomed to consider it today, and yet a crushing failure to the young author who would realize only $556.37 from royalties. Reviews were generally negative, some of them savagely negative, even in the U.K., where Melville's early, South Seas adventure romances novels were overnight best sellers. It was unfortunate that Melville's British publisher brought out the novel before his American publisher, and had not had time to incorporate Melville's new title, *Moby-Dick,* which was to replace

The Whale; yet more unfortunate, that the British publisher failed to include the last page of the novel, which includes the epilogue, and that some of the front matter of the manuscript was moved to the end of the book, as an unwieldy appendix of sorts. It was the case at this time that British publishers could remove from a manuscript anything politically questionable or "obscene"—not only without conferring with the author, but also without informing him. On the whole, American reviewers followed British reviewers' crushing opinions of the novel; not one American reviewer took time to note that the American edition differed from the British.

Like merely human-sized harpooners surrounding a mighty Leviathan, such crude reviewers had the power to kill sales of Melville's books, and to destroy the energies and hope of Melville's youth. He continued to write after *Moby-Dick* but never regained his old optimism. Even his attempt to cultivate a new career lecturing to lyceums soon ended when he couldn't resist mocking the quasi-intellectualism and pretention of the lyceum circuit. "Dollars damn me," Melville said—he had not enough of them.

By the time Melville died, in 1891, even his early best sellers were out of print and his name forgotten. (The account that Melville's name was printed in the *New York Times* obituary as "Henry Melville" is evidently not true; but a "Hiram Melville" seems to have crept into print a few days later.) Both his sons had predeceased him, the younger, Malcolm, by his own hand. His marriage seems to have been difficult—his wife's genteel parents kept urging her to leave Melville, on the grounds that he was a heavy drinker, and insane. It is significant that Melville's final work of fiction, the posthumously published novella *Billy Budd,* is a starkly imagined allegory of innocence, evil, and tragic atonement so Hawthornian in its prose and vision, it's as if Melville's beloved collaborator had assisted him a final time.

"Inspiration" in this instance was ravishing, irresistible, a double-edged sword. In the short run, it led to what seems unmistakably like failure, in the author's tragic experience; in the longer run, great and abiding posthumous success.

———

She was stalled in a new, ambitious novel, her seventh, that was to be a "study" of provincial English life. (Her most recent, novel *Felix Holt,* with a similar ambition, had been published two years before and had had disappointing sales.) She knew the setting well—in fact, intimately: the Midlands of England, in the 1830s. But after a desultory beginning in 1869, *Middlemarch* was set aside for a year following domestic distractions; uncharacteristically, the highly professional fifty-year-old George Eliot hadn't been writing on this new novel with much enthusiasm or inspiration.

And then, in May 1870, Eliot and her devoted companion, George Henry Lewes, visited Oxford, where they had lunch with the Rector of Lincoln College and his (conspicuously younger) wife, neither of whom they knew well. The Pattisons were perceived as an oddly matched husband and wife, not only because Francis Pattison was twenty-seven years younger than Mark Pattison but also because while Francis was beautiful, lively, and charming, Mark was a "wizened little man" without evident charm, "prone to depression," a highly private, reclusive scholar of classics and religion. Clearly, this marriage among unequals made a powerful impression upon George Eliot, who shortly afterward began *Middlemarch* anew, this time opening with the vivid portrait of Miss Dorothea Brooke: a beautiful, intelligent, and idealistic young woman who makes the grievous error of marrying a much-older clergyman-scholar, the pedantic, self-pitying Edward Casaubon. Just as the Rector's young wife Francis had hoped to assist him in his scholarly work, so too Eliot's Miss Brooke hopes to assist her husband in his quixotic effort to write "The Key to All Mythologies."

(Eventually, Francis Pattison would leave her dull, embittered husband, to live in close proximity to a male friend; after years of stoic resignation as Mrs. Edward Casaubon, Dorothea becomes a widow, and remarries, this time a far more suitable man. As Casaubon never completes "The Key to All Mythologies," so too Mark Pattison never completed his work of scholarly-historical ambition.)

Deciding to begin *Middlemarch* not as she'd originally planned, with the young physician Lydgate and the Vincy family into which he marries, but rather with Dorothea (and Casaubon), was indeed inspired, for with this stroke one of the great themes of *Middlemarch* is forged: the devastation of youthful female idealism under the heavy hand of (patriarchal) convention. Without the impetuous but always sympathetic Dorothea, who, like her American counterpart Isabel Archer (of Henry James's *The Portrait of a Lady*) makes a very bad mistake in marriage for which she pays dearly, it is difficult to imagine what Eliot would have made of the more conventional characters of *Middlemarch*. (It is not surprising, however, that George Eliot would always deny having modeled her fictional married couple on the Rector of Lincoln College and his young wife. Writers would far rather have us believe that they've imagined or invented rather than taken "from life"—in Eliot's case in particular, with her heightened sense of moral responsibility, she would have felt vulnerable to charges of having exploited the Pattisons, who had befriended her.)

"TRY TO BE ONE OF THOSE on whom nothing is lost"—this famous admonition of Henry James suggests the nature of James's own deeply curious, ceaselessly alert and speculative personality. His inspirations were myriad, and often sprang from social situations, typically for one who "dined out" virtually every night of his adult life. The most frequently recorded of these is James's inspiration for *The Turn of the Screw*, which he records in his notebook for January 1895:

Note here the ghost-story told me at Addington (evening of Thursday 10th) by the Archbishop of Canterbury . . . the story of the young children . . . left to the care of servants in an old country house, through the death, presumably, of parents. The servants, wicked and depraved, corrupt and deprave the children. . . . The servants *die* (the story vague about the way of it) and their apparitions, figures, return to haunt the house *and* children, to whom they seem to beckon. . . . It is all obscure and imperfect, the picture, the story, but there is a suggestion of a strangely gruesome effect in it. The story to be told . . . by an outside spectator, observer.

CN, Notebook, January 1895)

The "strangely gruesome effect" that most intrigued James was the presence of not one but two ghosts appearing to not one but two innocent children, thus the *turn of the screw*. It can't have been accidental that the Archbishop's tale gripped James when, by his account, in his early fifties, he was severely depressed following the (public) failure of his play *Guy Domville* (1895), for which James had had great hopes. (Is it a surprise to learn that Henry James, the very avatar of novelistic integrity, the darling of the most mandarin New Critics, in fact had wanted badly to be a popular playwright, and dared to fantasize success in the West End? Imagine poor James's grief when, at the opening of the play, a section of the audience cruelly jeered him as he stood onstage.) In this state of mind, the emotionally fragile James was particularly susceptible to the eerie "hauntedness" of the Archbishop's story; he let it gestate for more than two years, then began to write what would be *The Turn of the Screw* in as entertainingly dramatic and suspenseful way he knew how, to acquire, as he hoped, a new audience in the United States, where sales of his books had languished. Like so much that seems to spring at us from an accidental encounter, *The Turn of the Screw* had a powerful if perhaps unconscious significance to the author who claimed, in a letter to a friend, that when he was correcting proofs of the story he "was so frightened that I was afraid to go upstairs to bed." (Gosse 38)

What would be a disadvantage for a certain sort of writer, for whom the autobiographical is primary, was for James an enormous advantage: out of the emotional isolation of his bachelor-life, imagined by Colm Tóibín in *The Master* as a life of joyless restraint and denial, James was free to imagine the intense, intimate lives of others. The fascination of the governess of *The Turn of the Screw* for (sinister, sexual) Peter Quint, for instance, is given a particular charge by James's particular imagination: homoerotic energies so powerfully repressed, they emerge, they erupt, as agents of unspeakable evil. In this elegantly constructed gothic tale much is ambiguous but the atmosphere of yearning—of desperate, humiliating yearning—is unmistakable. We feel that the emotionally starved young governess is a form of the author himself, helpless in her infatuation with the (sexually charged) ghosts of her own imagination and forced, by this infatuation, to enter the tragic adult world of loss.

Another dinner party gave James the kernel for the gossipy/campy excess of *The Sacred Fount*.

———

"Where do you get your ideas?"—the question is frequently asked, and rarely answered with any degree of conviction or sincerity. And rarely is the answer, "A dream."

Written when Katherine Mansfield was thirty, her short, elliptical story "Sun and Moon" seems to have sprung virtually complete out of a dream. Lyric and fluid like ice melting, a shimmering impressionistic work of fiction, "Sun and Moon" suggests the haunting evanescence of a dream. In her journal for February 10, 1918, Mansfield wrote:

I *dreamed* a short story last night, even down to its name, which
was "Sun and Moon." It was very light. I dreamed it all— about
children. I got up at 6:30 and wrote a note or two because I
knew it would fade. . . . I didn't dream that I'd read it. No, I
was in it, part of it, and it played round invisible me. But the
hero is not more than five. In my dream I saw a supper table
with the eyes of five. It was awfully queer—especially a plate
of half-melted ice cream.

Mansfield's story, for all its delicate filigree, is a chilly prophecy of the destruction of childhood innocence—the "plate of half-
melted ice cream" is a little ice cream house that has melted away
amid the detritus of an adults' coarse party from which children are
excluded.

THE CHALLENGE WAS TO WRITE a "ghost story"—so Lord Byron had
suggested to his friends, with whom he was traveling in Italy in the
summer of 1816; and so Mary Wollstonecraft Godwin Shelley, eighteen at the time, recounts a nightmare:

I saw the pale student of unhallowed arts kneeling beside the
thing he had put together. . . . I saw the hideous phantasm of a
man stretched out, and then, on the working of some powerful
engine, show signs of life. . . . His success would terrify the artist; he would rush away [hoping] this thing . . . would subside
into dead matter. He sleeps, but he is awakened; he opens his
eyes; behold the horrid thing stands at his bedside, opening his
curtains.

Here is a dream-vision of singular vividness and strangeness. It
would seem almost, by the young writer's account, that the allegorical horror story/moral parable had not been imagined into being by

the author herself. Rather, Mary Shelley is the passive observer; the vision seems to come from a source not herself. Yet, we are led to think, knowing something of the biographical context of the creation of *Frankenstein*, that it can hardly have been an accident that a tale of a monstrous birth was written by a very young woman who'd had two babies with her mercurial and unpredictable poet-lover Percy Shelley, one of whom had died, and was very much pregnant again. And, they were not (yet) married.

Following this dream, Mary Shelley spoke of being "possessed" by her subject. (Though neither Byron nor Shelley responded fruitfully to Byron's challenge, their companion and friend John Polidori wrote one of the first vampire novels, *The Vampyre* [1819].) At first Mary Shelley had thought that her lurid gothic tale would be just a short story but, in time, as the manuscript evolved, the work became a curious, heavily Miltonic allegorical romance, rejected by both Shelley's and Byron's publishers, who knew that the author was a young woman; and finally published, anonymously, in 1818, when the author was twenty-one. Since then, *Frankenstein* has never been out of print and is surely the most extraordinary novel ever written by an eighteen-year-old girl in thrall to a brilliant but doomed Romantic poet.

Today, "Frankenstein" isn't identified as the doctor-creator of the monster, but the monster himself: the "hideous phantasm." And Mary Shelley's brilliantly deformed creation has been detached from the author, an iconic figure seemingly self-generated; one of the great, potent symbols of humankind's predilection for self-destruction, as significant in our time as in 1818.

Another horrific dream-inspiration some sixty years later is the great mythic parable of the Victorian era, *Dr. Jekyll and Mr. Hyde* by Robert Louis Stevenson (1885), the quintessential expression of humankind's tragic doubleness; or, at least, the criminal hypocrisy of Victorian gentlemen. Like numerous poets and writers of the Romantic and Victorian era, Robert Louis Stevenson, suffering from tuberculosis, "self-medicated" (as we would say today) with laudanum, an alcoholic tincture of opium with a trace of morphine. It is known that opium provokes astonishing dreams and nightmares, and so Stevenson experienced a "fine bogey tale" one night in 1885, from which his wife, Fanny, had to wake him; inspired by the dream, Stevenson wrote a story within three days, which his wife so disliked as "overly sensational," he destroyed it. But the story haunted him, and Stevenson composed another version, also feverishly, and also within three days; narrated by the "lean, long, dusty, dreary and yet somehow lovable" lawyer Utterson, the very emblem of Victorian propriety and dullness, the lurid tale of *Dr. Jekyll and Mr. Hyde* bursts free of its restraints in its final chapter, "Henry Jekyll's Full Statement of the Case"—the Victorian gentleman's acknowledgment of his animal-self, and the "condescension to evil that . . . destroyed the balance of my soul."

It seems significant that Stevenson's dream-inspired novel was written while the author was confined to his bed in an entranced state; that Jekyll speaks of Hyde as a being "within" him, as "intimate" as a wife, or an eye in its socket. It is a kind of miracle, though a hellish miracle—Jekyll gives birth to Hyde, as Stevenson the writer gives birth to both. We wonder who it is who speaks so passionately: "My devil had been long caged, he came out roaring."

———

Social injustice as inspiration. The wish to "bear witness" to those unable to speak for themselves, as a consequence of poverty, or illness, or political circumstances, which includes gender and ethnic identity. The wish to conjoin narrative fiction with the didactic and the preacherly. Above all, the wish to move others to a course of action—the basis of political, propaganda-art. Here we have such works as Harriet Beecher Stowe's *Uncle Tom's Cabin*; Charles Dickens's *Hard Times*, Stephen Crane's *Maggie: A Girl of the Streets*, Upton Sinclair's *The Jungle*. (Sinclair, an avid lifelong Socialist, wrote nearly one hundred books of which the majority are novels involving politics and social conditions in the United States; among these are *Oil!* [from which the much-acclaimed 2007 film *There Will Be Blood* was adapted] and the *Lanny Budd* series of eleven novels, each a best seller when it was published. *Dragon's Teeth* was awarded the 1943 Pulitzer Prize.) Frank Norris's *McTeague* and *The Octopus* are savage critiques of rapacious American capitalism; "class war" might be identified as the groundwork of such novels of Theodore Dreiser as *Sister Carrie* and *An American Tragedy* and of John Dos Passos's hugely influential *USA*. In the era of Dreiser there were few women writing of life in urban ghettos with the intelligence and emotional power of Anzia Yesierska whose *Bread Givers, Hungry Hearts*, and *How I Found America: Collected Stories* chronicle the lives of Jewish immigrants of New York City's Lower East Side with unflinching candor.

This is the sort of socially conscious "realistic" fiction that Nabokov scorned as vulgar ("Mediocrity thrives on 'ideas'") and of which Oscar Wilde would have said with a sneer ("No artist has ethical sympathies. . . . All art is quite useless") (Oscar Wilde, Preface, *The Picture of Dorian Gray*). Still, mainstream American literature with its predilection for liberal sympathies with the disenfranchised and impoverished, the great effort of the nineteenth- and twentieth-century novel to draw attention to social injustice and inequality, remains the most attractive of literary traditions even in our self-consciously postmodernist era. In Toni Morrison's *Beloved,* for instance, slave narrative sources have been appropriated and refashioned into an exquisitely wrought art that is both morally focused and aesthetically ambitious.

From his early novel imaginatively reconstructing the lives of the "atom bomb spies" Ethel and Julius Rosenberg, *The Book of Daniel,* through the much-acclaimed *Ragtime, Loon Lake, World's Fair,* and *The March* E. L. Doctorow has taken for his subject the volatile issues of class and race in America; his more recent novels have been shaped by oral histories. "Every writer speaks for a community." (Doctorow, *Paris Review* interview.)

No one has spoken more explicitly of his political/moral intention in writing a work of fiction than Russell Banks in his "Envoie" to the novel *Continental Drift,* which concerns itself, like most of Bank's fiction, with working-class and disenfranchised Americans caught up in the malaise of a rapacious capitalist economy:

> And so ends the story of Robert Raymond Dubus, a decent man, but in all the important ways an ordinary man. One could say a common man. Even so, his bright particularity, having been delivered over to the obscurity of death, meant something larger than itself. . . .
>
> Knowledge of the facts of Bob's life and death changes nothing in the world. Our celebrating his life and grieving over his death, however, will. . . . Sabotage and subversion, then, are this book's intentions. Go, my book, and destroy the world as it is.

———

James Joyce once remarked that *Ulysses* was for him essentially a way of "capturing the speech of my father and my father's friends"—an astonishing statement when you consider the complexity of *Ulysses,* but one which any writer can understand. So much of literature springs from a wish to assuage homesickness, a desire to commemorate places, people, childhoods, family and tribal rituals, ways of life—surely the primary inspiration of all: the wish, in some artists clearly the necessity, to capture in the quasi-permanence of art that which is perishable in life. Though the great Modernists—(Joyce, Proust, Yeats, Lawrence, Woolf, Faulkner)—were revolutionaries in technique, their subjects were intimately bound up with their own lives and their own regions; the Modernist is one who is likely to use his intimate life as material for his art, shaping the ordinary into the extraordinary. The Confessional poets—Robert Lowell, John Berryman, W. D. Snodgrass, Anne Sexton, Sylvia Plath—to a degree, Elizabeth Bishop—rendered their lives as art, as if self-hypnotized. Of our contemporaries, writers as seemingly diverse as Saul Bellow, Philip Roth, and John Updike created distinguished careers out of their lives, often returning to familiar subjects, lovingly and tirelessly reimagining their own pasts as if mesmerized by the wonder of "self." In his last, most obsessively self-reflective work, *Ada or Ardor: A Family Chronicle,* Vladimir Nabokov evokes the intense claustrophobia of a "super-imperial couple" who not only inhabit the same psychic realm but, boldly and audaciously, are also intimately related: sister and brother. Set in a whimsical counterworld, "Antiterra," Nabokov's commemoration of self is finally, and literally, incestuous.

No writer has been more mesmerized by the circumstances of his own, exceptional life than our greatest Transcendentalist poet Henry David Thoreau who wrote exclusively, obsessively of his "self" as an adventurer in a circumscribed world—"I have traveled much in Concord," as Thoreau famously said. *Walden* is the publicly revered text but it is Thoreau's *Journal,* in which he wrote daily from 1837 to 1861, eventually accumulating some seven thousand pages, that is the more remarkable document, as Thoreau is the most acute of observers of nature and of human nature; an analyst of his "self" in the Whitmanesque sense, the "self" that is all selves, the transcendent universal. Here is the essential Thoreau, in the essay "Ktaadn and the Maine Woods":

> I stand in awe of my body, this matter to which I am bound has become so strange to me. I fear not spirits, ghosts, of which I am one . . . but I fear bodies. . . . Talk of mysteries!—Think of our life in nature,—daily to be shown matter, to come into contact with it,—rocks, trees, wind on our cheeks! The *solid*

earth! The *actual* world! The *Common sense! Contact! Contact! Who* are we? *Where* are we? ""

———

The early Surrealists considered the world a vast "forest of signs" to be interpreted by the individual artist. Beneath its apparent disorder the visual world contains messages and symbols—like a dream? *Is the world a collective dream?* Not the hypnotic spell of the individual artist's childhood, family, regional life—(as in the inspiration of commemoration)—but rather its antithesis, the impersonal, the chance, the "found." The Surrealist photographer Man Ray wandered Parisian streets with his camera, anticipating nothing and leaving himself open to *disponibilité*, or availability/chance. The most striking Surrealist images were ordinary images made strange by being decontextualized—"Beautiful as the chance encounter of a sewing machine and an umbrella on a dissection table." (André Breton appropriating metaphor of Lautréamont.) When photography began to be an art that didn't depend upon careful staging in a studio, or even outdoors, it was discovered to be ideally suited to the caprices of opportunity; the artist wanders into the world, armed with just his camera, freed from the confines of the predictable and the controlled as in the work of Cartier-Bresson, Weegee, Bruce Davidson, Garry Winogrand, the newly discovered Vivian Maier, Diane Arbus (whose strategy was "to go where I've never been"), (quote from "Diane Arbus's 'Dark Secrets,'" *Daily Beast*, online), and numerous others.

Literature is not a medium that lends itself well to the Surrealist adventure of *disponibilité*. Even radically experimental fiction requires some strategy of causation, otherwise readers won't trouble to turn pages—unlike most visual art, which can be experienced in a single gaze, fiction is a matter of subsequent and successive gazes, mimicking chronological time, as it is locked into chronological time. (A rare exception is William Burroughs's *Naked Lunch* with its "cut-up" method of a discontinuous and disjointed narrative appropriate to a drug-addled consciousness for whom hallucination is more natural than coherence.) There is a very minor tradition of "found poems" discovered in unpoetic places like newspapers, magazines, advertisements and graffiti, instruction manuals, and brochures. Virtually all poets have experimented with "found po-ems" at some point in their careers, sometimes appropriating entire passages of prose into a poem, more often appropriating a few lines and constructing a poem around these lines, as in work by Howard Nemerov, Charles Olson, Blaise Cendrars, and Charles Reznikoff among others. A "found poem" gem is Annie Dillard's appropriation of a manual titled *Prehospital Emergency Care and Crisis Interven-tion* (1989) which the poet has fashioned into a suite of short poems titled *"Emergencies."*

"Answer"

If death is imminent either
On the scene or in the ambulance,
Be supportive and reassuring
To the patient, but do not lie.

If a patient asks, "I'm dying,
Aren't I?" respond
With something like, "You
Have some very serious injuries,
But I'm not giving up on you."

More often found poetry is meant to be satirical or witty, or mor-dantly ironic, as in Hart Seely's appropriated material titled *Pieces of Intelligence: The Existential Poetry of Donald H. Rumsfeld* (2003). Here is a complete poem by Rumsfeld/Seely:

"The Unknown"

As we know,
There are known knowns.
There are things we know we know.

We also know
There are known unknowns.
That is to say
We know there are some things
We do not know.

But there are also unknown unknowns.
The ones we don't know
We don't know.

———

If inspiration is many-faceted, out of what human need—or hunger—does inspiration spring?

That's to say, what is the motive for metaphor?

It seems clear that *Homo sapiens* is the only species to have anything like language, and certainly the only species to have written languages, "histories." Our sense of ourselves is based upon linguistic constructs, inherited, or remembered, and regarded as precious or at least valuable; our sacred texts are presumed to have been dictated by gods, and sometimes we are fired with murderous rage if these texts are challenged or mocked, or if our creator's name is uttered in the wrong way, or by the wrong lips. Perhaps literature in its broader sense, incorporating centuries, millennia, as a consequence of myriad individual inspirations across myriad cultures, relates to us as that part of the human brain called the hippocampus relates to memory.

The hippocampus is a small, sea horse-shaped part of the brain necessary for long-term storage of factual and experiential memory, though it is not the site of such storage. Short-term memory is transient—long-term memory can prevail for many decades: the last thing you will be able to retrieve in your memory may well be the first thing that came to reside there—a glimpse of your young mother's face, a confused blur of a childhood room, a lullaby, a caressing voice. If the hippocampus is injured or atrophied, there will be no further storage of memory in the brain—there will be no new memory. I have come to think that art is the formal commemoration of life in its variety—the novel, for instance, is "historic" in its embodiment in a specific place and time, and its suggestion that there is meaning to our actions; it is virtually impossible to create art without an inherent meaning, even if that meaning is presented as mysterious and unknowable.

Without the stillness, thoughtfulness, and depths of art, and without the ceaseless moral rigors of art, we would have no shared culture—no collective memory; as, if memory is destroyed in the human brain, our identities corrode, and we "are" no one—we become merely a shifting succession of impressions attached to no fixed source. As it is, in contemporary societies, where so much concentration is focused upon social media, insatiable in its fleeting interests, the "stillness and thoughtfulness" of a more permanent art feels threatened. As human beings we crave "meaning"—which only art can provide; but the social media provide no meaning, only this succession of fleeting impressions whose underlying principle may simply be to urge us to consume products.

The motive for metaphor, then, is a motive for survival as a species, as a culture, and as individuals.

THIS I BELIEVE:

Five Motives for Writing

It is a very self-conscious thing, to speak of one's "credo."

I think that most writers and artists love their work, which of course we don't consider "work"—exactly. As artists love the basic materials of their art—(paints, charcoal, clay, marble)—so writers love the basic materials of their art—(language).

Many visual artists have no "credo" at all. They offer no "artist's statement." And they consider those who do to be somewhat suspicious, if not frankly duplicitous.

The oracular, pontificating, self-aggrandizing vatic voice—how hollow it sounds, to others! There are great poets, including even Walt Whitman and Robert Frost, who might have known better, who have fallen into such hollowness, as one might fall into a bog.

Recall D. H. Lawrence's admonition—*Never trust the teller, trust the tale.*

Criticism, as distinct from literature, or "creative" writing, has often been aligned with a particular moral, political, religious sensibility. The 1950s were perceived, proudly and without irony, as an Age of Criticism—at least, by critics. (It does seem rather narrow to define the 1950s as an age of criticism when writers like Jack Kerouac, Allen Ginsberg, Eudora Welty and Flannery O'Connor among numerous others were publishing frequently.) Criticism is more naturally a kind of preaching, or propaganda; there are systems of belief underlying most criticism, intent upon rewarding those who confirm the critic's core beliefs and punishing those who don't. But "creative" artists resist defining their beliefs so overtly, as one might wish not to wear one's clothing inside out revealing seams and stitches.

However, considering my own life, or rather my career, I think it is likely that my credo, if I were to have one, involves several overlapping ideals.

Commemoration. Much of literature is commemorative. Home, homeland, family, ancestors. Mythology, legend. That "certain slant of light" in a place deeply imprinted in childhood, as in the oldest, most prevailing region of the brain.

Much of my prose fiction is "commemorative" in essence—it is a means of memorializing a region of the world in which I have lived, a past I've shared with others, a way of life that might seem to me vanishing, thus in danger of being forgotten. Not an "old" America but rather an "older" America—those years described as the Depression, through World War II, the Vietnam War, the 1960s, and so forward to the present time in upstate, quasi-rural America. Writing is our way of assuaging homesickness.

Commemoration is identical, for me, with setting. Where a story or a novel is set is at least as significant as what the story—the plot—"is." In my fiction, characters are not autonomous but arise out of the very physicality of the places in which they live, and the times in which they live. There is a spiritual dimension to landscape which gifted photographers can suggest, and gifted writers can evoke. Often, I am mesmerized by the descriptions of landscapes, towns, and cities in fiction—(obviously, the novels of Dickens, Hardy, Lawrence come to mind; it is difficult to name any novels of distinction that are not firmly imbued with "place"). And if the setting is antagonistic to the spirit, as in our environmentally devastated landscapes and cityscapes, this is a part of the story.

Bearing witness. Most of the world's population, through history, have not been able to "bear witness" for themselves. They lack the language, as well as the confidence to shape the language for their own ends. They lack the education, as well as the power that comes with education. Politically, they may be totally disenfranchised—simply too poor, and devastated by poverty and the bad luck that comes with poverty, like an infected limb turning gangrenous. They may be suppressed, or terrorized into silence. My most intense sympathies tend to be for those individuals who have been left behind by history, as by the economy; they are all around us, but become visible only when something goes terribly wrong, like a natural disaster, or an outburst of madness and violence. Particularly, I have been sympathetic with the plight of women and girls in a patriarchal society; I am struck by the ways in which weakness can be transformed into strength, and vulnerability into survival. If the writer has any obligation—(and this is a debatable issue, for the writer must remain free)—it's to give voice to those who lack voices of their own.

Self-expression. The "self" is, at its core, radically young, even adolescent. Our "selves" are forged in childhood, burnished and confirmed in adolescence. That is why there are great, irresistibly engaging writers of "adolescence"—for instance, Henry David Thoreau, Emily Dickinson, Ernest Hemingway (in his early short stories set in northern Michigan). Since I began writing fairly seriously when I was very young, my truest and most prevailing self is that adolescent self, confronting an essentially mysterious and fascinating adult world, like a riddle to be solved, or a code to be decoded. The essence of the adolescent is rebelliousness, skepticism. It is very healthy, a stay against the accommodations and compromises of what we call adulthood, particularly "middle age."

Propaganda, "moralizing." Once, it was not considered gauche for literary writers (Stowe, Upton Sinclair, Tolstoy, Eliot, Dickens) to address the reader more or less directly, and to speak of moral predilections; now, since the revolution in sensibility generally associated with the early decades of the twentieth century, which we call Modernism, it is virtually impossible to indicate a moral position in any dogmatic way. Ours is still, over all, an age of irony—indirection, obliquity. As Emily Dickinson advises, speaking of her own credo—- "Tell all the truth but tell it slant / Success in Circuit lies." And Virginia Woolf, in these thrilling, liberating words:

> Art is being rid of all preaching: things in themselves: the sentence in itself beautiful. . . . Why all this criticism of other people? Why not some system that includes the good? What a discovery that would be—a system that did not shut out.

Still, most of us who write hope to evoke sympathy for our characters, as George Eliot and D. H. Lawrence prescribed; we would hope not to be reducible to a political position, still less a political party—(though writers in other parts of the world are often adamantly political, and are political activists)—but we write with the expectation that our work will illuminate areas of the world that may be radically different from our readers' experience, and that this is a good thing. It is an "educational" instinct—one hopes it is not "preacherly."

Aesthetic object. Writing as purely gestural, as Woolf suggests—- "the sentence in itself beautiful." In fact it is very difficult to write a sustained work of fiction that is "purely gestural"—meaning emerges even out of the random, a moral perspective evolves even out of anarchy, nihilism, and amorality, the mere act of writing, still more the discipline of revision, seems to carry with it an ethical commitment to its subject. Yet most of us are drawn to art not because of its moral gravity but rather because it is "art"—that is, "artificial"—in some sort of heightened and rarefied and very special relationship to reality, which (mere) reality itself can't provide. Of course, "beauty" in art can be virtually anything, including even conventional ugliness, beautifully/originally treated. In choosing a suitable language for a work of prose fiction, as well as poetry, the writer is making an aesthetic choice: she is rejecting all other languages, or "voices"; she is gambling that this particular voice is the very best voice for this material. The truism "Art for art's sake" really means "Art for beauty's sake"—the content of any literary novel is of less significance than the language in which the novel is told.

Now that much of publishing is digital, the book as aesthetic object is endangered. Storytelling isn't likely to vanish, but physical, three-dimensional books comprised of actual pages (paper of varying quality)—with their "hard" covers and "dust" jackets—are in a perilous state. Many of us who love to write also love books—the phenomenon of books. We may have been initially drawn to writing because we fell in love with a very few, select books in childhood, which we have hoped to replicate somehow; we hoped, however fantastically, to join the select society of those individuals whose names are printed on the spines of books. It isn't to grasp at a kind of immortality—we fell into our yearning as children, long before immortality, or even mortality, was an issue. Rather, we yearn to ally ourselves with a kind of beauty, an object to be held in the hand, passed from hand to hand; an object to place upon a shelf, or to be stood upright, its beautiful cover turned outward to the world. As Freud said memorably in *Civilization and Its Discontents*, "Beauty has no obvious use; nor is there any clear cultural necessity for it. Yet civilization could not do without it."

Would the great writers of our tradition, James Joyce for instance, have labored quite so hard, and with such fierce devotion, if the end-product of their labor was to have been nothing more than "online" art—sustained purely by electricity, bodiless, near-anonymous, instantaneously summoned as a genie out of a bottle, and just as instantaneously banished to the netherworld of cyberspace? Like Joyce, most writers still crave the quasi-permanence of the book: not the book as idea but as physical, aesthetic object. This is as close as we are likely to come to the sacramental, which, for some of us, is wonderfully close enough.

ANATOMY OF STORY

Not that the story need be long, but
it will take a long while to make it
short.

HENRY DAVID THOREAU

It is a maxim: all stories are infinite. All stories have to be radically distilled. There is no "first cause" in a story as there can be no final line. Wherever the writer chooses to begin is arbitrary, *in medias res*. For—what came before the opening sentence? And before that? In an infinite regression, not to a beginning (for there is no beginning) but to an approximation of a beginning—*Once upon a time*.

THE KING DIED. THE *queen died*.

Is this a story, or is this an anecdote? Perhaps it is not even an anecdote, and not even a single statement but two (unrelated) statements.

The two brief statements so juxtaposed seem to suggest a temporal relationship. A geographical relationship. Some sort of familial relationship. Yet, the two statements are not actually linked, and so cannot constitute a "narrative."

The king died, the queen died.

The king died, soon then the queen died.

The king died, (and) soon then the queen died.

These three statements have entered the gravitational field of "narrative"—"story." For they are linked in a (seemingly) causal way.

(Though there is no evidence that the queen died because the king died, it is a natural human predilection to make this inference. The great eighteenth century Scottish philosopher/skeptic David Hume might not have agreed, out of a perverse sort of Scottish common sense: how can we know with absolute certainty that the sun will "rise" in the morning, based upon the (mere, empirical) fact that the sun has always "risen" in the morning, in memory? We think we know, we behave as if we know, but Hume is correct, *we cannot know* as we might know that one and one are two, or two times five is ten.)

The king died (and so) soon then the queen died.

In this compound statement, the relationship between the two phrases is unmistakable and irrefutable: we are told by the small determinate word "so" that the queen died because the king had died, and there is no margin now for speculation.

Is this a story? And if so, is it a subtle story? Or is it rather a too-explicit story, that announces its meaning before it has even begun, so that there is no mystery, and nothing for the reader to discover?

The king died, (but then) the queen did not die.

Here is an orthogonal narrative, that does/ does not spring from a causal relationship. The inference is that the queen *should die*, but in fact, we are told *but then* the queen did not die.

Such a narrative, that seems to spring in a perpendicular fashion from the *Once upon a time* opening, is more engaging, more problematic, as it is less conventional and expected, than *The king died, (and then) the queen died* or its variants.

The queen died. The king had died.

The queen died, (for) the king had died.

The queen did not die, (though) the king had died.

The queen will / will not die, (for/ though) the king had died.

All of these are variants on the original statements and each could be made interesting in its own (original, novel) way.

ONCE UPON A TIME is a (time-) honored way of beginning a story. For a story must begin *in time*; there is no story *out of time.*

Eudora Welty once said: "Time has to move through a mind."

As there can be no story without conflict, no forward momentum without disequilibrium, so there can be no story that does not move through time. Even in the distant, detached, oracular *Once upon a time* there is a storyteller, pretending to be anonymous. It may be a master of the faux fairy tale like Hans Christian Anderson: the highly conscious craftsman emulating the visionary distances and impersonality of the fairy tale, the voice of the people. Such faux fairy tales are bold appropriations of folk art, difficult to execute though (one might be led to think) appearing simple.

In great literature, the *simple, artless* is often the most brilliantly invented.

In tales beginning *Once upon a time* a narrator is telling a story in which he / she does not appear. Others appear, who are seen at a little distance—"characters." But these are like figures in a dream, each figure generated by the dreamer, and each a part of the dreamer, however (seemingly) unlike the dreamer.

In most contemporary fiction *Once upon a time* has been radically distilled and delimited. The time-setting is likely to be a recent time, a time within memory, a few years ago, yesterday. Unless it is the present time: the historic present. Our tenses are but two: *was, is.*

When the tense is *is,* the conceit is that the story is happening even as we read it. The story hasn't already *happened* but *is happening.*

Even a story that is *was* seems, to the reader, a story that *is happening*, whose outcome is unknown.

THE EXCITEMENT OF THE UNKNOWN!

Reading a story, the reader is the pursuer of the unknown—the not-yet-known. The reader is a kind of detective pursuing clues, trying to decipher a code, interpreting "tone"—"mood"—"language"—"meaning" which seem to flow beneath the surface of the story.

The "plot" is the vehicle bearing meaning. But if you summarize a plot, paraphrase a story, you will find that the reduction of a story to its plot yields no meaning. You will ask—"So what? What does it all *mean*?"

The first book I ever held in my hand was *The Gold Bug & Other Tales* by Edgar Allan Poe. With great fascination, though I could not yet read, I turned the mysterious and entrancing pages of this book, and studied the full-page illustrations that were intricately executed line drawings, "gothic" in nature. (Not that I had any idea of the "gothic.")

In the farmhouse of my childhood there were few books. Perhaps there were no other books until, a few years after my discovery of *The Gold Bug* on a shelf, my grandmother began to give me books for my birthday and for holidays, notably Lewis Carroll's *Alice in Wonderland and Through the Looking-Glass*. (From the approximate age of five onward, I became what is called a "voracious reader." A child happiest with a book in hand, or the prospect of a book.)

The experience of Poe in my life is a complicated one since it began, literally, before I could read. And then, when I began to read, in a childlike and stumbling way, the tales of *The Gold Bug* were utterly mysterious, unfathomable, and tantalizing; Poe's dense, tortuous prose was totally unlike the speech of the adults of my life, and bore virtually no relationship to the primer prose of my school books and to the newspaper and magazine articles my parents read, at which I glanced, or tried to read out of curiosity. It was a notion of mine that the early prose fiction I encountered, by Hawthorne as well as Poe, was "real"—"realistic"; that is, I took for granted that these writers were writing about real subjects, though totally strange to me, like those upsetting dreams of childhood in which I could not quite determine if I was awake or asleep or somehow both, simultaneously.

A child's sense of reality differs enormously from an adult's sense of reality which is informed by skepticism as well as experience. A child does not know enough to realize what she does not know and any voice of adult authority carries with it an air of the absolute, not to be questioned as (when a child is very young) she does not "question" the adults who surround her.

How many years passed, during which time I tried to read the short story "The Gold Bug"—five years? six? ten? Here as elsewhere in the more obscure works of Poe one encounters dense thickets of prose in the convoluted, overwrought style of the nineteenth century, in which nothing is stated clearly, or directly: all is filtered through the prism of a "gothic" sensibility, in the case of Poe often a narrator whose unreality is compounded by mania, paranoia, psychosis. (In other tales, notably "The Tell-Tale Heart," Poe is dazzling as any contemporary writer giving voice to extreme states of mind with obvious zest and virtuosity; but the denser, more "gothic" Poe tales outnumber the more fluid.) In fact I'm not sure that I ever comprehended what was happening in this awkward mixture of what Poe called "ratiocination" and nineteenth-century European gothic mystery involving the deciphering of an elaborate cryptogram message. (Though I recall as a young child being fascinated by "secret codes"—"secret languages." Very likely I felt a natural attraction to the act of writing in code [so that no adult could know what I was writing?]—which isn't very different from the writing of fiction generally.)

Found amid Poe's papers after his premature death on October 7, 1849, on a Baltimore street was a single-page manuscript titled

"The Light-House." It was a challenge to a writer of the twenty-first century to reimagine Poe in present-day terms: to transform nineteenth-century gothic into contemporary themes of ecology and evolution, male-female relations, a re-examination of the "Romantic." But "Poe Posthumous; or, The Light House" (originally titled "The Fabled Light-House at Vina de Mar" and written for a special edition of *McSweeney's* edited by Michael Chabon) is essentially a variant of the archetypcal Poe adventure story in which a hypersensitive protagonist confronts gothic horror and succumbs to it. In this story the Poe-like narrator lapses by degrees into an altered state of being, not madness, or not madness merely, but an aroused consciousness in which brute survival is the great, immediate and prevailing challenge. "Poe Posthumous" is intended as a nightmare tale, not without moments of comedy, depicting the ways in which human beings might adapt themselves to radically altered environments; how against the grain of their own "inborn" personalities they may discover themselves behaving. For it is not enough to maintain one's distinct identity—one must *survive* as a living organism.

The story is also an ironic portrait of the Romantic male, for whom the female is idealized and de-animalized. In Poe, as in gothic writers generally, there are no *bodies*, and no *bodily functions* including even *eating.* And so in this postmodernist appropriation, the Poe-like narrator realizes fully, and with some appetite, the range of his animal instincts, long suppressed in his former life in genteel Philadelphia literary circles. Rare among Poe, a happy ending!

THE FIRST GREAT WRITER whose work I read with avid interest, and set out as a young writer to emulate, was not the fevered Poe of childhood but the cool and understated Hemingway of early adolescence. In a tenth grade English class at Williamsville High School in Williamsville, New York, under the tutelage of a wonderful teacher named "Mr. Stein"—(Harold Stein?)—we were assigned short stories from an anthology of American classic stories dating back to Washington Irving, Hawthorne, Melville and Poe, and including such near-contemporaries as Ernest Hemingway, William Faulkner, Katherine Anne Porter, Irwin Shaw, Conrad Aiken ("Silent Snow, Secret Snow"—mesmerizing!). The Hemingway story in the anthology was "Soldier's Home"—sparely narrated, taut with irony (which I did not understand but certainly felt), a minimalist language that seemed to me very beautiful, if enigmatic. Soon then, I acquired a copy of Hemingway's early short stories *in our time* from the library, and set out to immerse myself in these elemental-seeming tales written when Hemingway was a young expatriate in his twenties, living in Paris, and already married, and a father. Oddly, these early stories are less accessible to the reader than the more famous stories of Hemingway's maturity—"The Snows of Kilimanjaro," "The Short Happy Life of Francis Macomber"—as they more resemble prose poetry than conventional prose fiction. The governing principle of Hemingway's prose in *in our time* is "less is more"—though only the hands of a master craftsman does this adage really apply. ("Indian Camp" is an ideal story for writing students to contemplate. Line by line, sentence by sentence, paragraph by paragraph this minimalist story, hard-cut as a diamond, yields a kind of shadow-story beneath its seemingly artless, idiomatic surface. Each element of punctuation is carefully chosen, with a mild, dramatic surprise in the final line.)

It is perhaps unexpected that my story "Papa at Ketchum 1961" is not at all in the tradition of Hemingway's minimalist stories, nor even in the tradition of his later, more expansive stories. It is rather more a meditative, introspective, postmodernist prose poem that builds through something like incremental repetition; the obsessions of the aging, ailing, near-paralyzed and deeply depressed "Nobel-prize winning author" constitute the plot, examining layers of motive and personality as Hemingway's fiction rarely did. Such inwardness would have dismayed Hemingway for it would seem to signal the kind of unmanly, self-exhibitionistic weakness more appropriate to Scott Fitzgerald (particularly in the memoirist "The Crack-Up") than to the hyper-manly Hemingway for whom the confession of weakness, any sort of intimate self-revelation or self-pity would be humiliating. The story moves back and forth in time as Hemingway's fiction, with its focus upon the present tense, and the present setting, resolutely did not. For the aging, ailing, deeply depressed and suicidal author (already in his late fifties an elderly man) the only way out of his quagmire was through writing—but writing was what he could not do, because (this is my theory) he could not confront his true subject, the paralysis of the spirit, the wellsprings of his own depression, the enigma of his own divided personality in which any sort of sentiment was softness, "feminine." That the portrait of Hemingway is clear-eyed does not mean that it is not wholly sympathetic: there is a sense in which, like James Joyce in a very different way, Hemingway is the essential writer's writer, a hero of writing, perhaps a martyr.

I take for granted the fact of Hemingway's genius—indeed, this is true for all of the subjects of *Wild Nights!*

Mark Twain's *Huckleberry Finn* was another of the great, influential novels of my adolescence, which I would subsequently teach as a university instructor so frequently, with such intensity, that decades later I've discovered, leafing through my old much-annotated copy the other day, that I had virtually memorized the novel; just to glance at a paragraph is to uncoil the familiar words, as a strain of music can precipitate an entire work of music once played on an instrument. Yet, the protagonist of the elegiac "Grandpa Clemens & Angelfish 1906" is not portrayed in anything like Twain's own prose. Here is a very different sensibility, not self-aggrandizing (in comic excess, in Twain's usual masterly vein) but obsessed with the self's guilt. (It is ironic that Twain would have considered such a story obscene and unfathomable. Though the writer was emotionally drawn to young, prepubescent girls he could not have confronted anything like the chastely modulated pedophilia depicted here, in himself; if he had, he could not have forgiven himself as we are moved to forgive Grandpa Clemens.)

It was my intention in these stories to present classic American writers in their "secret" lives. Not as they are usually perceived, and might have wished themselves perceived, but as, essentially, they really were in the coils of their own deep fantasies, in the last weeks, days, hours and minutes of their lives. The exception is Emily Dickinson who appears transmogrified, physically truncated and "distilled" as a computer-operated manikin, EDickinsonRepliLuxe—no longer mortal but immortal (as long as her owner doesn't destroy her in a fit of jealous rage); the author of the most exquisite verse, whose language is indeed iridescent—"Bright Knots of Apparitions/ Salute us, with their wings—" that is maddening to those who don't understand poetry (or, perhaps, women).

"The Master at St. Bartholomew's Hospital" is my homage to Henry James. It is an elegy for James's not often heralded courage, and for the vanished way of life of the Master; a depiction of a sudden flaring up of (sexual, spiritual) passion in an elderly gentleman-artist whose life has been almost totally repressed. This is the true subject of the story, that erupts in gothic excess in the Master's fever-dream of the demonic adversarial female, Nurse Edwards, who peers into his most secret longings. In life, Henry James behaved with extraordinary courage and generosity in volunteering to work with wounded soldiers at St. Bartholomew's Hospital in London, as noted by his friend and benefactor Edith Wharton; it would be good to think that, at the age of seventy-three, James died with his romantic fantasies intact—a fate all writers might wish for themselves.

THE WRITING ROOM

"No ideas but in dreams"—or rather, day-dreams.

A strange fact of my life is that I spend much of my time gazing out the window of any writing space I have inhabited. This is particularly true of my present study which overlooks, from the second floor of our house in a quasi-rural area four miles from Princeton, New Jersey, the rear of our property sloping down to a creek that flows into a nearby lake. (In Berkeley, where we sometimes live in the winter months in a house on Panoramic Hill, my writing table overlooks resplendent San Francisco Bay.)

There is surely some subtle connection between the vistas we face, and the writing we accomplish, as a dream takes its mood and imagery from our waking life.

Among my earliest memories are the fields, woods, and creeks of my childhood in western New York State where I grew up on a small farm on Transit Road in a rural community called Millersport, twenty miles north of Buffalo. We lived so close to the Tonawanda Creek that I could see it from the upstairs windows of our farmhouse.

This writing room replicates, to a degree, the old, lost vistas of my childhood. What it contains is less significant to me than what it overlooks though obviously there are precious things here—photographs of my parents Carolina and Fred Oates, and my grandmother Blanche Morgenstern (who is the inspiration for my novel *The Gravedigger's Daughter*). Photographs of my husband Raymond Smith, who died in February 2008, and of my second husband, Charlie Gross, who is a neuroscientist at Princeton University. Portraits of me by my artist-friend Gloria Vanderbilt, a collage by Gloria of photographs of my family and me, and a beautiful painting by Gloria—"*Joyce and Ray in the Rain*." A beautiful photograph of peacocks taken by Charlie in China. Like all writers, I have made my writing room a sanctuary of the soul.

Bookshelves contain copies of most of the books I have written from 1963 onward, along with selected paperback editions. How stunned I would have been to imagine, at the outset of my writing life, that, in time, I would write so many books!—when each day's work, each hour's work, feels so anxiously wrought and hard-won.

My writing begins in "long-hand" sketches and notes. Ideally, I write in this way seated at my beautifully carved little "antique" table where I can gaze dreamily toward the creek/lake in the near distance and be distracted by the activities of myriad birds at the feeders below. (Red cardinals in the snow are the heart's delight!) My larger and more utilitarian desk contains my laptop and it's here that I type seriously, often for hours; invariably I am expanding upon ideas that I've written by hand, in what is called, quaintly, "cursive"—soon to be a lost or even secret skill, like Gaelic.

I love my study and am unhappy to have to leave it for long.

Yet I think I most envy writers who look upon the sea, or upon rivers—I would be absolutely enthralled facing such a view where time would pass virtually unnoticed, in anticipation of something wonderful.

II

———————————

CLASSICS

MY LIFE IN MIDDLEMARCH:
REBECCA MEAD

Rarely attempted, and still more rarely successful, is the bibliomemoir—a subspecies of literature combining literary criticism and biography with the intimate, confessional tone of autobiography.

The most engaging bibliomemoirs establish the writer's voice in counterpoint to the subject, with something more than adulation or explication at stake. Nicholson Baker's quirkily inspired book-length essay *U and I* charts the young writer's obsession with the sensuous, poised prose and public career of John Updike, a curious double portrait that manages to be both self-effacing and arrogant; Geoff Dyer's *Out of Sheer Rage: Wrestling with D. H. Lawrence* is a very funny if despairing account of the writer's failure to write the "sober, academic study" of Lawrence's work he has hoped to write, before becoming overcome by distractions and inertia and creating a "wild book" in its place; Christopher Beha's *The Whole Five Feet: What the Great Books Taught Me About Life, Death, and Pretty Much Everything Else* is a warmly personal account of a young man's intensive summer's reading of the Harvard Classics Library (fifty-one volumes) amid a season of familial crisis and loss. Phyllis Rose's ironically titled *The Year of Reading Proust: A Memoir in Real Time* subordinates the magisterial *Remembrance of Things Past* to the busy, often trivial minutiae of the memoirist's daily life, while, as its ebullient title suggests, David Denby's *Great Books: My Adventures with Homer, Rousseau, Woolf, and Other Indestructible Writers of the Western World* is a zestful anecdotal account of an adult returning to the education he'd failed to appreciate as a Columbia undergraduate. And there is Rick Gekoski's chatty *Outside of a Dog: A Bibliomemoir,* which traces the influence of twenty-five books on the English bookseller-author's life. Each represents a risky appropriation of an exalted subject, and each fearlessly casts the memoirist's shadow over the text.

By contrast, Rebecca Mead's *My Life in Middlemarch* is a beguilingly straightforward, resolutely orthodox and unshowy account of the writer's lifelong admiration for George Eliot and for *Middlemarch: A Study of Provincial Life* (1874) in particular—the Victorian novel famously described by Virginia Woolf as "one of the few English novels written for grown-up people." There is no irony or Postmodernist posturing in Mead's forthright, unequivocal and unwavering endorsement of George Eliot as both a great novelist and a role model for bright, ambitious, provincially born girls like herself, eager to escape their intellectually impoverished hometowns—-"Oxford was my immediate goal, but anywhere would do." At the age of seventeen, when she first reads *Middlemarch,* Mead's identification with Eliot's nineteen-year-old heroine Dorothea Brooke is immediate, unqualified, and will last for decades:

> [Eliot's] theme—a young woman's desire for a substantial, rewarding, meaningful life—was certainly one with which Eliot had been long preoccupied. . . . And it's a theme that has made many young women, myself included, feel that *Middlemarch* is speaking directly to us. How on earth might one contain one's intolerable, overpowering, private yearnings? Where is a woman to put her energies? How is she to express her longings? What can she do to exercise her potential and

affect the lives of others? What, in the end, is a young woman
to do with herself?

Today, such earnest questions are more likely to be found in
young adult fiction for girls, but Victorian writers took seriously
their duties to "instruct and enlighten"; Mead notes how Eliot's
"guiding principle" was that of creating work that would "gladden
and chasten human hearts." Nor are these questions likely to have
been applicable to Victorian women of the working class: Dorothea
Brooke is the daughter of a well-to-do family, and financial concern
will not guide her life-choices. Instead, not unlike Henry James's
equally idealistic, naïve and well-to-do young heroine Isabel Archer
in *The Portrait of a Lady,* Dorothea makes a disastrous marriage
guided by bourgeois Victorian marital expectations: "The really de-
lightful marriage must be that where your husband was a sort of
father, and could teach you even Hebrew, if you wished it." Contemporary readers are likely to see the impossibly pompous, pedantic, and self-deluded pseudo-scholar Reverend Edward Casaubon
whom Dorothea marries as a caricature lacking even the subtlety
of the elderly professor in Chekhov's *Uncle Vanya*—another failed
pedant married to a young, beautiful and unhappy wife—but Dorothea is seduced by a kind of innocent self-aggrandizement in her
decision to marry the scholar who hopes to solve "The Key to All
Mythologies." Poor Casaubon! Eliot is unsparing of his pretensions
though the reverend's quixotic project resembles at least superficially James Frazer's *The Golden Bough* (1890). And contemporary readers are likely to feel, as feminists like Kate Millett have
observed, that Dorothea is a flawed heroine in that she chooses
marriage—and then remarriage—in place of a courageously ambitious life of her own or one that approximates the life of her
creator. It's as if Eliot did not dare, for all Dorothea's superiority,
conclude *Middlemarch* in a region beyond the "marriage plot"—the

formulaic conclusion to conventional romances for women which Eliot famously derided in her essay "Silly Novels by Lady Novelists." Mead notes the conjoining of "comedy" and "pathos" in Eliot's compromised world in which the novelist "makes Middlemarchers of us all."

Distilled from numerous biographies of Eliot including Rosemary Ashton's *George Eliot: A Life* and Rosemarie Bodenheimer's *The Real Life of Mary Ann Evans: George Eliot, Her Letters and Fiction*, enhanced by firsthand reports of travels to places where Eliot lived and worked, and suffused throughout with enormous sympathy for her subject, Rebecca Mead's' *My Life in Middlemarch* is an exemplary introduction to the work of George Eliot and a helpful and informed companion guide to *Middlemarch*. Its origins in what is suggested as a personal crisis on the author's part—"I wanted to recover the sense of intellectual and emotional immersion in books that I had had as a younger reader, before my attention was fractured by the exigencies of being a journalist"— connect with the perceived "natural history of yearning" which Mead sees in Eliot's work, as Mead's curiosity about the ill-fated friendship of Eliot and Herbert Spencer, the historical origins of the mismatched Dorothea and Edward Casaubon, and the relationship between Eliot and the infatuated Scots "fan" Alexander Main, who talked Eliot into allowing him to edit the cloyingly titled "Wise, Witty, and Tender Sayings, in Prose and Verse, Selected from the Works of George Eliot" (1873) provide emotional ballast. (Of the gushingly enthusiastic Scotsman, Mead says reprovingly: "Such an appeal to fiction—where do I see myself in here?—is not how a scholar reads, and it can be limiting in its solipsism.")

Mead is so reverent about her magisterial subject, and Eliot so solemn about the duties of the novelist to "enlarge sympathy" in her readers, it's a welcome surprise when the young Henry James arrives on the London scene to brashly proclaim: "(Eliot) is magnificently ugly—deliciously hideous. She has a low forehead, a dull grey eye, a vast pendulous nose, a huge mouth, full of uneven teeth and a chin and jaw-bone qui n'en finissent pas"; yet this first, crude impression is soon amended by the young American:

> Now in this vast ugliness resides a most powerful beauty which, in a very few minutes steals forth and charms the mind, so that you end as I ended, in falling in love with her. . . . You behold me literally in love with this great horse-faced bluestocking.

That the twenty-six-year-old Henry James was capable of such rhapsodic praise comes as something of a surprise for many of us, more familiar with the older, rather more circumlocutious Master.

The most evocative passages in *My Life in Middlemarch* are those in which the author hints at parallels with Eliot's domestic life as a loving stepmother (to longtime companion the critic George Henry Lewes's sons) in her own marriage to a man with children from a previous marriage: "From where I stand in the middle of my own home epic—my own mundane, grand, domestic drama, in which I attempt to live in sympathy with the family I have made—I now look upon the accomplishment of early-dawning, long-lasting love with something like awe." Not youthful romance but mature, abiding love amid the life of the everyday is Eliot's great subject: "*Middlemarch* gives my parents (who were married for sixty years) back to me." *My Life in Middlemarch* is a poignant testimony to the abiding power of fiction:

> I have grown up with George Eliot. I think that *Middlemarch* has disciplined my character. I know it has become part of my own experience and my own endurance. *Middlemarch* inspired me when I was young, and chafing to leave home, and now, in middle life, it suggests to me what home might mean, beyond a place to grow up and grow out of.

Yet it will strike some readers as debatable that Eliot is, as Mead states, "the great artist of disappointment"—rather more, Eliot strikes us as the great artist of bourgeois accommodation and compromise.

Admirable and endearing as *My Life in Middlemarch* is, there are virtually no surprises here; as Eliot's world view seems to confirm, for many, some approximation of their own, so too does *My Life in Middlemarch* confirm the general, uncontested view of this great Victorian novelist. There is something self-limiting if not solipsistic about focusing so narrowly upon a single novel through one's life, as if there were not countless other, perhaps more unsettling, more original, more turbulent, more astonishing, more aesthetically exciting and more intellectually challenging novels than *Middlemarch*— James Joyce's *Ulysses*, to name but one; Fyodor Dostoyevsky's *Crime and Punishment*, to name another. Does George Eliot, wonderful as she is, and certainly comforting in the unwavering sanity of her narrating voice, stir us to an awareness of the actual world with any of the authority of Franz Kafka? Isn't there a radiantly gifted Charles Dickens who transcends any of his Victorian contemporaries, including Eliot? Are not the radically experimental novels of Virginia Woolf more exciting, simply as aesthetic experiences? Like her genteel predecessor Jane Austen, George Eliot gives the impression of being utterly oblivious to the physical, physiological, sexual lives of women; far more insightful in the relations of the sexes is Thomas Hardy, not to mention the sexual visionary D. H. Lawrence. Clinging to *Middlemarch* isn't unlike clinging to an attractive but long-outdated map out of a stubborn predilection for the antique: an act of loyalty and fidelity, but perhaps disingenuous.

CHARLES DICKENS: A LIFE:
CLAIRE TOMALIN

The life of any man possessing great
gifts, would be a sad book to himself.

CHARLES DICKENS, 1869

Is Dickens the greatest of English novelists? Few would contest that
he is the most *English* of great English novelists, and that his most
accomplished novels, *Bleak House, Great Expectations, Little Dorrit, Dombey and Son, Our Mutual Friend, David Copperfield,* are
works of surpassing genius, thrumming with energy, imagination,
and something resembling white-hot inspiration; his gift for portraiture is arguably as great as Shakespeare's, and his versatility as
a prose stylist is dazzling, as in this famous opening of *Bleak House:*

London. Michaelmas Term lately over, and the Lord Chancel-
lor sitting in Lincoln's Inn Hall. Implacable November weather.
As much mud in the streets, as if the waters had but newly
retired from the face of the earth, and it would not be wonderful to meet a Megalosaurus, fifty feet long or so, waddling like
an elephantine lizard up Holborn Hill. Smoke lowering down
from chimney-pots, making a soft black drizzle, with flakes of
soot in it as big as full-grown snow-flakes—gone into mourn-

ing, one might imagine, for the death of the sun. . . . Fog everywhere. Fog up the river, where it flows among green aits
and meadows; fog down the river, where it rolls defiled among
the tiers of shipping, and the waterside pollutions of a great
(and dirty) city. Fog on the Essex marshes, fog on the Kentish
heights.

And, equally characteristic of Dickens, a chapter opening in the
lesser-regarded and uncompleted *The Mystery of Edwin Drood* in
which a natural observation acquires a portentous metaphoric significance:

Whosoever has observed that sedate and clerical bird, the rook,
may perhaps have noticed that when he wings his way home-
ward towards nightfall, in a sedate and clerical company, two
rooks will suddenly detach themselves from the rest, will re-
trace their flight for some distance, and will there poise and
linger; conveying to men the fancy that it is of some occult
importance to the body politic, that this artful couple should
pretend to have renounced connection with it.

Irresistibly the reader is drawn into the voice—exquisitely
lyric, yet with a profound melancholy beneath—of the child Philip
Pirrip—"Pip"—of *Great Expectations*:

Ours was the marsh country, down by the river, within, as the
river wound, twenty miles of the sea. My first most vivid and
broad impression of the identity of things, seems to me to have
been gained on a memorable raw afternoon towards evening.
At such a time I found out for certain, that this bleak place
overgrown with nettles was the churchyard; and that Philip
Pirrip, late of this parish, and also Georgiana wife of the above,
were dead and buried; and that Alexander, Bartholomew, Abra-

ham, Tobias, and Roger, infant children of the aforesaid, were also dead and buried; and that the dark flat wilderness beyond the churchyard, intersected with dykes and mounds and gates, with scattered cattle feeding on it, was the marshes; and that the low leaden line beyond, was the river; and that the distant savage lair from which the wind was rushing, was the sea; and that the small bundle of shivers growing afraid of it all and beginning to cry, was Pip.

Dickens is so brilliant a stylist, his vision of the world so idiosyncratic and yet so compelling, one might say that his subject is his unique rendering of his subject, in an echo of Mark Rothko's statement, "The subject of the painting is the painting"—except of course, Dickens's great subject was nothing so subjective nor so exclusionary, but as much of the world as he could render. If Dickens's prose fiction has "defects"—excesses of melodrama, sentimentality, contrived plots and manufactured happy endings—these are the defects of his era, which for all his greatness Dickens had not the rebellious spirit to resist; he was at heart a crowd-pleaser, a theatrical entertainer, with no interest in subverting the conventions of the novel as his great successors D. H. Lawrence, James Joyce, and Virginia Woolf would have; nor did he contemplate the subtle and ironic counterminings of human relations in the way of George Eliot and Thomas Hardy, who brought to the English novel an element of nuanced psychological realism not previously explored. Yet among English writers Dickens is, as he once called himself, part-jesting and part-serious, "the Inimitable."

EQUIPPED WITH PERIOD MAPS of Gad's Hill and Rochester (where Charles Dickens lived as a young child, from 1817 to 1822), Central London, and North London, an enormous cast of characters (relatives, friends, and acquaintances of Dickens spanning his lifetime), a generous gathering of photographs, and, in an appendix, a small selection of letters by Charles Dickens, Claire Tomalin's enormously ambitious biography of Charles Dickens begins *in medias res* in a dramatically rendered Prologue titled "The Inimitable: 1840." As in a Dickens novel, we are introduced to the twenty-eight-year-old householder as he takes his place on a jury convened by the Marylebone beadle to determine the probable guilt or innocence of a servant girl accused of infanticide. The narrative is present tense: the mood is suspenseful. We see the new young Marylebone resident Charles Dickens in his role as a responsible citizen, involving himself in the inquest with a hope of giving a "favorable turn to the case": "Dickens resolves to take on those who are ready to find her guilty of killing her child, and . . . he argues against them, so firmly and forcefully that he wins the argument." Not only does Dickens assure that the girl won't be vulnerable to a sentence of death, but he hires a lawyer for her and makes arrangements for her to be treated humanely as she awaits her trial in prison. In a narrative sleight of hand the biographer takes up Dickens's story from the perspective of a letter of his to a friend, telling of the troubling episode and its effect upon him. Tomalin notes that, twenty-three years later, the memory of the servant-girl charged with infanticide was still fresh to Dickens: "This is a very small episode in the life of Dickens, but it allows us to see him in action. . . . He is at his best as a man, determined in argument, generous in giving help . . . motivated by his profound sense that it was wrong that [the accused] should be victimized further."

What is impressive about Dickens's involvement in this case is that, in January 1840, the young author was leading a highly public, intense, and complicated life. In the past four years he'd written three commercially successful long novels (*The Pickwick Papers, Oliver Twist, The Old Curiosity Shop*) under the pressure of monthly installments; theatrical dramatizations were made of his work throughout England; "his success was unprecedented and thrilling"—but exhausting. Though he had no savings and lived from month to month, he'd already acquired a substantial household with a wife, young children, and family dependents as well as servants; he was an indefatigable giver of parties, an amateur actor, and a compulsive walker—his "expeditions" were often as many as twenty miles out of town. Here is a man over-committing himself to projects and responsibilities out of an insatiable interior restlessness that would leave him burnt out and exhausted in his fifty-ninth year. Like Honoré Balzac and Jack London, fellow obsessives and best-selling writers, Charles Dickens was a man of outsized energy, appetite, and ambition who in Tomalin's words "worked fast to give himself free time." It was said of him by an observer that he gave off "a sort of brilliance in the room, mysteriously dominant and formless. I remember how everyone lighted up when he entered."

The "most mysterious figure in Dickens's background"—in Tomalin's' words—is his father, John Dickens, who was twenty-seven when Dickens was born. The son of servants of a "grand household," John Dickens's ambitions lay beyond such service; at a young age, he secured a position in the Navy Pay Office in London that would pay him "a fortune compared with anything his (butler) father had ever earned." (Why was John Dickens so favored, and so careless with money through his life? Tomalin suggests that he may have been the illegitimate son of his father's employer or one of his gentlemen friends.) He owned a considerable library of "expensive" books, to which his son Charles would eventually be exposed; he was a "character"—"the model for his son's most famous character, Micawber." Through the decades Tomalin pursues the thread of John Dickens's relationship with his son who, as he ascends in fame, wealth, and influence, is yet burdened with his Micawber-father's feckless behavior and his confidence that Charles would pay his debts. (As indeed Charles paid his father's, his brother's, and eventually his numerous sons' debts, in exasperation, and repeatedly.)[1]

The great drama—which is to say, the abiding trauma—of Dick-

ens's childhood was his year-long stint in a rat-infested blacking factory near the Thames, when he was twelve years old, following the
arrest of John Dickens for debt in 1824 and his incarceration in
the debtors' prison at Marshalsea. Much has been written about
this long-secret episode in Dickens's life, including, most recently,
the heavily documented *Charles Dickens and the Blacking Factory*
by Michael Allen, a work of nearly three hundred pages of interest primarily to Dickens scholars, but very likely impenetrable to
Dickens readers in its concentration upon historical minutiae only
tenuously related to Dickens and his novels; see also *Dickens &
the Workhouse: Oliver Twist and the London Poor* by Ruth Richardson, for a more intimately evoked view of Dickens's childhood and
the New Poor Law of 1834 by which workhouses became "a sort
of prison system to punish (the poor)." For the child Dickens, the
shock of this change of fortune was all the more in that his seemingly loving parents so readily agreed to the enslavement of their
bright young son: "No one made any sign. My father and mother
were quite satisfied. They could hardly have been more so, if I'd
been twenty years of age, distinguished at a grammar-school, and
going to Cambridge." At the factory—which manufactured blacking for men's and boys' boots—Dickens had a relatively light job,
covering and labeling the pots of blacking; he was known there as
"the young gentlemen"; but the horror of his situation never altered:
"No words can express the secret agony of my soul . . . the sense I
had of being utterly neglected and hopeless; of the shame I felt in
my position. . . . My whole nature was penetrated with grief and
humiliation." And when Dickens was released from his servitude,
neither his father nor his mother ever spoke of the blacking factory
again: "From that hour . . . my father and mother have been stricken
dumb upon it. I have never heard the least allusion to it, however
far off or remote, from either of them." His parents' betrayal was
unforgivable, and his year in the factory humiliating, yet, twenty
years later, recounting the episode to his first biographer, his be-

loved friend John Forster, Dickens acknowledged that the blacking factory had given him the determination to persevere, with "a sense that everything was possible to the will that would make it so." And, of course, servitude as a child-worker would provide the author with both material and a sharply informed perspective as well as a natural empathy for the enslaved working poor of all ages, that remained with Dickens through his life.

Surprisingly, Dickens wasn't an outstanding student at even the mediocre Wellington House Academy to which his parents eventually sent him; when his father couldn't any longer pay his tuition, Dickens's formal education ended at fifteen, at which time he began to be a "serious smoker"—an addiction that would grip Dickens through his life, and was very likely a factor in his premature death. Dickens's first employment was in a law office; his early interest in the law soon dissipated, as he began to write and to publish— initially, as an ecclesiastical reporter, then as reporter at the *Morning Chronicle,* where the blithely composed sketches of London scenes by "Boz" began to appear, and to attract a wide readership. Soon, the energetic young writer was covering politics and elections for · the newspaper, even as he was assembling *Sketches by Boz* (1836), and publishing the *Pickwick Papers* in monthly installments, which quickly became a best seller. He was soon to become involved with the theater and with performing as an amateur actor. He turned down several invitations to stand for Parliament.

By this time Dickens had fallen in love desperately, and been rejected, by an "enchantingly pretty" young woman named Maria Beadnell; he was eighteen, and Maria twenty; his intense romantic feeling for Maria wasn't requited, and Dickens was, by his account, at the time and many years later, devastated. The "wasted tenderness" of those hard years caused him to suppress emotion, he said, "which I know is no part of my original nature, but which makes me chary of showing my affections, even to my children." Maria Beadnell is immortalized in two portraits in Dickens's fiction: as the pretty feather-headed Dora of *David Copperfield* (1850), who dies young; and the fat, fatuous, garrulous middle-aged Flora Finching of *Little Dorrit* (1857).[2]

Despite the cruelty of his parents and his father's chronic irresponsibility, like any Victorian Dickens seems to have conceived of family life as an ideal. Still besotted with Maria Beadnell, he quickly decided to marry Catherine Hogarth, the daughter of his newspaper employer, within six months of meeting her in 1835, an impulsive decision which he came to regard as "the worst decision" of his life. Though Dickens would impregnate Catherine more than ten times, resulting in a daunting number of children both loved and not-so-loved by their father, in a way that strikes the contemporary reader as outrageously and obtusely sexist Dickens seems to have blamed his wife for their numerous progeny, as if this plain, placid, passive woman had been a siren to tempt her husband into sexual intercourse against his will.[3] Casually and belatedly, after having sired ten children, Dickens remarked that he had not wanted "more than three children." Not so casually, and cruelly, in the final year of his life he would speak and write of his ill-suited marriage as a "skeleton in the closet"; luckless Catherine, cast aside by her husband when, at the age of forty-six, he fell in love with the eighteen-year-old actress Ellen Ternan, was transformed in Dickens's imagination into that most horrific of Victorian villainesses—the unmotherly mother: "She does not—and she never did—care for the children; and the children do not—and they never did—care for her. . . . I want to forgive and forget her." ["A Selection of Letters," in Tomalin, under the title "A Skeleton in a Closet"] Yet Dickens never divorced Catherine, for divorce would have been a scandal for one of Dickens's presumed moral stature; pragmatically, if perhaps hypocritically, he lived with Nelly Ternan until his death, in quasi-secret locations, sometimes under the name "Charles Tringham." But amid the myriad entanglements of his life Dickens never ceased writing—not only his fiction but his extraordinary letters, estimated to be beyond fourteen thousand[4]—and, with ever-increasing compulsion in the last decade of his life, giving "paid readings" of his work to large, adoring audiences in both the U.K. and in the United States.

The vicissitudes of Dickens's visits to the United States are tracked in detail in Tomalin's biography, suggesting a curious admixture of innocent authorly vanity, a shrewd desire to make as much money as possible, and what comes to seem to the reader a malignant, ever-metastasizing desire for self-destruction. Dickens's delight in his massive and uncritical audiences shifts by degrees to an addiction to public performing; like Mark Twain, Dickens quickly came to see that public performance paid more than writing, and was much easier, at least in the short run. Dickens's greed for the immediate gratification of public performing is both tonic and masochistic; consumed by vanity, the celebrated writer is consuming his very self. In 1868 the exhausted author would write triumphantly in a letter to one of his daughters:

> I not only read last Friday, when I was doubtful of being able to do so, but read as I never did before, and astonished the audience quite as much as myself. You never saw or heard such a scene of excitement.

One must not think that Dickens was reading "authentic" Dickens to these mass audiences. Instead, yielding to the predilection for emotional hysteria among his fans, Dickens prepared "scripts" showcasing his and his audience's favorite characters—Micawber, Dora, Little Em'ly, Steerforth, Mrs. Gamp, Bill Sikes and his victim Nancy; half of the readings were from inferior Christmas stories, though *A Christmas Carol* was always a favorite. (Dickens read the lurid murder of Nancy by Sikes twenty-eight times between January 1869 and March 1870, "exciting and horrifying his audiences.") In America, Henry James, possibly rebuked by the sheer size and volume of the rival-novelist's crowds, spoke of Dickens's "hard charmless readings"; decades later Edmund Wilson summed up the phenomenon succinctly: "Dickens had a strain of the ham in him, and in the desperation of his later life, he gave in to the old ham and let him rip."

When, in 1842, the much-acclaimed author of *Oliver Twist, Nicholas Nickleby* (1839), *The Old Curiosity Shop* (1841) and *Barnaby Rudge* (1841) went to America for the first time, though lionized by the gentry and swooned-over by audiences—("People *eat* him here," an observer remarked)—he found America, on the whole, disappointing; and American publishers, who had been pirating his novels for years with impunity, intransigent on the matter of honoring international copyright. Despite ecstatic receptions in Boston and New York City (where a "Boz Ball" with some three thousand paying guests was arranged to celebrate Dickens like visiting royalty as Dickens was presented on the arm of a U.S. army general in full-dress uniform and Catherine was escorted by the mayor of the city in a grand march twice around the ballroom), Dickens was not impressed with the United States: he was repelled by the slave state of Virginia, and thought the Mississippi River "the beastliest river in the world"; Ohio was a region of "invariably morose, sullen, clownish, and repulsive (individuals) . . . destitute of humor, vivacity, or the capacity of enjoyment." He wrote to his friend John Forster, "I don't like the country. I would not live here, on any consideration. It goes against the grain with me. I think it is impossible, utterly impossible, for any Englishman to live here, and be happy." He found here "follies, vices, disappointments." Nor was Toronto, Ontario, any improvement, for there "the wild and rabid toryism . . . is . . . *appalling.*" Unexpectedly, Dickens thought Cincinnati a "very beautiful" city —unfortunately, populated by "bores." Niagara Falls evoked rhapsodic emotions, perhaps predictably: "It would be hard for a man to stand nearer to God than he does there." But there was nothing romantic about the continued defiance of American publishers, who not only refused to pay the author royalties for the many thousands of his books which they sold, but took offense that the author should expect any recompense at all. America was "a low, coarse, and mean Nation driven by a herd of rascals. Pah! I never knew what it was to feel disgust and contempt, 'till I travelled in America." (Tomalin notes that international copyright was not sorted out until 1891, long after Dickens's death.) Dickens's *American Notes* appeared soon after the trip, a haphazard assemblage of sardonic observations and unmediated rancor—as Edgar Allan Poe called it, "One of the most suicidal productions, ever deliberately published by an author, who had the least reputation to lose."

Yet, Dickens persevered. Within the span of seventeen years, even as his personal life threatened to disintegrate, and public readings took up more and more of his time and energy, he would write his inimitable masterworks: *Dombey and Son* (1848), *David Copperfield* (1850), *Bleak House* (1853), *Hard Times* (1854), *Little Dorrit* (1857), *A Tale of Two Cities* (1859), *Great Expectations* (1861), *Our Mutual Friend* (1865). His was a frantic and yet fecund energy. "If I couldn't walk fast and far, I should just explode and perish."

BIOGRAPHY IS A LITERARY CRAFT that, in the hands of gifted practitioners, rises to the level of art. Yet even its most exemplary practitioners are frequently left behind, like hunters on the trail of elusive prey, in the tracking of genius. Claire Tomalin's biography is likely to be one of the definitive Dickens biographies in its seamless application of "the life" to "the art"—and what a perilous balancing act it is, in which, just barely, Dickens's art isn't lost amid a smothering welter of facts. "This may be more detail than one normally wants about anyone's life," Tomalin acknowledges. And indeed there is an inordinate amount of detail in this biography, particularly in regard to Dickens's frantically busy social life, his scattered interests, and grinding public career. (How many reading tours Dickens embarked

upon before, finally, his "last farewell to the London reading public" in 1870! The reader begins to be as fatigued as Dickens.) The
problem with such assiduously recorded lives of great artists is that
one is drawn to an interest in the artist's life because of his or her
accomplishments, primarily; the "life" in itself is of interest as it il-
luminates the work, but if the often banal details of the life detract
from the work, the worth to the biography is questionable. Even an
ordinary life, cataloged in every detail, will bloat to Brobdingnagian
girth, distorting the human countenance. Only a very few encyclopedic biographers—Richard Ellmann most illustriously, in his
massive yet never dull biographies of James Joyce and Oscar Wilde
in particular—transcend the weight of their material, and make
of it an intellectual entertainment commensurate with its subject.
Admirable as it is, warmly sympathetic and often eloquent, Tomalin's *Charles Dickens* frequently moves like a vehicle with concrete
wheels set beside, for instance, the rapid, deft, conversational and
confiding short life *Charles Dickens* (2002) by the novelist Jane Smiley. There is nothing here resembling the flamboyant idiosyncrasies
of the controversial thousand-page Dickens biography by Peter Ackroyd (1991), with its many risks and rewards, which must squat, like
the proverbial eight-hundred-pound gorilla, in the peripheral vision
of subsequent Dickens biographers. (Tomalin can bring herself to
reference Ackroyd only once, as if dutifully: Ackroyd, alone of contemporary biographers, believes that the highly fraught relationship
between Dickens and Ellen Ternan was "never consummated.") The
most engaging writing in Tomalin's biography is inspired by a critical
appreciation of Dickens's novels, as one might expect: *Bleak House*
("Dickens's imagination, always bold, now offers scenes as odd and
inspired as Shakespeare's"), *David Copperfield* ("a masterpiece built
on Dickens's ability to dig into his own experience, transform it,
and give it the power of myth"), *Great Expectations* ("a great book,
delicate and frightening, funny, sorrowful, mysterious"), *The Mystery of Edwin Drood* ("the achievement of a man who is dying and

refusing to die, who would not allow failing powers to keep him from exerting his imagination, or to prevent him from writing: and as such it is an astonishing and heroic enterprise"). And Tomalin is very convincing in her discussion of the abiding secret of Dickens's later life—his relationship with the ex-actress Ellen Ternan, about whom, in 1990, Tomalin devoted a book aptly titled *The Invisible Woman*.

Dickens's end, though protracted, and painful to contemplate, comes with startling abruptness, on June 8, 1870, in his home in Gad's Hill—(not in the residence he shared with Ellen Ternan):

> He sat down and [Georginia Hogarth] asked him if he felt ill and he replied, "Yes, very ill; I have been very ill for the last hour." On her saying that she would send for a doctor, he said no, he would go on with the dinner, and go afterwards to London. He made an effort to struggle against the fit that was coming on him. . . . In every version she gave their final exchange, her "Come and lie down," and his reply, "Yes, on the ground."

"He left a trail like a meteor," Tomlin says, "and everyone finds their own version of Charles Dickens." How Tomalin's version will compare, with the passage of time, with such previous "definitive" biographies as those by Peter Ackroyd, Michael Slater (2009), and Robert Douglas-Fairhurst (2011), all of which spring from John Forster's renowned three-volume biography of Dickens (1872, 1873, 1874) is an open and intriguing question.

NOTES

1. And yet, Dickens's fabled generosity could burn out, as in this startling outburst in a letter of 1870, the year of his death, regarding the debts of his son Sydney, which he was obliged to pay: "I fear Sydney is much too far gone for recovery, and I begin to wish that he were honestly dead."

2. Unwisely, yet with characteristic emotional abandon, in 1855 Dickens arranged for a romantic re-encounter with Maria Beadnell, now Mrs. Winters, who had written to him, and drew from him an impassioned response—"It is a matter of perfect certainty to me that I began to fight my way out of poverty and obscurity, with one perpetual idea of you" [in "A Selection of Letters," appendix, under the title "Heartache Again"]. At their meeting, Dickens was astounded by the alteration of his old love, for here was a very middle-aged, heavyset, toothless and vacuous female scarcely different in girth and temperament from his own wife Catherine. It isn't so much revenge upon poor Maria for having so crushed the author's romantic delusion but a droll sort of self-mockery in Dickens's portrait of Flora Finching of *Little Dorrit*.

3. Though his experience with Maria Beadnell was a rebuke to his romantic fantasies, Dickens remained susceptible to the charms of "innocent"—(that is, virginal)—young women, through his life. Shortly after his marriage to the ever-pregnant Catherine, Dickens seems to have been smitten with Catherine's younger sister Mary, who died when she was seventeen of a mysterious collapse, and left Dickens bereft: "Thank God she died in my arms, and the very last words she uttered were of me." (Dickens removed a ring from the dead girl's finger and wore it for the remainder of his life. He declared his wish to be buried in Mary's grave, a wish that would prove impractical, in time.) Tomalin is very funny, in writing of Dickens's fantastical romanticizing of his young sister-in-law when he visited Niagara Falls several years later, weirdly imagining that "the dear girl whose ashes lie in Kensal-green" had accompanied him and Catherine to such a wildly beautiful place: "But she has been here many times, I doubt not, since her sweet face faded from my earthly sight." The exasperated biographer appeals to us: "Did he actually believe (that Mary's) spirit wandered the world visiting selected beauty spots?" and concluding that, however practical-minded Dickens was in life, he allowed himself to wander into "feeble fancies" when he approached spiritual matters. Another abiding, if seemingly undeclared love of Dickens's life was another sister-in-law, Georgiana, who came to live with Dickens and Catherine at the age of fifteen, as a sort of genteel au pair, eventually housekeeper, and never left; "Georgy" adored her celebrity brother-in-law and seems to have

acted as his public companion upon numerous occasions, when poor pregnant Catherine was at home with the brood of Dickens children that soon came to include "five more unwanted sons."

4. Drawn from the twelve-volume British Academy Pilgrim Edition of more than 14,000 letters of Dickens addressed to 2,500 known correspondents, the 450 included in *The Selected Letters of Charles Dickens* edited by Jenny Hartley are more revealing and more intimate than any biography as a record, in the editor's words, not so much of the "inner Dickens" as of the "Dickens in motion."

BOOKS CITED IN THIS REVIEW:

Charles Dickens and the Blacking Factory
By Michael Allen

*Dickens & The Workhouse: Oliver Twist
and the London Poor*
By Ruth Richardson

Charles Dickens: A Life
By Jane Smiley

The Selected Letters of Charles Dickens
Edited by Jenny Hartley

"THE KING OF WEIRD":
H. P. LOVECRAFT

"Though in many of its aspects this visible world seems formed in love, the invisible spheres were formed in fright."
Herman Melville, *Moby-Dick*

1.

How mysterious, how unknowable and infinitely beyond their control must have seemed the vast wilderness of the New World to the seventeenth-century Puritan settlers! The inscrutable silence of Nature—the tragic ambiguity of human nature with its predilection for what Christians call "original sin," inherited from our first parents Adam and Eve. When Nature is so vast, man's need for control—for "settling" the wilderness—becomes obsessive. And how powerful the temptation to project mankind's divided self onto the very silence of Nature.

It was the intention of those English Protestants known as Puritans to "purify" the Church of England by eradicating everything in the Church that seemed to have no Biblical justification. The more radical Puritans, "Separatists" and eventually "Pilgrims," settled Plymouth, Massachusetts, in the 1620s; others who followed in subsequent years were less zealous about defining themselves as "Separatists." Yet all were characterized by the intransigence of their faith, their fierce sense of moral rectitude and self-righteousness. The intolerant theology of the New England Puritans could not have failed to breed paranoia, if not madness, in the sensitive among them. Consider, for instance, the Covenant of Grace, which taught that only those men and women upon whom God sheds His grace are saved, because this allows them to believe in Christ; those excluded from God's grace lack the power to believe in a Savior, thus are not only not saved, but also damned. *We never had a chance!* those so excluded might cry out of the bowels of Hell. *We were doomed from the start.* The extreme gothic sensibility springs from such paradoxes: that the loving, paternal God and His son Jesus are nonetheless willful tyrants; "good" is inextricably bound up with the capacity to punish; one may wish to believe oneself free but in fact all human activities are determined, from the perspective of the deity, long before one's birth.

It comes as no surprise, then, that the very titles of celebrated Puritan works of the seventeenth and early eighteenth centuries strike a chord of anxiety. *The Spiritual Conflict, The Holy War, Day of Doom, Thirsty Sinner, Groans of the Damned, The Wonders of the Invisible World, Man Knows Not His Time, Repentant Sinners and Their Ministers, Memorable Providences Relating to Witchcraft and Possessions*—these might be the titles of lurid works of gothic fiction, not didactic sermons, prose pieces, and poetry. The great Puritan poet Edward Taylor was also a minister; much of Taylor's subtle, intricately wrought metaphysical verse dwells upon God's love and terror, and man's insignificance in the face of God's omnipotence: "My will is your Design." Here is the gothic predilection for investing all things, even the most seemingly innocuous (weather, insects), with cosmological meaning. Is there nothing in the gothic imagination that can mean simply—"nothing"?"

The first American novelist of substance, Charles Brockden Brown, was born of a Philadelphia Quaker family; but his major novel *Wieland; or The Transformation* (1798) is suffused with the spirit of Puritan paranoia—"God is the object of my supreme passion," the fanatical Wieland declares. Indeed, the very concept of rational self-determinism is challenged by this dark fantasy of domestic violence. The novel is a nightmare expression of the fulfillment of repressed desire, anticipating Edgar Allan Poe's similarly claustrophobic tales of the grotesque. Wieland is a disciple of the Enlightenment who is nonetheless driven mad by "voices" urging him to destruction.

Such assaults upon individual autonomy and identity characterize the writings of Washington Irving, Nathaniel Hawthorne, Edgar Allan Poe, Charlotte Perkins Gilman, Ambrose Bierce, H. P. Lovecraft, and more recent twentieth-century writers for whom the "supernatural" and the malevolent "unconscious" have fused. Even in the more benign "enchanted region" of Washington Irving's Sleepy Hollow (of *The Sketch Book,* 1820), an ordinary, decent man like Ichabod Crane is subjected to an ordeal of psychic breakdown.

In the work of our premier American gothicist, Edgar Allan Poe, from whose *Tales of the Grotesque and Arabesque* (1840) so much of twentieth-century horror and detective fiction springs, there are no fully realized female characters, indeed no fully realized characters at all; but the female is likely to be the obsessive object of desire, and her premature death, as in "The Fall of the House of Usher," "Ligeia," and "The Black Cat," is likely to be the precipitating factor. "The Black Cat" presents a madman's voice with such mounting plausibility that the reader almost—*almost*—identifies with his unmotivated and seemingly unresisted acts of insane violence against the affectionate black cat Pluto, and eventually his own wife. Like "The Tell-Tale Heart," with which it bears an obvious kinship, "The Black Cat" explores from within a burgeoning, blossoming evil; an evil exacerbated by alcohol, yet clearly a congenital evil unprovoked by the behavior of others.

The canonical writers of the gothic-grotesque were all born, fittingly, in the nineteenth century. As realism began to dominate prose fiction in the late nineteenth century in Europe and America, along with the more radical, more grindingly materialist school of "naturalism" derived from Flaubert and Zola, educated readers turned to the work of such writers as Stephen Crane, Frank Norris, Jack London, Hamlin Garland, and Theodore Dreiser. In the toughly Darwinian masculine-urban worlds of such writers, with their exposure of social and political corruption and their frank depiction of adult sexual relations, there would seem to have been no place, still less sympathy, for the introspective, brooding idiosyncrasies and metonymic strategies of the gothic imagination.

2.

"The most merciful thing in the world . . . is the inability of the human mind to correlate all its contents. We live on a placid island of ignorance in the midst of black seas of infinity, and it was not meant that we should voyage far."

> H. P. Lovecraft, "The Call of Cthulhu"

In writers like Henry James and Edith Wharton who experimented with gothic forms of fiction, the gothic tale may compensate for a conventional, restrictive life; in others, notably Edgar Allan Poe and H. P. Lovecraft, the gothic tale would seem to be a form of psychic autobiography.

The American writer of the twentieth century most frequently compared with Poe, in the quality of his art (bizarre, brilliant, inspired, and original, yet frequently hackneyed, derivative, and repetitive), its thematic preoccupations (the obsessive depiction of psychic disintegration in the face of cosmic horror perceived as "truth"), and its critical and commercial reception during the writer's truncated lifetime (dismal), is H. P. Lovecraft of Providence, Rhode Island (1890–1937). Like Poe, Lovecraft created a small body of work carved by monomaniacal passion out of a gothic tradition that had already become ossified in the mid-nineteenth century. Like Poe, though more systematically than Poe, Lovecraft set forth an aesthetics of the art to which, by temperament and family history, he was fated. (Lovecraft's frequently updated essay "Supernatural Horror in Literature" [1927] is a pioneering effort in tracing the history of the gothic sensibility from Ann Radcliffe, Hugh Walpole, "Monk" Lewis, and Charles Maturin through Emily Brontë, Hawthorne, Poe, and Lovecraft's contemporaries Algernon Blackwood, Arthur Machen, Lord Dunsany, M. R. James and others.) Both tried to sell their writing and editing skills in a debased and demeaning marketplace, with little financial reward, burning themselves out in the process. Both were beset by dreams, nightmares, "visions." Both entered upon brief, disastrous marriages (though there are bleakly comical overtones to Lovecraft's marriage to a woman seven years his elder). Both left no heirs. Both died prematurely, Poe at forty, Lovecraft at forty-six, having egregiously mistreated their bodies.

Though Poe is far more renowned than Lovecraft, indeed, and ironically, now a canonical figure in American literature—he who died penniless and scorned!—both writers have had an incalculable influence on succeeding generations of writers of horror fiction, and Lovecraft is arguably the more beloved by contemporary gothic aficionados.[1] Poe is credited with the invention of the "mystery-detective" story and with the perfection of a certain species of ahistoric, claustrophobic, and boldly surreal monologue (of which "The Tell-Tale Heart" is the masterwork); Lovecraft with the fusion of the gothic tale and what would come to be defined as "science fiction," and with the development of a species of horror fantasy set in meticulously described, historically grounded places (predominantly, in Lovecraft, Providence, Rhode Island, Salem, Massachusetts, and a region in northern central Massachusetts to which he has given the name "the Miskatonic Valley"), in which a seemingly normal, intelligent scholar or professor, usually a celibate bachelor, pursues a mystery it would be wiser for him to flee. The remarkably detailed, intensely imagined "The Dreams in the Witch-House" (set in "Arkham"/Salem), "The Colour Out of Space" (set in the "blasted heath" west of "Arkham"), and "The Shadow over Innsmouth" (set in "Innsmouth"/Newburyport, Massachusetts) are of this type, in which place itself would seem to generate horror.

Where Poe's settings are minimally if hysterically depicted, like brushstrokes laid on with a trowel, Lovecraft's most evocative stories are set in regions that seem "real" enough at the outset, like photographs just perceptibly blurred. Lovecraft's mystical identification with his settings in rural Massachusetts and colonial-antiquarian towns like Salem, Marblehead, and Providence, Rhode Island, suggests a mock Transcendentalism in which "spirit" resides everywhere except possibly in human beings.

> To all intents and purposes I am more naturally isolated from mankind than Nathaniel Hawthorne himself, who dwelt alone in the midst of crowds. . . . The people of a place matter absolutely nothing to me except as components of the general landscape and scenery. . . . My life lies not in among people but among *scenes*—my local affections are not personal, but topographical and architectural. . . . It is *New England I must have*—in some form or other. Providence is part of me—I am Providence.
>
> *From a letter of 1926*

In the celebrated opening of "The Picture in the House" (1920), the nature of Lovecraft's infatuation with landscape is vividly rendered:

> Searchers after horror haunt strange, far places. For them are the catacombs of Ptolemais, and the carven mausolea of the nightmare countries. They climb to the moonlit towers of ru-

ined Rhine castles, and falter down cobwebbed steps beneath the scattered stones of forgotten cities in Asia. The haunted wood and desolate mountain are their shrines. . . . But the true epicure in the terrible, to whom a new thrill of unutterable ghastliness is the chief end and justification of existence, esteems most of all the ancient, lonely farmhouses of backwoods New England; for there the dark elements of strength, solitude, grotesqueness, and ignorance combine to form the perfection of the hideous.

In Lovecraft, as frequently in Poe, style and self-parody are indistinguishable.

3.

Howard Phillips Lovecraft, who boasted of having descended from "unmixed English gentry," was the only son of an ill-fated marriage between a traveling salesman for a Providence silversmith company and the daughter of a well-to-do Providence businessman. His father began to exhibit symptoms of dementia, paranoia, mania, and depression when Lovecraft was two years old; a victim of untreated syphilis, he died in an insane asylum when Lovecraft was seven. Lovecraft's mother was an emotionally unstable person who seems to have been, according to biographers, both abnormally attached to her only child and critical of him; her fear of change, and of the world beyond her household, was extreme.

Already in early childhood, Lovecraft suffered from violent dreams and nightmares; he called these afflictions, to which he would give minute expression in his tales, the "night-gaunts." Many of Lovecraft's stories read like pitilessly transcribed dreams. Of these "The Dreams in the Witch-House" is the most elaborate account of a descent into hallucinatory madness. In this nightmare fantasy, a student of mathematics and folklore rents a room once inhabited by a witch fleeing the Salem Gaol in 1692, and is sub-sequently destroyed by demonic forces—his heart literally eaten out by a gigantic species of rat. (Lovecraft seems to have taken for granted that Salem "witches" existed, not considering whether they were perhaps victims of others' malevolent misuse of power.)

Like Poe, Lovecraft focuses upon interiors, the interior of the soul. His subject is the continuous assault on the person of un-conscious forces of dissolution, disintegration; the collapse of sanity beneath the weight of chaos; the triumph of mindless entities like the subterranean deities Azathoth and Nyarlathotep and the "mad faceless god [who] howls blindly in the darkness to the piping of two amorphous idiot flute-players" ("The Rats in the Walls"). It was Lovecraft's observation that the successful gothic tale replicates the paralysis and horror of a certain kind of dream:

> I believe that—because of the foundation of most weird con-cepts in dream-phenomena—the best weird tales are those in which the narrator or central figure remains (as in actual dreams) largely passive, & witnesses or experiences a stream of bizarre events which . . . flows past him, just touches him, or engulfs him utterly.
>
> *From a letter of 1936*

Yet this matter-of-fact statement gives no idea of the remarkable simulacra Lovecraft frequently evokes in his dreamscapes, which linger in the reader's visual memory like those horrific yet somehow natural-seeming monsters of Hieronymus Bosch.

Bravely Lovecraft claimed that his dreams were not personal but "cosmic," just as his tales drew upon no personal experience. Again like Poe, Lovecraft had a mind too pure to be violated by any idea of mere mundane reality.

S. T. Joshi's meticulously researched *H.P. Lovecraft: A Life* sug-gests that Lovecraft, for all his championing of independent think-

ing, was much in thrall to his widowed, ailing mother Susie, who
seems to have made of her son's personal appearance (tall, gaunt,
with a long, prognathous jaw and frequently blemished skin) an image of moral degeneracy. A neighbor recounts that "Mrs. Lovecraft
talked continuously of her son who was so hideous that he hid from
everyone and did not like to walk upon the streets where people
would gaze at him," a statement the neighbor considered "exagger-
ated." (Mrs. Lovecraft was believed not to have been told the cause
of her husband's syphilitic dementia and death, and associated
Lovecraft with his father. Yet it must have been she who encouraged her son to wear his deceased father's clothes as a young man.)
It would not be until Mrs. Lovecraft died while institutionalized,
when Lovecraft was thirty-one years old, that he would try to free
himself, at least sporadically, from his housebound, claustrophobic
existence.

Yet no fathers or mothers appear in Lovecraft's work, excepting
the comically grotesque Mr. Whately of "The Dunwich Horror," who
consorts with demonic forces and arranges for his daughter to mate
with a creature named Yog-Sothoth; virtually no women appear in
the work, for to Lovecraft, the most asexual of men, for whom Eros
manifested itself primarily in landscape and architecture, "male"
and "female" have no more vital relationship with each other than
atoms. In the lushly overwritten "The Thing on the Doorstep," an
unfortunate marriage between a precocious scholar-poet and a
young woman with mysterious hypnotic powers is revealed to be, in
fact, a marriage between the scholar-poet and the young woman's
deceased father, who had seized demonic possession of her body
at the time of his death, and manages at last to seize possession of
the scholar-poet's body as well. What seems initially to be a tale of
vampiristic erotic obsession turns out very differently indeed.

Is Lovecraft's life a tragedy of a stunted, broken-off personality,
severely traumatized in childhood, and never to "mature," or is there
a poignant triumph of a kind in the way in which the aggrieved,

terror-ized child refashions himself, through countless nocturnal-insomniac sessions of writing, into a purely cerebral being?

> I could not write about "ordinary people" because I am not in the least interested in them. Without interest there can be no art. Man's relations to man do not captivate my fancy. It is man's relations to the cosmos—to the unknown—which alone arouses in me the spark of creative imagination. The humanocentric pose is impossible to me, for I cannot acquire the primitive myopia which magnifies the earth and ignores the background.
>
> *From a letter of 1921*

This is the resolute, defiant note so frequently struck in the American visionary imagination: the very voice, surely, of Edgar Allen Poe and Emerson; the voice we might well imagine of Hawthorne, Emily Dickinson, even the exuberant Walt Whitman ("one of the roughs, a kosmos"). For how can the merely personal be of galvanizing interest to the *imagination*?

The fascination for the historical past we might interpret, in Lovecraft, as a profound wish that the present might not yet have happened, if the clock and calendar be turned back far enough. To love the past, to extol the past, to yearn in some way to inhabit the past is surely to misread the past, purposefully or otherwise; above all, it is to select from the past only those aspects that accommodate a self-protective and nourishing fantasy. What is "past" tempts us to reconstruct a world rather like a walled city, finite and contained and in the most literal sense predictable. For the writer, the (selected, edited) "past" is in itself a form of fiction, though the writer will set as his idealized task its "coming to life" and credulous readers will respond to its "authenticity."

Already as a child of eight, by his own account, Lovecraft perceived time as "some especial enemy of mine." Repeatedly he speaks of his art as a "defeat of time"; as an adult he was irresistibly drawn to those city- and landscapes (particularly Quebec City) in which the past seems to coexist, dreamlike, with the present. The "continuity from the past" was, for Lovecraft, the defeat of time. Yet in many Lovecraft tales the intellectual protagonist is lured to his doom or disintegration by the prospect of transcending time, by attempting a Faustian "entry to many unknown and incomprehensible realms of additional or indefinitely multiplied dimensions—be they within or outside the given space-time continuum"—as in "The Dreams in the Witch-House," where the young protagonist meets his grisly fate. (Despite Lovecraft's ardent proselytizing for the weird fiction of Lord Dunsany, Algernon Blackwood, Arthur Machen, and Ambrose Bierce, he acknowledged Proust as the greatest contemporary writer, for the subtlety and beauty of his treatment of time.)

Such extended adventures as "The Shadow Out of Time" and the novella-length "At the Mountains of Madness" collapse millennia within the cataclysmic experience of individuals whose lives intersect with those of the Great Old Ones, alien creatures of immense intelligence from a distant galaxy, until now unknown to *Homo sapiens.* In the former, a professor at Miskatonic University deduces that he has been kidnapped psychically by aliens for purposes of research and hurtled back into prehistory; while in the latter story the surviving members of an expedition to Antarctica, fellow faculty members of Miskatonic, discover the mummified bodies of these fantastical aliens as well as the awesome ruins of their lost civilization, which would seem to have been patterned by Lovecraft on ancient Egypt. "The Rats in the Walls," Lovecraft's most frequently reprinted tale, ironically reverses the much-lauded progress of *Homo sapiens,* as the civilized American hero helplessly descends the evolutionary ladder to become, like his despised ancestors, a cannibal.

In attempting to defeat time, such protagonists are defeated by

it; they may discover to their horror, or mad glee, that they are in fact related genetically ("by blood") to monster-ancestors and that these ancestors live in them. The ponderous, meandering, yet fascinating long story "The Shadow over Innsmouth" ends with the student-hero turning by degrees into a subhuman Innsmouth being (a sort of humanoid fish, or fishy humanoid), as one might succumb to madness. Investigating the ancient seaport of Innsmouth, though physically repelled by its inhabitants, the young hero ironically turns into one of them, and comes to rejoice in his subhumanity:

> I shall plan my cousin's escape from the Canton madhouse, and together we shall go to marvel-shadowed Innsmouth. We shall swim out to the brooding reef in the sea and dive down through the black abysses . . . and in that lair of the Deep Ones we shall dwell amidst wonder and glory forever.

In such a reversal, the tension of resisting sadness is abruptly eased; the dreaded "night-gaunts" may be embraced like literal kin. To expunge the drama of having witnessed a parent's descent into madness one may join the madness oneself. And perhaps time can only be "defeated" by madness.

Unlike Poe's fevered tales, which appear unrelated to one another, isolated in essential ways, Lovecraft's mature work, the cycle of horror/fiction tales to which his disciples have given the title the "Cthulhu Mythos," springs from a common source of invented legend. Lovecraft was one of those accursed, or blessed, writers who ceaselessly work and rework a small nuclei of scenarios, as if to force a mastery over the unconscious compulsions that guide them; such "mastery" for the writer may exist during the composition of the work, but fades immediately afterward, so that a new work, a new effort of organization and control, must be undertaken.

As a child, according to his own account, Lovecraft repudiated his mother's family's Baptist faith. For Lovecraft, who was proud of his life-long atheism, the Cthulhu Mythos was an "anti-mythology"; an ironic inversion of traditional religious faith. It constitutes an elaborate, detailed working-out of an early recurring fantasy of Lovecraft's that an entire alien civilization lurks on the underside of the known world; as a "night-gaunt" may lurk beneath a child's bed in the darkness, or as mankind's tragically divided nature may lurk beneath civilization's veneer. (Lovecraft was writing during and after World War I.) In the Cthulhu Mythos, there are no "gods" but only displaced extraterrestrial beings, the Great Old Ones, who journeyed to Earth many millions of years ago, bringing with them, disastrously, their slaves, called "shoggoths," protoplasmic creatures that gradually overpower and defeat their masters. Deluded human beings mistake the Great Old Ones and their descendants for gods, worshiping them out of ignorance.

Among the sacred (and "forbidden") texts that chronicle the exhaustively protracted history of the Great Old Ones is the *Necronomicon* of the Arab Abdul Alhazred, so frequently cited in Lovecraft that the title becomes a sort of running joke. One can see why Jorge Luis Borges was drawn to Lovecraft and inspired, in such Lovecraftian tales as "Tlön, Uqbar, Orbis, Tertius," to create for his own purposes a fictitious library of mythical, cross-referenced, ancient cabbalistic texts.

In the frequently anthologized Grand Guignol "The Dunwich Horror," we learn by degrees that the virgin Lavina Whateley has been forced by her brutal father to mate with Yog-Sothoth, a "god"-creature from another dimension, giving birth to male twins. One of them seems initially a self-parody of the young Lovecraft, seven feet tall by the age of thirteen and haplessly bookish, doomed to be killed by a ferocious guard dog while breaking into the Miskatonic University library in his search for such texts as the *Necronomicon*. The other twin, for a time invisible, grows enormous as a barn, an obscene ravenously hungry ropy-tentacled monstrosity that shouts, in its death throes atop Sentinel Hill, ". . . ff-ff—ff—FATHER! FA-THER! YOG-SOTHOTH!"

Most of Lovecraft's tales are not so luridly sensational as "The Dunwich Horror," but rather develop by way of incremental detail, beginning with quite plausible situations—an expedition to Antarctica, a trip to an ancient seaside town, an investigation of an abandoned eighteenth-century house in Providence, Rhode Island, that still stood in Lovecraft's time ("The Shunned House"—a novelty in Lovecraft's oeuvre in that it ends happily, with "one of the earth's nethermost terrors perished forever" and ordinary springtime commencing). One is drawn into Lovecraft by the very air of plausibility and characteristic understatement of the prose, the question being, *When will weirdness strike?*

Readers of genre fiction, unlike readers of what we presume to call "literary fiction," assume a tacit contract between themselves and the writer: they understand that they will be manipulated, but the question is how? and when? and with what skill? and to what purpose? However plot-ridden, fantastical, or absurd, populated by whatever pseudo-characters, genre fiction is always resolved, while "literary fiction" makes no such promises; there is no contract between reader and writer for, in theory at least, each work of literary fiction is original, and, in essence, "about" its own language; anything can happen, or, upon occasion, nothing. Genre fiction is addictive, literary fiction, unfortunately, is not.

Lovecraft's simulation of "reality" was deliberate. In the essays "In Defence of Dagon" (1921) he divides literature into romantic, realistic, and imaginative, placing "weird fiction" in the last category, but aligning it with realism in its treatment of human psychology and emotion; in technique, "a tale should be plausible—even a bizarre tale except for the single element where supernaturalism is involved." Romance is pointedly unreal, but fantasy is something altogether different. Here we have an art based on the imaginative life of the human mind, *frankly recognized as such;* and in its way as natural and scientific—as truly related to natural (even if uncommon and delicate) psychological processes as the starkest of photographic realism.

"Weird fiction" can only be a product, Lovecraft saw, of an age that has ceased to believe collectively in the supernatural while retaining the primitive instinct to do so, in eccentric, atomized ways. He would hardly have been surprised, but rather confirmed in his cynicism regarding human intelligence, could he have foreseen how, from the 1950s onward, hundreds of thousands, perhaps millions, of purportedly sane Americans would come to believe in UFOs and "extraterrestrial" beings with particular, often erotic designs upon them.

For all his intelligence and aesthetic theorizing, Lovecraft was, like Poe, a remarkably uneven writer. Read chronologically, his tales stand in bewildering juxtapositions: the richly detailed, artfully constructed "The Call of Cthulhu" followed by the trashy "Pickman's Model," both of 1926; the subtly modulated "The Colour Out of Space" followed by the overwrought sensationalism of "The Dunwich Horror." Like Melville, Lovecraft was "damned by dollars"—except, in Lovecraft's case, the writer was forced to sell his stories, first-rate and otherwise, usually for no more than one cent a word, to the pulp magazine *Weird Tales* (launched in 1923, and destined to survive for a surprising thirty-one years). His work would never be published in book form during his lifetime.

Lovecraft's most effective tales are those in which atmosphere is predominant and plot subordinate; in which a richly detailed, layered narrative circles about a numinous, indefinable image. In the early, Poe-inspired "The Outsider," the unwittingly monstrous speaker moves as though in a dream to confront his own reflection inside "a cold and unyielding surface of glass"; even should we know nothing of the thirty-one-year-old author's bleakly cramped life, we respond to the story as a codified *cri de coeur:* "Unhappy is he to whom the memories of childhood bring only fear and sadness. Wretched is he who looks upon lone hours in vast and dismal chambers with . . . maddening rows of antique books. . . ." Despite Lovecraft's expressed contempt for mysticism, clearly he was a kind of mystic, drawing intuitively upon a cosmology of images that came to him unbidden, from the "underside" of his life: all that was repressed, denied, "defeated." There is a melancholy, operatic grandeur in Lovecraft's most passionate work, like "The Outsider" and "At the Mountains of Madness"; a curious elegiac poetry of unspeakable loss, of adolescent despair, and an existential loneliness so pervasive that it lingers in the reader's memory, like a dream, long after the rudiments of Lovecraftian plot have faded. A hybrid of the traditional gothic and "science fiction," Lovecraft is clearly gothic in temperament; his "science" has its own fictional logic, yet it is never future-oriented, but directed obsessively into the distant past. In Lovecraft's cosmos, some tragic conjunction of the "human" and the "nonhuman" has contaminated what should have been natural life; there is no logic, no reason for such a fate, any more than there is reason for lightning to strike.

In one of Lovecraft's best stories, the parable-like "The Colour Out of Space," with its vivid rendering of a once-fertile and now etiolated New England landscape, we see the obverse of American destiny, the repudiation of American-Transcendentalist optimism, in which the individual participates in the divine and shares in nature's divinity. And how prophetic the story seems to us decades later, in its depiction of ecological disaster as a powerful, seemingly nuclear/toxic force emanating from a meteor fallen to Earth on a farmer's land, utterly mysterious and unknowingly deadly.

> They had uncovered what seemed to be the side of a large coloured globule embedded in the [meteor]. The color, which resembled some of the bands in the meteor's strange spectrum, was almost impossible to describe. . . . Aside from being almost plastic, having heat, magnetism, and slight luminosity, cooling

slightly in powerful acids, possessing an unknown spectrum, wasting away in air, and attacking silicon compound with mutual destruction as a result, it presented no identifying features whatsoever. . . . It was nothing of the earth, but a piece of the great outside.

In the gothic imagination there is a profound and irreconcilable split between mankind and nature in the Romantic sense, and a tragic division between what we wish to know and what may be staring us in the face. So "The Colour Out of Space" ends, not sensationally, but with elegiac understatement: "It was just a colour out of space—a frightful messenger from unformed realms of infinity beyond all Nature as we know it." But the Massachusetts heath is permanently blighted, and all who have come into contact with the "colour" suffer neurological and bodily afflictions not dissimilar to those suffered by the victims of radioactivity and Agent Orange.

4.

Like a dictionary, a definitive biography will always tell us more than we need to know. But that is hardly ground for criticism. S. T. Joshi's *H. P. Lovecraft: A Life* overflows with information, both in and out of footnotes and appendixes; in addition to a virtually day-by-day account of Lovecraft's life, it contains a history of gothic literature, excerpts from Lovecraft's unpublished letters, essays, and travel pieces, and, among other inspired passages, a description of New York City in 1924 and how it must have looked to Lovecraft's wondering eyes when he first journeyed there, embarked upon his brave and unlikely marriage. The biography is so organized that, as Joshi suggests in his introduction, a reader may skim or skip entirely sections of relatively little interest to him or her. This is an admirable, pragmatic solution to the *longueurs* of the "definitive" biography.

Admirers of Lovecraft's fiction will certainly be interested in this reclusive author's unusually eloquent, frank letters (of which it's estimated he wrote between sixty thousand and a hundred thousand, most of them now lost), but it seems unlikely that any will be equally interested in the "amateur journalism" organizations and activities to which Lovecraft, ever the gentlemanly amateur, gave so much of his time; nor will most readers be interested in the endless stream of long-forgotten or never-known "amateur writers" of the day who came to know Lovecraft or corresponded with him, and whose lives receive perfunctory thumbnail sketches from the biographer. Joshi suggests skimming, too, some of the many passages on Lovecraft's philosophy—more accurately, philosophizing—but these are among the biography's most engaging features. How rare to encounter, in life or literature, a person for whom the mental life, the *thinking* life, is so suffused with drama as Lovecraft.

Like his idol Friedrich Nietzsche, Lovecraft could write little that was not a *cri de coeur*; in ordinary matters, he gives the impression of struggling for his life. Joshi notes Lovecraft's lifelong attraction to suicide, as in this letter of 1930 to the young acolyte August Derleth, who would become his posthumous publisher:

I am perfectly confident that I could never adequately convey to any other human being the precise reasons why I refrain from suicide—the reasons, that is, why I still find existence enough of a compensation to atone for its dominantly burthensome quality. These reasons are strongly linked with architecture, scenery, and lighting and atmospheric effects, and take the form of vague impressions of adventurous expectancy coupled with elusive memory.

Yet, much earlier in his life, in a letter of 1918 written when he was twenty-eight:

I am only about half alive—a large part of my strength is consumed in sitting up or walking. My nervous system is a shattered wreck, and I am absolutely bored & listless save when
I come upon something which peculiarly interests me. However—so many things *do* interest me. . . . that I have never
actually desired to die.

If we are to believe Lovecraft's account, by the age of thirteen
he was convinced of "man's impermanence and insignificance," and
by the age of seventeen, having studied astronomy, he was struck by
"the futility of all existence."

Even for a reader relatively familiar with Lovecraft's work and
with the gothic legend of his life, *H. P. Lovecraft: A Life* will contain
illuminating surprises. That Lovecraft was a solitary, nocturnal personality we might know. But that his solitude was, after his mother's fortuitous death in 1921, frequently interrupted by socializing
of a kind in amateur journalism circles; that his hermetic, quasi-
invalided existence was periodically rejuvenated by fanatic trips by
bus or train to places as remote from his bachelor's sanctuary in
Providence as St. Augustine, New Orleans, and Quebec City;[2] that,
with his stark melancholy eyes, his peculiar stiff conduct, and the
"archaic" cut of his clothes, not to mention his asexuality, he was
nonetheless attractive to a number of women—all this is wholly
unexpected. We learn that a "Junoesque" and quite vibrant writer-
businesswoman, Sonia Greene, fell in love with Lovecraft for his
intelligent conversation, and pursued him for three Platonic years
before, misguidedly, he consented to marry her. (The marriage
faded by degrees, and after two years, Sonia Greene asked for a
divorce.)

We learn that Lovecraft, scourge of conventional piety in his
writing, was for much of his life a self-styled "Tory" in homage to
his "unmixed English gentry" ancestors, and became an adamant
if purely theoretical Socialist in his forties, during the Depression.

How strange to know that Lovecraft was unfailingly kind, patient, generous, unassuming, and gentlemanly in his personal relations; yet, in keeping with his Tory sensibility, an anti-Semite (despite his deep affection for Sonia Greene and other Jewish friends), racist, and all-purpose Aryan bigot.[3]

Following a nervous breakdown at the age of eighteen from which, Joshi suggests, he never fully recovered, Lovecraft never sought to formally educate or train himself for serious employment. Less worldly even than Poe, who had worked as an editor at several magazines, he eked out a meager living by doing revisions for other, mostly terrible writers, and occasional ghostwriting (once, for Harry Houdini). Though he prided himself on writing for the "sensitive," a small circle of like-minded persons, in fact all of Lovecraft's work was published in trashy magazines; and even after he became known for his numerous stories in *Weird Tales,* no contribution of his, no matter how atrocious, was honored with a lurid cover. Stories of the quality of "The Colour Out of Space" were summarily rejected. Most surprisingly, though Lovecraft's much-declared vision of life was as bleak as Ambrose Bierce's ("Life is a hideous thing, and from the background behind what we know peer demonical hints of truth which make it a thousand-fold more hideous"), he seems, on a day-to-day basis, very often to have enjoyed it.

Lovecraft's career, however, was increasingly disappointing to him. Even as he became more admired in the cultist world of gothic fiction, he became ever more impoverished, eccentric. One of his Tory handicaps was a misguided noblesse oblige: whoever wrote to him, he believed, deserved a thoughtful reply, so his time was consumed in writing to a daunting number of eager young writers and readers (among them a teenaged protégé named Robert Bloch, one day to write *Psycho*). With the publication of a cruelly mangled "The Shadow Out of Time" in the pulp *Astounding* in 1936, when Lovecraft was forty-six, he seems to have burnt himself out. Locked into idiosyncratic habits like one of his hapless protagonists in a nightmare scenario, Lovecraft took ascetic pride in eating frugally, estimating that he could subsist on thirty cents a day, $2.10 a week; often he ate unheated food out of cans and aged, even spoiled food. A lifelong phobia against doctors and hospitals prevented his intestinal cancer from being diagnosed until it was too late; but, in true Lovecraftian fashion, despite being in terrible agony he kept a "death diary" until he could no longer hold a pen.

Like Poe, Lovecraft died believing himself an ignominious failure. In his most fantastical musings this artist of "cosmic pessimism" could not have foreseen his posthumous fame; still less that, within a decade of his death, the very book he could not get published, *Lovecraft's Best Supernatural Tales*, would sell more than 67,000 copies in hardcover in a single year.

1. It is something of a tradition for writers of horror and dark fantasy to emulate Lovecraft. See, for instance, the anthology *Lovecraft's Legacy*, edited by Robert E. Weinberg and Martin H. Greenberg (Tor Books, 1990). Thomas Ligotti's novella "The Last Feast of Harlequin" has the dedication "In homage to H. P. Lovecraft." And should you be needful of a Lovecraft calendar, *The Lovecraft Horror Calendar* with "Mythos art" is available from Artefact Publications.

2. Can there be an Eros of the landscape, or place? The feverish intensity with which Lovecraft traveled, sleeping on buses and trains to save hotel expenses, forgetting to eat, the indefatigable sightseeing that wore out companions in better physical condition than he—what is this but the seeking of the beloved object, embodied in the yet-unknown? A friend of Lovecraft's comments on the man's manic traveling habits:

   "Howard arrived back from Quebec. I have never before nor since seen such a sight. Folds of skin hanging from a skeleton. Eyes sunk in sockets like burnt holes in a blanket. Those delicate, sensitive artist's hands and fingers nothing but claws. The man was dead except for his nerves."

But the forty-two-year-old Lovecraft reports having had an ecstatic visit to Quebec!

3. Certain of Lovecraft's tales, notably "The Shadow over Innsmouth" with its debased, subhuman race of fishy-reptile folk with staring, unblinking eyes, are clearly paranoid fantasies of miscegenation. Over the course of his life, Lovecraft retreated from the most blatant claims of Aryan superiority ("No anthropologist of standing insists on the uniformly advanced evolution of the Nordic as compared with that of other Caucasian and Mongolian races. . . . It is freely conceded that the Mediterranean race turns out a higher percentage of the aesthetically sensitive and that the Semitic groups excel in sharp, precise intellection," he concedes in 1931); yet he persisted in a belief in the biological inferiority of "blacks and Australian aborigines."

H. P. Lovecraft: A Life
By S. T. Joshi

The Dunwich Horror and Others
Selected by August Derleth, with texts
edited by S. T. Joshi

At the Mountains of Madness & Other Novels
Edited by S. T. Joshi

Dagon and Other Macabre Tales
Edited by S. T. Joshi

Miscellaneous Writings
Edited by S. T. Joshi

Selected Letters Vol. I: 1911–1924
Edited by S. T. Joshi

Selected Letters Vol. II: 1925–1929
Edited by S. T. Joshi

Selected Letters Vol. III: 1929–1931
Edited by S. T. Joshi

Selected Letters Vol. IV: 1932–1934
Edited by S. T. Joshi

Selected Letters Vol. V: 1934–1937
Edited by S. T. Joshi

MY FARAWAY ONE:
SELECTED LETTERS OF GEORGIA
O'KEEFFE AND ALFRED STIEGLITZ

Is there an alternative, diminished universe in which Herman Melville failed to meet Nathaniel Hawthorne, whose influence changed his life; a universe in which the young T. S. Eliot failed to meet Ezra Pound, and Hemingway never met Gertrude Stein; in which Elizabeth Barrett Browning and Robert Browning, Virginia Stephen and Leonard Woolf, George Eliot and George Henry Lewes didn't meet, fall in love, and live together in richly productive domestic arrangements that have taken on some of the qualities of romantic myth? These gifted writers would have written in any case—but not so well, perhaps; and not so happily. And so too, Georgia O'Keeffe and Alfred Stieglitz who met in 1916 when O'Keeffe was a young, unknown artist of twenty-nine and Stieglitz, famous for his entrepreneurial work as a promoter of avant-garde art in his Fifth Avenue gallery 291 as well as for his own, distinctive photography, was fifty-two, the exact age of O'Keeffe's mother. Stieglitz's influence on O'Keeffe is known to be immeasurable, both on her art and her career; less known is the considerable influence the younger O'Keeffe had upon Stieglitz, as evidenced in these newly published letters as in Katherine Hoffman's sympathetic biography of Stieglitz—which is, in essence, a partial biography of O'Keeffe, and of the American "avant-garde" in the early decades of the twentieth century as well.

At the time of her death in 1986, at the age of ninety-eight, Georgia O'Keeffe had already passed into myth, as an icon of American art, an inimitable commingling of the austerely "primitive" and the aesthetically rendered, bearing the sort of relationship to her younger, uncertain, and ambitious self that the posthumous, iconic Vincent van Gogh might be said to bear to his historic self: the latter is a consequence of the former, but the latter could hardly have been discerned in the former. Apart from the strong, striking, starkly original visual images with which O'Keeffe is associated— her elegantly stylized oil paintings *Cow's Skull: Red, White, and Blue, Black Abstraction, Black Iris, Black Place II*, among others that have become nearly as famous in our popular culture as certain key paintings by her contemporary Edward Hopper—much of the mythologizing of Georgia O'Keeffe has to do with our familiarity with her as a visual "image" originally recorded by her lover Stieglitz in a remarkable sequence of intensely intimate, yet compositionally studied, mostly nude photographs taken in the 1920s and consisting of 350 mounted prints. It is rare in art history that one individual is so meticulously and beautifully recorded by another, still more rare that an artist of O'Keeffe's gifts would be the model. (One thinks of Andrew Wyeth's just slightly scandalous *"Helga"* paintings of 1971 to 1985, but Helga was not a fellow artist. Through her career O'Keeffe would rage against condescendingly "sexual" interpretations of her work which she insisted was purely aesthetic and not at all determined by "womanliness.") Only think if Picasso, Matisse, Rembrandt had posed in the nude for other artists, and so many times! The identity of the female model in Stieglitz's photographs was allegedly not revealed at the time of the exhibit, yet everyone in Stieglitz's circle, which was considerable in New York City in the early decades of the twentieth century, would have known who she was. So too, in her later years, when O'Keeffe emerged as a "pioneer painter" in popular magazines like *Life* and *Time*—("pioneer" is particularly ludicrous, since O'Keeffe had been born in Wisconsin, not the Southwest; on a dairy farm, and not a ranch; and her art was highly stylized, in the way of the American avant-garde of the early twentieth century, hardly the equivalent of "pioneer" or "outsider" work)—her plain, sun-wizened, androgynous and resolutely unsmiling face seemed to suggest a being from another era, a kind of desert prophet, or prophetess, quite the material for American mythologizing, as the more accessible, less exotic of her female-artist contemporaries (Imogen Cunningham, Dorothea Lange, Isabel Bishop, Alice Neel, Lee Krasner, Helen Frankenthaler) apparently were not. In such iconic-female-artist terms, only Mexico's gorgeously exotic Frida Kahlo is a (posthumous) rival to O'Keeffe's acclaim.

These three beautifully produced and exhaustively researched "coffee table" books, each by way of Yale University Press, weigh in at over thirteen pounds in all and are not for the faint of heart or the casual browser, particularly the seven-hundred-page *Selected Letters*—which is only the first volume of the O'Keeffe-Stieglitz letters. In all, the lovers, married in 1924 but frequently living apart, Stieglitz in New York City and Lake George, in the Adirondacks, and O'Keeffe in New Mexico, exchanged more than five thousand letters, which comprise more than twenty-five thousand pages; the present volume contains letters written between 1915 and 1933. The reader will learn, from Hoffman's biography of Stieglitz, that Stieglitz was an indefatigable letter-writer to many friends, acquaintances, and associates, not only to Georgia O'Keeffe; he seems to have been a virtual graphomaniac, whose handwritten letters sometimes ran to as many as forty pages which, as he said, he never reread or revised.

"Finally, a woman on paper. A woman gives of herself. The miracle has happened." So Stieglitz allegedly exclaimed, seeing a portfolio of abstract drawings by the then-unknown Georgia O'Keeffe, for consideration in his Fifth Avenue gallery 291, in 1915. So enthusiastic was Stieglitz, he arranged to exhibit O'Keeffe's work in the spring of 1916 without consulting her; at first the young woman artist was upset by the gallery owner's impetuousness, then, meeting Stieglitz she was mollified, and un-characteristically deferential: "Nothing you do with my drawings is 'nervy.' I seem to feel that they are as much yours as mine"—an extraordinary statement from O'Keeffe who so prized her inde-pendence and self-reliance.

O'Keeffe left New York City, eventually moving to Canyon, Texas, where she had a position teaching art at West Texas State Normal College, and so begins the massive, astonishing correspondence between O'Keeffe and Stieglitz—then married, and the father of a daughter whom he'd once photographed obsessively; a daughter who would suffer a mental breakdown in her early twenties, regress to "the mentality of a young child," and was institutionalized for the remainder of her life. In their fascination with each other, both O'Keeffe and Stieglitz hardly seem aware of other people, let alone of their responsibility to others; their letters are extravagantly nar-cissistic, exhibitionistic, often brilliant, uncensored cries from the heart that more resemble stream-of-conscious journal entries than composed letters. Breathless single-sentence paragraphs careen down the page of O'Keeffe's letters to Stieglitz, at times reminiscent of the seemingly dashed-off lines of Emily Dickinson:

> Of course it is all right for you to put me in *Camera Work* if you want to—but it hurts—Do you understand how? Oh it's very bad—Then—my hard crust gets to the top—and I don't care— Write a whole book about me if you want to— I guess I hate myself when I don't care—Then I look around helplessly at my disgusting independence—and find myself asking—what can I do about it— And have to laugh—for there is nothing— And tonight—let me ask you something else—I don't know— There is never anyone to ask the things we most need to ask—I'm get-ting to like you so tremendously that it some times scares me—

(NOVEMBER 4, 1906)

In his typical grandiloquent manner Stieglitz writes to O'Keeffe:

You are a very, very great Woman. You have given me—I can't tell you what it is—but it is something tremendous—something so overpowering that I feel as if I had shot up suddenly into the skies & touched the stars—& found them all women— Women like you are a Woman. . . . There never was a letter like the one here before me—a Woman's Soul laid bare in all its beauty—pulsating—crying out into the starlight night.

(NOVEMBER 4, 1906)

Stieglitz is a romantic visionary, in his art and in his life; it seems reductive to say that he was a notorious womanizer, for his religion seems to have been Woman as Muse, first formed by his reading of *Faust* as a young man: the concept of a woman who might embody all Women, "whose purity might redeem a man's soul."

Soon, Stieglitz confides in O'Keeffe that he has been married for twenty-three years without believing in marriage—"Nor have I believed it since." He isn't fit for marriage, he says; even as his appeal to O'Keeffe is frankly sexual, as well as visionary and idealistic; often, startlingly intimate:

I hope you haven't had that headache.—But being a woman you are probably damned to those periodic headaches, frightful ones, that so many women must stand. And you with your nature are doomed to the worst kind. . . . One ought to sleep during the day—When one is mad as I am.

By nature Stieglitz is an enthusiast; his truest nature is celebratory, Whitmanesque. Repeatedly in his letters he describes New York City, or Lake George, or his own interior weather, in exclamatory terms: "What a magnificent day for me!"—"Power— Color—Vision—Elemental Force—Greatest Delicacy—Intensest

Passion—Killing Love!!—" "I wish I wasn't so damn sane—It borders on insanity to see too straight—"

O'Keeffe is most intriguing when she writes, ostensibly to Stieglitz but perhaps primarily to herself, about herself as a rebel and iconoclast:

> *I'll be damned* and I want to damn every other person in this little spot (Canyon, Texas)—like a nasty pretty little sore on the wonderful plains. The plains—the wonderful great big sky— makes me want to breathe so deep that I'll break—There is so much of it—I want to get outside of it all—I would if I could— even if it killed me.

Yet more intriguing are O'Keeffe's spontaneous remarks about her art:

> I don't understand—I get the shapes in my head—can never make them exactly like I want to—but there is a fascination about trying— And then too—there is the delicious probability that I don't know anything about what Art is—so it's fun to make the stuff—

> The next one is already whirling in my mind—

> You know—I'm just living—I just sort of plunge from one thing into another—so often—so very much afraid—

After Stieglitz separates from his wife, he and O'Keeffe live together for several years until his divorce is final; but their marriage doesn't alter their fundamental relationship, nor even the flood of letters they write to each other when they are apart. One feels that for each, the other was a kind of alter ego, or soul mate; in confiding in the other, one confides in oneself, in terms other-wise inaccessible. For years, the mutual tone is both operatic and tender; though the initial romance becomes qualified by marital problems, primarily Stieglitz's penchant for becoming infatuated with (and obsessively taking pictures of) ever younger women, it is difficult not to believe that Stieglitz writes sincerely to O'Keeffe, in explanation of one or another heartbreak he has caused her:

> You suffered when I didn't want you to suffer—& through me. I suffered as horribly as you Sweetheart—& didn't understand—suffered because I did not understand & saw your face! . . . but I suppose I was "hurt"—& stupid—wounded vanity maybe— (September 3, 1926)

And, at a time when O'Keeffe had moved to Taos, New Mexico, to pursue a life of art largely independent of her aging husband:

> Eleven years have passed by.—I see all its phases—all the days and hours & moments of ecstasy & pain—the growth—of something very exceptional & very beautiful between us—I see the studio in 59th St.—291 (no man's room)—our sitting there that first Sunday afternoon—Yes all those days & hours & really minutes still existing vividly for me, All the wonder & beauty & life—& all the terrible ordeal.—Life—your innocence—Emmy [Stieglitz's wife]—Kitty [his daughter]. . . . And I see myself—And you. . . . My Holy Mountain invisible within.—Another part of me tossed about like the waters of the sea. And yet quiet. A contradiction ever. (June 8, 1929)

And, in Whitmanesque grandiloquence, shading perhaps into bombast:

You grand Woman—You say you are my Woman. Yes I know
on Aug. 9th it will be 11? Years that you gave me your virginity.
During Thunder and Lightning. It's as if it were yesterday. It's
a wonder I didn't give you a child. We were made to have one,
but it was not to be. . . . You gave me your virginity, that's the
reason you are my Woman for all time. You are not like other
women—and I am your man for all Time for I am not like other
Men . . . you gave me your virginity. . . . I love you my wild
Georgia O'Keeffe. (August 5, 1929)

And, a few years later, when Stieglitz is sixty-eight:

Good morning my ever unsettled body—beautiful—
Gentle—so—lovely soft one—ever sacred.

(AUGUST 29, 1932)

Except now, the beloved isn't Georgia O'Keeffe but a young
woman named Dorothy Norman, forty years Stieglitz's junior, whose
presence in her husband's life would precipitate a nervous breakdown in O'Keeffe in February 1933, and cause a permanent rift in
their marriage. Norman, who assisted Stieglitz in his gallery, An
American Place, and worked with him closely on a number of publishing projects, was Stieglitz's model for another series of intimate
photographs, of the 1930s, not nudes, and none so strikingly sensual
as those of O'Keeffe a decade before. (For some reason, one of the
least interesting photographs of Dorothy Norman is reproduced on
the cover of A Legacy of Light, when clearly the cover photograph
should have been of Stieglitz himself, who was a strikingly photo-
genic man; or, indeed, of one of the famous O'Keeffe nudes. The
photograph of Norman depicts a woman in black, her back to the
camera, head bowed, shoulders slightly hunched and a row of singularly ugly large buttons down her back—a curious choice of an im-

age for a book celebrating Stieglitz's career as a great photographer.) Perhaps the single cruelest thing that Stieglitz did was to exhibit recently taken photographs of Dorothy Norman as a young, beautiful, "adoring" woman side by side with recently taken photographs of Georgia O'Keeffe that depict her as older, wary, plain, "sexless." If O'Keeffe could forgive Stieglitz for his love affair with Norman, about which he allegedly talked openly, to anyone who would listen, including O'Keeffe herself, it isn't likely that she could forgive him for an act of such thoughtlessness, which had the effect of embarrassing this dignified woman artist publicly. Dorothy Norman, married and the mother of several children, would nevertheless remain in Stieglitz's life until his death in July 1946, at the age of eighty-two. At this time O'Keeffe, still Stieglitz's legal wife, returned to take over his estate as his executrix, summarily banishing Norman from the scene in what must have been a kind of belated triumph. O'Keeffe would spend years going through Stieglitz's immense collections of art, personal documents, and memorabilia, and would give away most of his collected work to museums, primarily to the National Gallery and the Metropolitan Museum of Art. O'Keeffe was extraordinarily generous in giving away such priceless work: "I did not wish to keep the collection and preferred not to sell it. I had no choice but to give it to the public." Of course, O'Keeffe had had a choice: she could certainly have kept some of Stieglitz's work and some of the highly valuable art he'd collected over a period of more than fifty years.

In speaking of her brilliant, charismatic, loving and yet chronically unfaithful and impetuous husband, O'Keeffe said:

> There was a constant grinding like the ocean. It was as if something hot, dark, and destructive was hitched to the highest, brightest star. For me he was much more wonderful in his work than as a human being. I believe it was the work that kept me

with him—though I loved him as a human being. . . . I put up
with what seemed to me a good deal of nonsense because of
what seemed clear and bright and wonderful.

[*Legacy of Light*]

——

As *A Legacy of Light* and *Stieglitz and His Artists: Matisse to O'Keeffe*
make abundantly clear, Alfred Stieglitz had a life and a career
wholly distinct from his relationship with Georgia O'Keeffe. If she
had not met him, one can only speculate whether she would have
acquired the reputation she did; certainly, she would not have attracted such early, exhilarating attention, resulting in early commercial success, if she hadn't been showcased in Stieglitz's highly
regarded "avant-garde" gallery at 291 Fifth Avenue. Yet, if Stieglitz
hadn't met O'Keeffe, it seems likely that his reputation as a major American photographer would be more or less the same; if he
hadn't photographed O'Keeffe obsessively in the 1920s, he would
have photographed another young woman, or women, very likely
with comparable results. Certainly, the photographs of Stieglitz
contained in these books are surpassingly beautiful, some of them
strange, eerie, and arresting: winter scenes in New York City of
snow falling in the streets, the early "sky-scrapers" and building
construction of *Old and New New York* (1910) and *The City of Ambition* (1910); the famous *The Steerage* (1907), which Stieglitz photographed on an ocean crossing in which he was traveling, of course,
in first-class accommodations; moody sky-scenes, *The Aeroplane*
(1910), *A Dirigible* (1910), *Songs of the Sky* (1923), and the ambitious
sequence of abstract cloud pictures, *Equivalents* (1920s); meticulous, near-mystical photographs of Stieglitz's beloved Lake George,
titled *Later Lake George* (1930s); brilliant photographs of Stieglitz's
artist- and writer-friends Arthur Dove, Marsden Hartley, Charles
Demuth, Francis Picabia, Sherwood Anderson, Waldo Frank, Jean

Toomer, with whom O'Keeffe had an intensely romantic friendship for a brief while in November 1933, writing to him afterward: "I like knowing the feel of your maleness. I wish so hotly to feel you hold me very tight and warm to you." Stieglitz also took numerous photographs of friends, companions, and associates, including the wife of his friend Paul Strand, Rebecca Strand, with whom both he and O'Keeffe seem to have shared a romantic infatuation in the early 1920s.

One has the impression, studying Stieglitz's work, of a man of genius inventing, or helping to invent, an entirely new art form, photography, at a time when only paintings, drawings, and sculpture were considered serious art. With his younger photographer-friend Edward Steichen, Stieglitz helped to formulate what became known as Pictorialist photography with its dreamlike subjects, soft-focus nocturnal scenes and atmospheric weather reminiscent of French Impressionism and of certain of the effects of Whistler. "My photographs are born of an inner need . . . an Experience of Spirit. I have a vision of life and I try to find equivalents for it sometimes in the form of photographs. . . . There is art or not art. There is nothing in between."

Quite apart from his creative gifts, Stieglitz had a perhaps equally rare charismatic gift for gathering first-rate artists to him, showcasing and selling their art, persuading wealthy collectors to collect them, and creating "public relations" for photography as a new, vital, exciting art-form very different from ordinary "picture-taking." *Stieglitz and His Artists,* which documents a recent exhibition of that name at the Metropolitan Museum of Art taken from the Alfred Stieglitz Collection that took "decades to complete," suggests the astonishing range of Stieglitz's interests as an American-born but German-educated follower of European and avant-garde trends: these include early works of Kandinsky, drawings and watercolors by Matisse, ink-on-paper drawings by Picasso, paintings and drawings by Toulouse-Lautrec, Félicien Rops, Charles Demuth,

Arthur Dove, Marsden Hartley, John Marin, and of course Georgia O'Keeffe, among many others originally exhibited in his gallery at 291 Fifth Avenue. (Despite its fame, Stieglitz had to close 291 in 1917, with the economic downturn after the start of the war; he would open other galleries, and continue with art publications, through the remainder of his long life.)

Stieglitz: A Legacy of Light is fact filled, like a compact encyclopedia of Stieglitz's era; it contains photographs of places and scenes vital to Stieglitz's life, like Lake George, taken by the biographer— (and inadvertently providing a sharp contrast to the "artistic" photographs of Stieglitz); clearly, Katherine Hoffman knows her subjects intimately, and is excellent at drawing together seemingly disparate aspects of their lives. Still, her staid, tidy, resolutely "academic" prose seems inadequate to convey the sheer vitality of the remarkable Stieglitz, whose erotic attachment to his art might require a different sort of perspective. And the sheer quantity of breathless, dashed-off, hyperbolic and repetitive letters collected by Sarah Greenough in *My Faraway One* has the effect of those enormous magnified portraits by Chuck Close that are so dauntingly close-up, they can barely be seen for their disintegration into pixels. *Less is more* might have been a principle for collecting the letters, which are fascinating to read at the start, but soon become much less fascinating as the years pass; there is an epic journey here, a tumultuous love affair settling into a kind of long-distance marriage of mutual regard and respect, but significance is lost in a welter of details, and the prospect of hundreds more of these letters is indeed daunting. Fortunately, Greenough provides helpful transitional passages and footnotes to aid in our understanding of what might be really going on, beneath and behind the letters.

The last letter in *My Faraway One* is this touching, typically breathless one from Stieglitz in New York City to Georgia O'Keeffe in Lake George, where she has retreated to recover from a breakdown that was very likely precipitated by Steiglitz's love affair with Dorothy Norman:

> Midnight. It's New Year—1934—the City is agog with whistles & bells—sirens—I have been in bed—I jumped up to say Hello—If I didn't feel you were asleep I'd phone now. . . .
>
> Oh Georgia.—And I am seventy finally.—I never expected to see that age. Yes seventy. And you on the road to full recovery.—That's my gift from you. Again much, much love— I'll hop into bed again.—Another kiss—the first in 1934!
>
> There is shouting—still bells & whistles—all sorts of noises—1934—January 1st—Do be careful.

My Faraway One: Selected Letters of
Georgia O'Keeffe and Alfred Stieglitz
Volume I. 1915–1933
Edited by Sarah Greenough

Alfred Stieglitz: A Legacy of Light
By Katherine Hoffman

Stieglitz and His Artists: Matisse to O'Keeffe
Edited by Lisa Mintz Messinger
The Metropolitan Museum of Art, New York/ Yale University Press

SIMENONS

A "simenon" is a sparely written and tautly constructed novella by the phenomenal Belgian-born Georges Simenon (1903–1989), author of hundreds of works of prose fiction under his own and assumed names, in addition to countless screenplays, short stories, and the multivolume autobiographical *Dictées* (1975–1981) and *Memoires Intimes* (1981).

A "simenon" may or may not be a crime/suspense novella, but it will always move swiftly and with seeming inevitability from its opening scene to its final, often startling and ironic conclusion; a "simenon" is the antithesis of the elaborately literary, infinitely digressive, and relatively plotless prose fiction of twentieth-century European modernism, notably Proust's monumental seven-volume *Remembrance of Things Past* (published in its entirety in 1927). More temperamentally akin to such fluidly composed, radically distilled, and mordantly "existential" works of fiction as Camus's *The Stranger* (1942), the experimental novellas of Alain Robbe-Grillet and Marguerite Duras, and such films as Jean-Luc Godard's *Breathless* (1960) and Alain Resnais's *Hiroshima Mon Amour* (1959), the quintessential "simenon" makes no effort to establish a detailed, catalogued social world; its structure is a sequence of cinematic confrontations in which an individual—male, middle-aged, unwittingly trapped in his life—is catapulted into an extraordinary adventure that will leave him transformed, unless destroyed:

> He was waiting for something to which he aspired and which had not yet come. . . . He was a man who, for a long time, had endured the human condition without being conscious of it, as others endure an illness of which they are unaware.
>
> *Monsieur Monde Vanishes, translated by Jean Stewart*

> For all these years it had been a strain playing [his] part, and watching himself incessantly to make sure that he didn't say or do the wrong thing. Now all that was ended.
>
> *The Man Who Watched the Trains Go By,*
> *translated by Stuart Gilbert*

All "simenons" have in common the language of understatement, which gives to the subgenre an air of the parable or allegory. As we read of the vertiginous plunge from stultifying bourgeois respectability to murder, moral chaos, and lunacy in, for instance, the much-admired *The Man Who Watched the Trains Go By* (1938), or the laconic *récit* of *The Man with the Little Dog* (1964), we come to feel that we are in the presence not of specific individuals so much as allegorical human types, as in those obsessively repeated two-dimensional images of bourgeois male anonymity in the canvases of Magritte. The characteristic glissando of Simenon's prose, skillfully rendered in this new translation of a somewhat atypical "simenon," provides, as in the smooth surface of ice, a reflecting movement that hints—subtly, mysteriously—of depths of secret feeling available to the protagonist, to be revealed only by degrees to the reader. *Three Bedrooms in Manhattan* is the most existential of love stories, stripped to skeletal urgency, highly cinematic yet underlaid by the desperation of François Combe, the most autobiographical of Simenon's protagonists:

He was going too fast. He knew that he'd traveled, in almost
no time at all, a long, steep path that men can take years to
complete, often their whole lives, if they reach the end
at all.

In most "simenons," as in the nouveau romans of Robbe-Grillet,
Duras, and others, there is a cinematic intensity to the observed
world: Simenon is renowned for the succinctly rendered yet powerfully evocative atmospheres of his fiction. In his Parisian-set novellas, the weather in the streets is often bleak, overcast, pelting rain.
Elsewhere, in Manhattan for instance, the atmosphere is similarly
brooding, mysterious:

> Two wide streets, almost deserted, with garlands of luminous
> globes running down the sidewalks.
>   On the corner, its high windows lit violently, aggressively,
> with boastful vulgarity, was a sort of long glass cage where peo-
> ple could be seen as dark smudges and where he went in just
> so as not to be alone.
>   Stools anchored to the floor along an endless counter made
> of something cold and plastic. Two sailors swayed drunkenly,
> and one of them shook his hand solemnly, saying something
> Combe failed to understand.
>   It wasn't on purpose that he sat down beside the woman. He
> realized it only when the white-coated black waiter was stand-
> ing in front of him, impatient for his order. The place smelled
> of fairgrounds, of lazy crowds, of nights when you stayed out
> because you couldn't go to bed, and it smelled like New York,
> of its calm and brutal indifference.

Despite hostile weather, a Simenon character, in a state of anxious exhilaration, can walk for hours, miles:

It was cold and drizzling. The sky hung low with heavy gray clouds. The East River was covered with angry white crests of waves, the tugs sounded shrill whistles, and ugly flat-bottomed brown ferryboats carried passengers back and forth on unchanging routes, like trams. . . . That one last worry, which he dragged past block after block of buildings, brick cubes with iron staircases outside in case of fire, where the question was not how people had the strength to go on living there—that was easy enough—but how they had the strength to die there.

It's rare to discover in Simenon a complex sentence, let alone a soaring, even grandiloquent flight of prose:

A magnificent sight, magnificent and sordid, met [Monsieur Monde's] eyes: the soaring blocks of blackened houses between which the train was threading its way, with hundreds and thousands of windows open or closed, linen hanging out, aerials, a prodigious accumulation, in breadth and in height, of teeming lives, from which the train suddenly broke away after a glimpse of the last green-and-white bus in a street that already seemed like a highway.

Monsieur Monde Vanishes

Though there are notable exceptions, most of Simenon's sentences are spare and without adornment, and his paragraphs are generally short, even staccato; that Simenon began his writing career as a journalist and the pseudonymous author of hundreds of pulp fictions comes as no surprise. "Be simple. Never try for a literary effect. Leave out every word and syllable you can," Colette advised the younger writer, who seems to have followed her advice throughout his career.

Perhaps not surprisingly, Simenon's more conventional crime/detective novels, featuring the laconic Inspector Maigret, have always been more popular than the others. Maigret is an irresistibly engaging character, middle-aged, pipe smoking, a lover of good food and drink, rather gruff, no-nonsense, and the antithesis of the world's most famous amateur sleuth, the Englishman Sherlock Holmes, whom Simenon disdained. Like his creator, Inspector Maigret prefers to understand than to judge; he has a knack for putting himself in the minds of others, especially criminal others.

Universal to Simenon's work, whether a Maigret title or one of his less formulaic novels, is a concentration on behavior that might be considered obsessive. As the novels are formally prescribed, so too the circumstances of their composition were formally prescribed, ritualistic and obsessive. A self-declared fetishist, Simenon required absolute privacy from interruptions; specific notebooks, pencils, pipes filled and lined up on his desk; manila envelopes, white paper, maps, dictionaries, such stimulants as coffee and Coca-Cola. In the mid-1960s he seems to have decided that writing a manuscript with a pencil was too self-conscious a technique, and switched to a manual typewriter: "With a pencil you feel too much like a writer. It elicits elegant turns of phrase, lovely images, and so on." Writing a "simenon" usually took no more than nine or ten days, including three days for revisions, but these were obviously days of extraordinary concentration, a kind of controlled manic frenzy that brought the author close to breakdown, exhaustion.

Simenon spoke openly, perhaps boastfully, of his "neurotic" nature; in *When I Was Old* (1971), one of twenty-seven autobiographical titles by Simenon, as well as in numerous interviews, he describes himself as an "obsessive"—a "psychopath." (Rivaling Don Giovanni, Simenon once claimed to have had sex with as many as ten thousand women, the majority of them prostitutes.) Biographers suggest a narcissistic personality skilled in the manipulation of others, but hardly a psychopath; the circumstances of Simenon's private life may seem to some of us rather more pragmatic and self-serving than clinically psychopathic, just as Simenon's output, invariably described as "prodigious," is perhaps not so exceptional measured against the achievements, quantitative as well as qualitative, of Balzac, Dickens, Trollope, Dostoevsky, Henry James. (The typical "simenon" is fewer than two hundred smaller-than-average pages.) Simenon's biographer Pierre Assouline asserts that Simenon lied about himself compulsively, but that his lies were a "novelist's lies," told with all his characteristic genius. They were solicitous, too: lies that told the truth, lies by omission, selective amnesia. . . . By middle age [Simenon] was no longer able to tell truth from falsehood, real from imaginary."

As he grew older, his self-intoxication grew to the point where he sincerely believed everything he said and wrote about himself. He became the worst source of information about Georges Simenon until finally author and readers alike were lost in a hybrid form of autobiographical fiction.

Allowing even for self-aggrandizement, Georges Simenon was certainly the great best seller in the French language of the twentieth century, and surely one of the great international best sellers of all time. His books are said to have been translated into fifty-five languages, and to have sold as many as two hundred million copies. Since Simenon wrote his early books under pseudonyms, no one seems to know precisely how many book-length titles he published, but the estimate of four hundred–plus seems plausible. There have been as many as sixty feature films and nearly three hundred television adaptations, predominantly in Europe and featuring Inspector Maigret. Though, unfortunately, relatively few of Simenon's titles are in print in the United States at present, his books continue to sell in Europe. By the time of his death in 1989, the income from Simenon's printed work had been long eclipsed by the income from subsidiary rights.

Despite his "difficult" personality, and charges of wartime collaboration with the Nazis, Simenon has been admired by a remarkable

diversity of his fellow writers, among them Henry Miller, Thorn-
ton Wilder, Somerset Maugham, John Cowper Powys, Ian Flem-
ing, Dashiell Hammett ("Simenon is the best author of the genre").
André Gide (the publisher's reader who had headed the Gallimard
committee notable for having rejected Proust's *Swann's Way*, the
first volume of *Remembrance of Things Past*, in 1912) made the extravagant claim that Simenon was perhaps the best French writer
of the twentieth century, though, astonishingly, Gide believed that
Simenon had "not really fulfilled his promise."

Three Bedrooms in Manhattan, originally published in France,
in 1946, as *Trois chambres à Manhattan*, is both a typical and an
atypical "simenon." It belongs to that category of his work to which
Simenon gave the generic name *dur*, or "hard," to distinguish it
from the Maigret novels. One of the most overtly autobiographical of Simenon's novels, *Three Bedrooms* is a fictionalized account
of Simenon's impassioned love affair with Denyse Ouimet, whom
he met in Manhattan in November 1945 (Simenon interviewed
the strong-willed young woman, seventeen years his junior, for a
secretarial position) and would marry in June 1950 in Reno, Nevada, after his divorce from his current wife. In *Three Bedrooms*,
the wife of the forty-eight-year-old protagonist is reimagined as an
adulteress who has humiliated her husband by having eloped with a
much younger gigolo; the protagonist, a Frenchman named François
Combe, is not a best-selling writer but a famous Parisian actor who
has fled to Manhattan to escape his past. Though *Three Bedrooms*
is constructed like most "simenons," sparely and urgently written,
impressionistically atmospheric, with a middle-aged protagonist approaching a crisis in his life, it is considerably different in tone.
Though set in the "calm and brutal indifference" of Manhattan,
Three Bedrooms evolves by quirky degrees into an unexpected romance.

Unlike the typical Simenon protagonist, François Combe manages to resist the downward spiral of mere contingency and seems

to will himself to establish a permanent relationship with Kay Miller, whom he has very casually met in a Greenwich Village diner. Though Kay Miller exhibits mannerisms that annoy Combe, the two are drawn together and consummate their mutual attraction, after hours of compulsive walking on Manhattan streets, in a seedy hotel room. Not long afterward, they make love in Combe's rented room, which seals Combe's sense of destiny:

> For months now, Combe's life had been going nowhere. But, until two days ago, he had at least been walking stubbornly in one direction. On this chilly October morning, he was a man who had cut all the threads, a man approaching fifty, without ties to anything—not to family, profession, country, himself, and definitely not to a home. His only connection was to a complete stranger, a woman sleeping in his room in a seedy hotel.

The third room in Manhattan will be Kay Miller's room, to which the lovers come as at the end of an arduous pilgrimage. *Three Bedrooms* is a departure for Simenon, in that his protagonist isn't an ordinary bourgeois jolted out of his routine, stuporous life, but a "famous" man fleeing humiliation. (At this time, Simenon had been accused of wartime collaboration, charges which would later be dropped.) Where most of Simenon's novellas are set in Europe, *Three Bedrooms* is pointedly set in several selected Manhattan bars, Greenwich Village, Rockefeller Center, on Fifth Avenue, and in a cheap hotel called the Lotus. These settings, deftly rendered, are cinematic backgrounds for the lovers' escalating, if somewhat mysterious, relationship, which endures through Combe's obsessive jealousy (a trait of Simenon's) and Kay Miller's distracting mannerisms (perhaps in emulation of the real-life Denyse, Kay Miller eats, drinks, and smokes cigarettes with exasperating slowness). The author is considerably challenged to make the reader feel the intensity of his lovers' attraction for each other. Lacking overt drama, *Three*

Bedrooms is perhaps best described as a memoirist work: it's as if Simenon, master of irony, is overcome by wonder at what is happening to him, succumbing to romantic infatuation in jaded middle age. There is something very Gallic about *Three Bedrooms,* in the mode of the fated lovers of, for instance, Truffaut's *Jules et Jim.* For here, for once, male skepticism is countered by female resiliency and good humor. The drift toward entropy and disaster is subverted. Though in the author's own turbulent life his relationship with Denyse Ouimet would end tragically, as Denyse lapsed by degrees into psychosis, and their daughter Marie-Jo committed suicide, in *Three Bedrooms* all is new, yet to be discovered:

> Tomorrow would be a new day. Now it was dawn, and far off, you could hear the city coming to life.
>
> Why hurry? The day was theirs, and the days that would follow. The city no longer frightened them, not this one and not any other.

TWO AMERICAN PROSE MASTERS

John Updike, Ralph Ellison

Could two stories by contemporary American male writers of the mid-twentieth century be more dissimilar? At least, at first glance.

John Updike's brilliantly condensed, intensely lyric homage to the voice of another American contemporary, J. D. Salinger, has long been the Updike story most anthologized, as it is likely the Updike story that is the most readily accessible to young readers. Ironically, or perhaps appropriately, in its very brevity and colloquial lyricism "A & P" isn't characteristic of Updike's short stories, which tend to be much longer, richer in detail and background information, slow-moving and analytical; this is a story told exclusively from the perspective of a teenaged boy, in the boy's mildly sardonic, droll voice—"In walks these three girls in nothing but bathing suits."

The boy is a checkout cashier at an A & P store in the (fictitious) small town of Tarbox, Massachusetts, an old New England settlement that dates to 1634, close enough to the Atlantic Ocean that, as Updike notes in another Tarbox story ("The Indian"), "You find you must drive down toward the beach once a week or it is like a week without love."

This proximity to the beach—(and perhaps the wild sensuous beauty of the ocean)— figures crucially in "A & P," for the girls who have entered the store are in bathing suits, and such casual wear is forbidden by the priggish store manager: "Girls, this isn't the beach." And, yet more priggishly, "We want you decently dressed when you come in here."

Immediately there is tension: drama. Immediately we are in the presence of a generational standoff: on one side, the girls in bathing suits and Sammy the admiring cashier, on the other the store manager Lengel, who happens to be an old friend of Sammy's parents ("Sammy, you don't want to do this to your mom and dad"—typically, a remark to make a rebellious adolescent feel guilty).

Sammy makes his gallant, if quixotic gesture—impulsively, he quits his job, in protest of the store manager's behavior: "You didn't have to embarrass them." And when Sammy leaves the store, the girls are gone. "My stomach kind of fell as I felt how hard the world was going to be to me from here on."

"A & P" is a wonderfully visual story. It is no surprise to learn that John Updike studied art, and that his fiction abounds with vividly realized and minutely delineated scenes. Though only a high school boy, Sammy has a sharp, droll eye: a middle-aged woman customer is seen as "a witch about fifty with rouge on her cheekbones and no eyebrows"—"if she'd been born at the right time they would have hung her over in Salem"; housewife-shoppers in the A & P he sneers at as "houseslaves in pin curlers." His intense interest is in the girls, or rather one of the girls who is wearing a "kind of dirty-pink—beige maybe, I don't know—bathing suit with a little nubble all over it and, what got me, the straps were down. They were off her shoulders looped loose around the cool tops of her arms . . . all around the top of the cloth there was this shining rim . . . I mean, it was more than pretty."

We note that Sammy recounts the story as an anecdote that occurs both in the present tense ("In walks . . .") and the past tense ("The one that caught my eye first . . ."): why? Is this an error on the author's part, or a shrewd decision? When we write/read/think in the present tense, we are literally *not yet in possession of what comes next;* like a horse with blinders, yoked in place, unable to turn our heads and look back, we can only look forward, and we are helpless to "analyze" what is happening, since such a perspective can only come retrospectively. The present tense is the very tense of things unfolding—it's the present tense in which we actually live, though our wandering, questing, ruminating minds can take us very far even as we remain, in the eyes of an observer, in one place. Updike's narrator is retelling this story of how his life was changed when he was sixteen or seventeen, in the Tarbox "A & P" one momentous day— he's older now, and we might assume he is less impulsive. The reader is left to wonder: Did Sammy regret quitting his job in the A & P?

Ralph Ellison's "Battle Royal" is also the most frequently anthologized story by this distinguished black American writer, most famous for his novel *Invisible Man* (1952); it is also recounted by a narrator looking back upon his boyhood—"It goes a long way back, some twenty years." Both stories depict boys who make dramatic decisions that have affected their subsequent lives, and it's suggested in "A & P" that Sammy will always be an outsider in his smug, provincial society. But the (unnamed) narrator of the harrowing "Battle Royal" is truly an outsider in the white racist society in which he must live, and his horrific experience is virtually the antithesis of the quite mild, unthreatening experience of the (white) boy Sammy. (Indeed, we don't think of Sammy as "white" when we read "A & P"—we take for granted that he is of the majority race, which happens to be "white" in the United States. Only when we contrast Sammy with Ellison's teenaged boy do we realize the profound abyss between them.)

In 1948, when this story was first published, American blacks were called "Negroes"—this was the polite, proper designation, in vernacular speech often diminished and degraded to the racist slur with which, daringly, Ellison ends his story: "Keep This Nigger-Boy Running." At the outset, Ellison's narrator is shocked by his seemingly meek grandfather's instructions to him on his deathbed: "I never told you, our life is a war. . . . Live with your head in the lion's mouth. I want you to overcome 'em with yeses, undermine 'em with grins, agree 'em to death and destruction, let 'em swoller you till they vomit or burst wide open." (By "'em" the grandfather means, of course, "white folks.")

Where "A & P" is a sweetly melancholy/comic story, "Battle Royal" is a horror tale all the more horrible for being historically "real." (Though once, when I taught this famous story in a Princeton writing workshop, an undergraduate said, "This never happened. Nothing like this ever happened." The student was not of the white racial majority, and the rest of us simply sat stunned, in silence. How to reply? We said nothing—we did not defend Ralph Ellison's authority. My feeling was that Ellison's brave story was the only valid reply—the witnessing of truth by one who has experienced it, not one who is only summarizing it.)

Both "A & P" and "Battle Royal" are dramatic, and riveting. Both focus upon turning points in teenaged boys' lives. Both are beautifully written, though Ellison's is the richer in its background exposition, as it is the more profound in its indictment of the very complacency of the white society to which, we can assume, Updike's Lengel belongs. The experience of racist harassment and cruelty could not be more succinctly focused than in "Battle Royal" in which black boys are forced to fight one another for the amusement of ignorant but powerful white men in a segregated city (very likely Oklahoma City, where Ellison grew up in the early years of the twentieth century) in which a Negro high school valedictorian is instructed by a racist to "keep developing as you are and some day [this prize briefcase] will be filled with important papers that will help shape the destiny of your people."

It is a delicious irony. But it is a painful irony. For who among the simpering white racists could have foreseen that indeed, the "important papers" of Ralph Ellison would one day be published as *Invisible Man,* among the greatest of American novels of the twentieth century?

A VISIT WITH DORIS LESSING

It is a bright, fresh, cold day in London, one of those excellent winter days that seem to promise spring. But it is already spring here, by the calendar, the spring of 1972, not winter, and one's expectations are slightly thrown off—everything has been blooming here for months, and now trees are in full leaf, the sun is a very powerful presence in the sky, but still it is strangely cold, as if time were in a permanent suspension. Walking along Shoot-Up Hill in Kilburn, London, I am aware of people's steamy breaths—in mid-May!—and as always I am a little disconcerted by the busyness of main thoroughfares, the continual stream of taxis and shiny red double-decker buses and private automobiles, and the quiet that attends this commotion. It seems so unexpected, the absence of horns, the absence of noise. Americans in London are disoriented by the paradox of such enormous numbers of people crowded into small areas without obvious intrusions upon one another, or even obvious visual displays of their crowdedness. It is usually the case that a one-minute walk off a busy road will bring one to absolute quiet—the pastoral improbability of Green Park, which is exactly like the country and even smells like the country, a few seconds stroll from Piccadilly on one side and the Mall on the other—and Doris Lessing's home, only a few hundred yards from Kilburn High Road, incredibly quiet and private, as remote a setting as any home deep in the country. She lives in the top-floor flat of a handsome, sturdy, three-storied house on Kingscroft Road, a short, curving street of single and semi-detached homes, with brick or stone walls that shield their gardens from the street. There is a fragrant smell of newly mown grass in the air, and the profusion of flowers and full-leafed trees seem out of place in the cold. Upstairs, the large room that serves Mrs. Lessing as both a dining room and a workroom looks out upon a yard of trees, delicate foliage that is illuminated by sunshine just as I am shown into the room.

It is a room of spacious proportions: at one end a wide window-sill given over to trays of small plants, at the other end an immense writing desk covered with books and papers. The flat—fairly large by London standards—is well-lived-in and comfortable, filled with Mrs. Lessing's own furniture, rugs, pillows, and many shelves and tables of books.

Doris Lessing is direct, womanly, very charming. She wears her long, graying black hair drawn into a bun at the back of her head; her face is slender and attractive, exactly the face of the photographs, the "Doris Lessing" I had been reading and admiring for so long. Meeting her at last I felt almost faint—certainly unreal—turning transparent myself in the presence of this totally defined, self-confident, gracious woman. I had arrived at Kilburn half an hour early, in order to wander around, to see the neighborhood in which she lived; and now, meeting her at last, I marveled at how easily the space between us had been crossed. Surely everything must seem to me a little enchanted.

When I had left the Kilburn Underground station, however, I had paused at a news agent's stand to read in amazement of the attempted assassination of George Wallace. I explained to Mrs. Lessing that I was still stunned by the news—that I hardly knew what to think—that I felt depressed and confused by this latest act of violence. And, like many Americans in foreign countries, I felt a sense of shame.

Lessing spoke very sympathetically of the problems of violence in contemporary culture, especially in America. "But everyone had guns when I was a child, on the farm," she said, referring to her childhood in Southern Rhodesia. "They went out and shot snakes; it seemed quite natural, to kill. No one ever seemed to ask: Why? Why kill? It seemed entirely natural." She asked me some very perceptive questions about the political climate in the United States: whether anyone would take Wallace's place (since it seemed, this morning, that Wallace might not recover), whether I thought the long, courageous years of effort of the antiwar protesters had really done much good? She seems more sympathetic, generally, with the United States—or with the liberal consciousness of the United States—than with England; when I remarked upon this, she said that her writing seemed to her better understood in the United States.

"In England, if you publish regularly, you tend to be written off," she said. "In America, one has the impression of critics scrutinizing each performance—as if regarding one's efforts at leaping hurdles, overcoming obstacles, with interest."

I asked about the response in England to a recent novel, the very unusual *Briefing for a Descent into Hell* (1971). "The readers who best understood it were the young," she said.

Briefing for a Descent into Hell is "inner space fiction" (Lessing's category), and shows a remarkable sympathy with the "broken-down" psyche. It is the record of the breakdown of a professor of classics, his experience of a visionary, archetypal world of myth and drama, his treatment at the hands of conventional psychiatrists, and his subsequent—and ironic—recovery into the mean, narrow, self-denying world of the "sane." An afterword by the author makes the fascinating observation that the defining of the "extraordinarily perceptive" human being as abnormal—he *must* have "something wrong with him"—is the only response one can expect, at present, from conventional medical practitioners. I asked Mrs. Lessing if she were sympathetic with the work of Ronald Laing, whose ideas resemble her own.

"Yes. We were both exploring the phenomenon of the unclassifiable experience, the psychological 'breaking-through' that the conventional world judges as mad. I think Laing must have been very courageous, to question the basic assumptions of his profession from the inside. . . . In America, the psychiatrist Thomas Szasz, in *The Manufacture of Madness,* has made similar claims. He has taken a very revolutionary position."

(Szasz, radical indeed, has demanded that the "mentally disturbed" be given full civil rights, including the right to be arrested and tried for their crimes, not treated as "sick"; he believes that "medical intervention" is simply a method of control of individuals at odds with the system, and that it is altogether too easy for psychiatrists and other powerful individuals to diagnose as "mentally ill" people whom they simply dislike.)

Lessing has known people who have experienced apparently "mystical" insights. After the publication of that iconoclastic book *The Golden Notebook* (1962), she received many letters from people who have been in mental asylums or who have undergone conventional psychiatric treatment but who, in Lessing's opinion, were not really insane—not "sick" at all.

I asked whether the terms "mystical" and "visionary" weren't misleading, and whether these experiences were not quite natural—normal.

"I think so, yes," she said. "Except that one is cautioned against speaking of them. People very commonly experience things they are afraid to admit to, being frightened of the label of 'insane' or 'sick,' and there are no adequate categories for this kind of experience."

Because this is a problem I am encountering in my own writing, I asked Lessing whether she felt it was extremely difficult to convey the sense of a "mystical" experience in the framework of fiction, of any kind of work intended to communicate naturalistically to a large audience. She agreed, saying that in England, at least, there is a tendency for reviewers to dismiss viewpoints that are not their own, that seem outside the ordinary response. I mentioned that Colin Wilson, in treating most sympathetically the writings of the American psychologist Abraham Maslow (in his *New Pathways in Psychology: Maslow and the Post-Freudian Revolution*), received at least one review that attempted to dismiss him as "clever," and that I believed this quite symptomatic of English literary reviews in general. Lessing, who has met Colin Wilson, said that reviewers and critics have been intent upon paying him back for his early, immediate success with *The Outsider,* written when he was only twenty-three; but that he is erudite, very energetic, and an important writer. However, critical response to a book like his, or any book which attempts to deal sympathetically with so-called "mystical" experiences, will meet opposition from the status quo.

One of the far-reaching consequences of Doris Lessing's two recent books, *Briefing* and *The Four-Gated City,* will be to relate the "mystical" experience to ordinary life, to show that the apparently sick—the "legally insane"—members of our society may, in fact, be in touch with a deeper, more poetic, more human reality than the apparently healthy. But both novels are difficult ones, and have baffled many intelligent readers. When I first read *The Four-Gated City,* in order to review it for the *Saturday Review,* I was impressed by the author's audacity in taking a naturalistic heroine into a naturalistic setting, subjecting her to extraordinary experiences, and bringing her not only up to the present day but into the future—to her death near the end of the twentieth century. I could not recall ever having read a novel like this. And it is the more iconoclastic in that the novel is the last of a five-part series, *Children of Violence,* begun in 1952, tracing the life of Martha Quest, an obviously autobiographical heroine.

I asked Lessing what she was working on at present, if she were continuing this exploration of the soul; but she said that, no, in a way she might be accused of a slight "regression," in that the novel she has just finished concerns a woman whose marriage has disintegrated and whose life is suddenly hollow, without meaning. "The title is *The Summer Before the Dark,* and the woman in it, the woman who loses her husband, goes to pieces in a way I've witnessed women go to pieces." Her own marriages, she mentioned, were not very "permanent," and did not permanently affect her; but this phenomenon of a woman so totally defined by her marriage has long interested her. More immediately, she was planning a collection of short stories: the American edition to be called *The Temptation of Jack Orknay,* and the English edition *The Story of an Unmarrying Man.* She was arranging a visit to the United States for a series of five lectures, to be delivered at The New School, and she was very much looking forward to the trip—she wanted to visit friends, and to travel, if possible, to the Southwest.

Her last trip to the United States was in 1969, when she gave a number of lectures at various universities. At that time she met Kurt Vonnegut, "a bloke I got on with very well," whose writing she admires immensely. This struck me as rather surprising, since to me Doris Lessing's writing is of a much more substantial, "literary" nature than Vonnegut's; but their similar concerns for the madness of society, its self-destructive tendencies, would account for her enthusiasm. She spoke of having heard that Vonnegut did not plan to write anymore—which I hadn't heard, myself—and that this distressed her; she thought he was very good, indeed. She mentioned *Slaughterhouse Five* as an especially impressive book of his.

Less surprisingly, she felt a kinship with Norman Mailer, and believed that the critical treatment he received for *Barbary Shore* and *The Deer Park* was quite unjustified; "they're good books," she said. I mentioned that the exciting thing about Mailer—sometimes incidental to the aesthetic quality of his work—was his complete identification with the era in which he lives, his desire to affect radically the consciousness of the times, to dramatize himself as a spiritual representative of the times and its contradictions, and that this sense of a mission was evident in her writing as well. "In beginning the Martha Quest series, you could not possibly have known how it would end; and the sympathetic reader, following Martha's life, cannot help but be transformed, along with Martha," I said. Lessing was understandably reticent about her own writing—and perhaps I embarrassed her by my own enthusiasm, though I did not tell her that she was quite mistaken in her feeling that her writing might not have the effect she desired: *The Golden Notebook* alone has radically changed the consciousness of many young women. Was there anyone else with whom she felt a kinship? She mentioned Saul Bellow, and of course D. H. Lawrence, and the African writer Nadine Gordimer (Lessing cannot return to the country of her childhood and girlhood, Southern Rhodesia, because she is a "prohibited immigrant"; homesick for the veldt, she had her daughter send her several color photographs of African flowers, which are on display in her flat). At the back of her mind, she said, is a work "about two men in prison" which she is not writing (as Kurt Vonnegut was "not writing" for decades the story of the Dresden fire bombing which is the ostensible subject of *Slaughterhouse Five*); perhaps this work, which she may someday do, is related to her South African background.

What most excited her about America was, during her visit, the spirit of liberality and energy in the young. She gave a lecture at the State University of New York at Buffalo in 1969, when that university was in a state of turmoil (a condition that the national press unaccountably overlooked, focusing news stories on Columbia and Berkeley), then flew to Stony Brook, which, though hardly a radical institution at the time, immediately erupted into student riots and rampages, brought on by a long history of police harassment over drugs. After visiting these two universities, Lessing was scheduled to fly to—of all places—Berkeley, where she gave another lecture. She was most favorably impressed by the students, and young people in general, with whom she became acquainted. I asked her if she might like to teach full-time, but she said she would hesitate to take on a position of such responsibility (she had been offered a handsome job at City College, which she declined with regret), partly because she considered her own academic background somewhat meager. "I ended my formal education at the age of fourteen, and before that I really learned very little," she said. It struck me as amazing: a woman whose books constitute a staggering accomplishment, who is, herself, undisputably a major figure in English literature of the twentieth century—should hesitate to teach in a university! It is rather as if a resurrected Kafka, shy, unobtrusive, humble, should insist that his works be taught by anyone else, any ordinary academic with ordinary academic qualifications, sensing himself somehow not equal to what he represents. Perhaps there is some truth to it. But I was forced to realize how thoroughly oppressive the world of professional "education" really is; how it locks out either overtly or in effect the natural genius whose background appears not to have been sufficient.

Lessing said that connections between English writers and universities were quite rare, but that in the United States it seemed very common. I explained that this was because of the existence of creative writing programs in the United States, which were not narrowly "academic," but which allowed a writer-in-residence to meet with students once or twice a week, giving him much time for his own work. In England, many writers are forced to work in publishing houses or on magazines. The publishing world in London, Lessing said, is always changing; editors are always switching publishers, publishing houses disappear and new ones appear. In fact, she told me news I hadn't heard (and probably would not have heard, since I am in a kind of dream world here, strangely out of contact with local literary events), concerning the paperback reprint house which publishes us both, Panther: the two top editors quit this week and are going to form their own publishing house. When I expressed surprise, she told me that this sort of thing is always happening. New York City, though also restive, is not quite so bad.

Lessing's American publisher is Knopf, and her editor the well-known Bob Gottlieb, with whom she enjoys working very much. She moved with Gottlieb when he left Simon & Schuster, and thinks he is an excellent editor; he helped arrange for her lecture series. I asked her if she was pleased, generally, with her writing and with its public response. Strangely, she replied that she sometimes had to force herself to write—that she often was overcome by the probable "pointlessness" of the whole thing. I asked Lessing if she meant that her own writing seemed to her sometimes futile, or was it the role of literature in society.

"I suppose one begins with the idea of transforming society," she said, "through literature and then, when nothing happens, one feels a sense of failure. But then the question is simply *why* did one feel he might change society? Change anything? In any case, one keeps going."

I told Lessing that her writing has worked to transform many individuals, and that individuals, though apparently isolated, do, in fact, constitute society. Her own writing, in my opinion, does not exist in a vacuum, but reinforces and is reinforced by the writing of some of her important (and nonliterary) contemporaries—Ronald Laing, Abraham Maslow, Buckminster Fuller, Barry Commoner—and many other critics of the "self-destructing society."

"Yet one does question the very premises of literature, at times," Lessing said. "Has anything changed? Will anything change? The vocal opposition to the war in Vietnam, in America—has it forced any real change?"

"I think there have been changes, alterations of consciousness," I said.

Lessing received my opinion respectfully, but it seemed clear that she did not share it. She went on to remark that she felt rather out of touch with current writing, since she kept to herself, generally, and did not make any attempt to keep up with all that was being written. She asked me about the English writers I admired. When I told her that I very much liked Naipaul's *In a Free State*, she agreed that Naipaul was an excellent writer. "But somehow I don't feel a rapport with him, the kind of sympathy I feel for someone like Vonnegut, even though he writes about a part of the world, Africa, I know very well."

Of the younger English writers I admired, only Margaret Drabble was a familiar name to Lessing. She liked Miss Drabble's writing but had not yet read *The Needle's Eye;* I told her that I thought this novel shared some important themes with her own work—the conscious "creating" of a set of values by which people can live, albeit in a difficult, tragically diminished urban world.

"Well, whether literature accomplishes anything or not," Mrs. Lessing said, "we do keep going."

When I left Lessing's flat and walked back down the hill to the Underground station, I felt even more strongly that sense of suspension, of unreality. It seemed to me one of the mysterious paradoxes of life, the inability of the truly gifted, the prophetic "geniuses" (an unforgivable but necessary word) to comprehend themselves, their places in history: rare indeed is the self-recognized and self-defined person like Yeats, who seems to have come to terms not only with his creative productivity but also with his destiny. Doris Lessing, the warm, poised, immensely interesting woman with whom I had just spent two hours, does not yet know that she is *Doris Lessing,* one day to win the Nobel Prize in Literature.

Yet it is natural, I suppose, for her not to know or to guess how much *The Golden Notebook* (predating and superseding even the most sophisticated of all the "women's liberation" works) meant to young women of my generation; how beautifully the craftsmanship of her many short stories illuminated lives, the most secret and guarded of private lives, in a style that was never self-conscious or contrived. She could not gauge how *The Four-Gated City,* evidently a difficult novel for her to write, would work to transform our consciousness not only of the ecological disaster we are facing, the self-annihilating madness of our society which brands its critics as "mad," but also of the possibilities of the open form of the novel itself. Never superficially experimental, Lessing's writing is profoundly experimental—exploratory—in its effort to alter our expectations about life and about the range of our own consciousness.

Her books, especially the Martha Quest series, *The Golden Notebook,* and *Briefing for a Descent into Hell,* have traced an evolutionary progress of the soul, which to some extent transforms the reader as he reads. I think it is true of our greatest writers that their effect on us is delayed, that it may take years for us to understand what they have done to us. Doris Lessing possesses a unique sensitivity, writing out of her own intense experience, her own subjectivity, but at the same time writing out of the spirit of the times. This is a gift that cannot be analyzed; it must only be honored.

III

———————————

CONTEMPORARIES

THE CHILDHOOD OF JESUS:
J. M. COETZEE

Like J. M. Coetzee's richly symbolic early novels *Waiting for the Barbarians* (1980) and *Life & Times of Michael K.* (1983), the starkly narrated *The Childhood of Jesus* plunges us at once into a mysterious and dreamlike terrain. Where the early novels evoke Coetzee's native South Africa and the madness of apartheid, and immerse the reader in situations of near-unbearable intensity, *The Childhood of Jesus* is set in a sort of posthumous limbo in which a haze of forgetfulness has enervated most of the characters, as in a paralyzing smog. We arrive by boat in a city called Novilla, in an unnamed but possibly southern European country, in the company of a middle-aged man named Simon, who has taken under his protection a child named David—"Not my grandson, not my son, but I am responsible for him." It would appear that the travelers are refugees: they have come from a "camp" at Belstar, where they were given Spanish lessons and new passports. The child has been separated from his parents. Simon seems to have no family at all. Having been shorn of his memory on the ocean voyage, like all his fellow travelers, Simon arrives in unknown territory and must establish himself as a citizen; he must find shelter, and he must find work to support himself and the boy. If Simon has had a profession or a trade in his former life, he can't recall it; he is grateful to find work as a stevedore, for which he is barely qualified. It will be Simon's obsession to locate David's mother, whose name he doesn't know, and of whom he knows nothing, not even that she has arrived in this strange, nameless country.

In time we learn that "Simon" and "David" are arbitrary names; no one in this place knows his or her birth-name; even ages and birth dates have been given out arbitrarily:

> The names we use are the names we were given . . . but we might just as well have been given numbers. Numbers, names—they are equally arbitrary, equally random, equally unimportant.

It's an unusual dystopian fiction in which a protagonist is so passive in his acceptance of his fate, but Simon exhibits virtually no curiosity about such decisions or who the anonymous authorities are who administer them; just possibly, the enigmatically titled *The Childhood of Jesus* isn't a dystopian fiction at all.

Though Spanish is the official language of the new country, it is not a native but an arbitrarily chosen language. As Simon tries to explain to David, who has begun to take refuge in jabbering to himself in a private, nonsense-language:

> Everyone comes to this country as a stranger. . . . We came from various places and various pasts, seeking a new life. But now we are all in the same boat together. So we have to get along with each other. One of the ways in which we get along is by speaking the same language. That is the rule. It is a good rule, and we should obey it. . . . If you refuse, if you go on being rude about Spanish and insist on speaking your own language, then you are going to find yourself living in a private world.

The conflict between the "private" world of individual, childish fantasy (suggested by an illustrated copy of *Don Quixote* to which David clings) and the larger, public, impersonal world which demands conformity of all citizens would seem to be a predominant theme of *The Childhood of Jesus*.

Here is not the chill, mounting terror of Orwell's *1984,* nor even the somnolent haze of Huxley's *Brave New World,* but rather a quasi-socialist state in which conformity, mediocrity, and anonymity are both the norm and the highest values. There appear to be no threats of punishment—the very term "police" is used only once, as a warning when David refuses to attend school like other children; no "police officers" ever appear. The indistinctly dreamlike, minimally described atmosphere suggests a Kafkaesque cityscape or a near-barren Beckett stage. (The penultimate chapter of Coetzee's 2003 novel *Elizabeth Costello* is an "appropriation" of several fabled prose pieces of Kafka. Coetzee wrote his Ph.D. dissertation on Samuel Beckett, and has clearly been influenced by Beckett.) Where an invisible but benign bureaucracy oversees individual lives at a considerable distance, most citizens are grateful for sustenance and accommodations in uniform housing blocks; some watch football on TV, and others attend night-school classes in the hope of self-improvement. All appear content to live lives somewhere below the level of what Henry David Thoreau has called quiet desperation. Boredom? Sexual yearning? Suffering, dying, death? Why be concerned? As a citizen typically remarks, "If he died he will go on to the next life."

Simon has difficulty adjusting to his new life. He has lost his memory yet retains a discomforting "memory of having a memory." Though he tries to conform to the worker-ant society, he feels alienated from the very atmosphere of Novilla—a generalized "benevolence"—"a cloud of goodwill." Nothing seems urgent here, nothing is "privatized." All is generic, universal, impersonal. In uniformly plain, flat, unadorned prose, in which nothing so luxurious as a metaphor emerges, or a striking employment of syntax, or a word of more than one or two syllables, Coetzee never suggests any sort of nationalism or religious tradition—there are no churches, synagogues or mosques in this exhausted country. It would appear to be a wholly secular state, a non-nation, with a non-native-language and a quasi-socialist agenda lacking history; all its citizens are amnesiacs. Love, desire, even intense friendships are virtually unknown. When Simon complains that goodwill, a "universal balm for our ills," is no substitute for "plain old physical contact" he's met with a bemused rejoinder—"If by sleeping with someone you mean sex—quite strange too. A strange thing to be preoccupied with."

Surrounded by benevolent zombies, plaintively Simon demands, "Have you ever asked yourself whether the price we pay for this new life, the price of forgetting, may not be too high?" He is the only person to rage against the loss of a fuller humanity: "When we have annihilated our hunger, you say, we will have proved we can adapt, and we can be happy for ever after. But I don't want to starve the dog of hunger. I want to feed it!" Literally, Simon wants to eat meat—-"Beefsteak with mashed potatoes and gravy . . . Beefsteak dripping with meat juices." He is deeply unhappy that the diet in Novilla is mostly crackers, bread, and a tepid sort of bean paste; there is no salt in Novilla, as there is no irony. "It is so bloodless. Everyone I meet is so decent, so kindly, so well-intentioned. No one swears or gets angry. No one gets drunk. . . . How can that be, humanly speaking? Are you lying, even to yourselves?" As a militant vegetarian, Coetzee has written passionately and scathingly of the custom of eating meat; in the mock-autobiographical/confessional *Elizabeth Costello,* he has suggested that the Holocaust of 20th-century Europe is not essentially different from the Holocaust of daily animal slaughter, and that meat-eaters are not to be distinguished from the Nazis who made soap of human beings and fashioned lamp shades of their skin. (Delivered as a "fable-lecture" at Princeton University in the 1997–1998 Tanner Lecture series, this excerpt from Coetzee's work-in-progress created a ripple of unease and indignation among the mostly meat-eating academic audience; if it was Coetzee's intention to unsettle them, he succeeded brilliantly. At the official dinner that followed, no meat was served to any guest.) Yet, in this scene, as in others in *The Childhood of Jesus,* the reader is inclined to assume that Simon is speaking for the author, in a rare and welcome display of feeling in a novel so generally muted in emotion.

Perhaps the issue of Simon's unhappiness is essentially a philosophical one, however: not sex or love per se but the very phenomenon of "passion" needs to be examined, as in this rather prissy lecture put to Simon by the "gaunt" woman with whom he has been having a perfunctory affair:

> In the old way of thinking, no matter how much you may have, there is always something missing. The name you choose to give this *something-more* that is missing is passion. . . . This endless dissatisfaction, this yearning for something-more that is missing, is a way of thinking we are well rid of . . . *nothing is missing.* The nothing that you think is missing is an illusion. You are living by an illusion.

This is the very vocabulary of Buddhist and Hindu epistemology: the world of transient attachments and desires is an illusion, and to free oneself from such is to free oneself from illusion. Yet, to attain this enlightenment is, in a sense, to renounce what is fully human; it is a kind of death. Like an obtuse naïf Simon is frequently rebuked: "This isn't a possible world—it is the only world."

Starved for "feminine beauty" as well as for beefsteak, Simon tries to register with a service called Salon Comfort, where he will have sessions with sex-workers; his application is denied, with the tactless suggestion that he "withdraw from sex. You are old enough to do so." In this, Simon is clearly akin to the emotionally starved "professor of communications" of Coetzee's best-known, best-selling novel *Disgrace* (1999), whose rejection by an escort-for-hire whom he has been seeing routinely for years precipitates the disaster—the "disgrace"—of his life.

One day, abruptly, in a display of irrationality that seems out of character, Simon decides that a woman he has seen playing tennis, a stranger, is David's mother—"I recognized her as soon as I set eyes on her." The woman, Ines, is a "blank slate, a virgin slate," upon which Simon can project his private, highly idiosyncratic meaning. Except that *The Childhood of Jesus* is a fable of the Absurd and not a realistic novel, it's difficult to see how or why Simon would act so brashly. He duly arranges for the "stolid, humorless" Inez to live with David in his flat, supported by Simon. In this way, a quasi-family is created, *ex nihilo*. The reader might wonder at this point: If David is, in some sense, the child "Jesus," is the stolid Ines meant to suggest, or in some way to be, the Biblical "Virgin Mary"? In which case, is Simon an avatar of the Biblical St. Joseph? Given the solemnity of this far-fetched development it is also possible that Coetzee is gently parodying messianic delusions among people who have nothing else to sustain them.

The remainder of *The Childhood of Jesus* is taken up with the protracted struggle of David's pseudo-parents over the boy, not unlike the ongoing struggle of ordinary parents with "difficult" children. Ines infantilizes David as "the light of my life" and wants to keep him with her at home, while Simon wants to send him to school. Both are adamantly certain that David is "exceptional." Not a very convincing child, David would seem to be a symbol in the author's imagination of "childness" in the Romantic, Wordsworthian, sense—that is, the child as close to God, "trailing clouds of glory" (Wordsworth's "Ode: Intimations of Immortality"). Consequently, the reader has difficulty forming a coherent picture of him: at times David seems emotionally disturbed, possibly autistic, or mildly schizophrenic; he has no friends at school and his teacher finds him essentially unteachable, as he is a disruptive presence in the classroom, yet his immature behavior might be a consequence of adult over-indulgence. He is unusually bright at times, then again obstinate, exasperating. If David is indeed meant to be the child

Jesus, Coetzee has not fashioned an appropriate early life for him, for David's concerns are exclusively for himself, and not for others; indeed, David seems to have no sense of others' existences, stubbornly convinced that whatever he thinks, is true. (Told that things have to have value before they can be placed in a museum, David typically rejoins, "What is value?" His argument is, in a sense, irrefutable: "I prize it. It's my museum, not yours.") Soon, the five-year-old begins to make grandiloquent pronouncements: "I haven't got a mother and I haven't got a father. I just am." "*Yo soy la verdad.* 'I am the truth.'" (225) A child psychologist diagnoses him as maladjusted: "The real . . . is what David misses in his life. This experience of lacking the real includes the experience of lacking real parents. David has no anchor in his life." Yet, no one in Novilla has any "anchor" in life, since no one has any memory of a life before Novilla; in fact, Novilla seems scarcely to exist, a sketchily imagined fictitious place that might well be a bare, Beckett stage in which actors are reading scripts they don't fully understand, at the bequest of a director who remains elusive and has relinquished the very responsibility of "direction." In this existential stalemate even Simon is reduced to a primitive *cri de coeur*: "The life I have is not enough for me. I wish someone, some savior, would descend from the sky."

The Childhood of Jesus is clearly an allegory—some might say, echoing Herman Melville, "a hideous and intolerable allegory" (see chapter 45, *Moby-Dick*)—but it isn't an allegory with the transparency of Plato's *Allegory of the Cave,* Bunyan's *Pilgrim's Progress,* or Orwell's *Animal Farm;* nor is it an allegory of the emotional, psychological, and visceral density of *Waiting for the Barbarians* and *Life & Times of Michael K.* which, along with *Disgrace,* set in a recognizably "real" post-apartheid South Africa, constitute J. M. Coetzee's major works of fiction. With few cues the reader is left to wonder: Is Novilla a socialist utopia, or rather a parody of a socialist utopia? Does it represent the realization of Buddhist asceticism, the triumph of spiritual detachment over sensual appetite?

Or, given the title *The Childhood of Jesus,* is this the Christian renunciation of the flesh? Are the inhabitants of Novilla political refugees? Are they even alive, and not rather lost, wandering souls? Is this a Bardo state, following death, as imagined in *The Tibetan Book of the Dead*? But why have they lost their memories? (In mimicry of José Saramago's allegorical novel *Blindness* [1995], which dramatizes the effects of an epidemic of blindness in an unnamed city?) For a while I wondered if *The Childhood of Jesus* might be a novel of ideas in which the stillness of the Buddhist vision of enlightenment and the striving of Christian salvation are contrasted: the one essentially cyclical, the other "progressive"; the goal of one the annihilation of the individual personality in a sort of universal void, and the goal of the other the "salvation" of a distinctly individual personality and its guarantee of everlasting life and reunion with loved ones in Heaven. The Buddha is a universal, the "Christ" is an actual, historical figure who is unique as the son of both God and humankind.

More plausibly, *The Childhood of Jesus* is a Kafka-inspired parable of the quest for meaning itself: for reasons to endure when (secular) life lacks passion and purpose. Only an arbitrary mission—searching for the mother of an orphaned child, believing in a savior who descends from the sky—can give focus to a life otherwise undefined and random. It's a bleak and intransigent vision in which the possibility of a "new life" seems just another delusion, however idealistic.

THE DETECTIVE AS VISIONARY:
DEREK RAYMOND

What shall we be,
When we aren't what we are?

Minimalism in fiction is rarely conjoined with outbursts of passionate lyricism, and still more rarely is the formulaic crime/detection novel conjoined with the novel of philosophical quest. Derek Raymond's much-admired *"Factory"* novels are bold and intriguing hybrids: idiosyncratic police procedurals narrated by an unnamed Detective Sergeant of the London Metropolitan Police who so identifies with the victims of his investigations that he becomes involved in their (imagined) lives and is drawn, often at great risk to himself, into their (imagined) suffering. Raymond's milieu is the chill of Thatcher-era London, and his atmosphere is an unrelenting existentialist *noir*—as if the most brutal of crime fictions had been re-cast by Sartre, Camus, or Ionesco while retaining something of the intimate wise-guy tone of Raymond Chandler and Dashiell Hammett. Chapters in the *"Factory"* novels are likely to be short, blunt, fevered: "Every day you amass knowledge in a frantic race against death that death must win."

The unnamed Detective Sergeant is also a sort of novelist, or poet, obsessed with his fictitious characters and with his own, ever-shifting relationship to them as if, as he learns astonishing truths about them, they are helping to create him; rare for a veteran police officer, especially one so difficult with his fellow officers, he's susceptible to extremes of emotion, and vulnerable to the near-literal "absorption" of every hellish detail of a crime scene. He sends other police officers away—he insists upon being alone with the dead. In *I Was Dora Suarez,* Raymond's most excruciatingly horrific novel, we learn that, having been married to a psychopath-murderer, the detective credits his experience with having made him a skilled detective:

> Now, having passed through what I was hard taught, I have for a long time made use of it in my work to judge and place the actions and motives of others and see how the catcher, to be a true arrow against assassins, must at some time in his own life had personally had to do with one.

(Note the curiously formal tone, as if the passage had been translated from a foreign, slightly archaic language.)

Still, we know very little about the man except that, in *He Died with His Eyes Open* (1984), the first of the series, the irascible and indomitable investigator is forty-one years old and lives alone in a "dreadful little bachelor's flat" in Earlsfield, central London, on a "raw scar" of a block called Acacia Circus. He'd once been married, and is subject to sudden memories of his daughter, whom the reader infers he hadn't seen in some time. (In *I Was Dora Suarez* [1990], the fourth novel in the series, we learn that the daughter's name is Dahlia; his wife, Edie, is a psychopathic murderer who killed the nine-year-old and has been institutionalized since then.) As a police officer the Detective Sergeant is grimly obsessive, "obstinate," sarcastic and unpredictable; he's both highly professional and unprofessional when it suits him, beating up an insolent skinhead, or breaking into a suspect's residence without a warrant; provoked, he has even attacked one of his superior officers. His commitment to solving murders is a commitment to avenging the dead, and leads him into reckless acts; the reader is startled to realize that this British police officer isn't armed, yet places himself in positions of extreme danger, with the expectation that he can talk his way out of danger. (He can't.) Formerly he'd been with the Vice Squad of the Metropolitan Police but now works in the Department of Unexplained Deaths—"the most unpopular and shunned branch" where low-ranking police officers labor on "obscure, unimportant, apparently irrelevant deaths of people who don't matter and who never did"; but where, nonetheless, "no murder is casual to us." Career advancement lies elsewhere, in the classier CID (Criminal Investigation Department) or SIB (Special Intelligence Branch) where victims aren't near-anonymous welfare recipients found beaten to death and tossed like trash into the shrubbery in front of the Word of God House in Albatross Road, West Five, "eyes open."

The influence of Raymond Chandler is considerable in Derek Raymond, notably in the very surname "Raymond"—("Derek Raymond" is the pseudonym of the British writer Robin Cook (1931–1994), who changed his name in the early 1980s to distinguish himself from the best-selling American writer Robin Cook)—and the Chandleresque drollery of his language. The character of the unnamed detective conforms almost entirely to the knightly ideals as set forth in Chandler's "The Simple Art of Murder" (1950):

> In everything that can be called art there is a quality of redemption. It may be pure tragedy, if it is high tragedy, and it may be pity and irony, and it may be the raucous laughter of the strong man. But down these mean streets a man must go who is not himself mean, who is neither tarnished nor afraid.
>
> The detective in this kind of story must be such a man. He is the hero; he is everything. He must be a complete man and a common man and yet an unusual man. He must be, to use a

rather weathered phrase, a man of honor. . . . He is a relatively poor man, or he would not be a detective at all. He is a common man or he could not go among common people. He has a sense of character, or he would not know his job. He will take no man's money dishonestly and no man's insolence without due and dispassionate revenge. He is a lonely man. . . .

The story is the man's adventure in search of a hidden truth.

Like Chandler's Philip Marlowe, ("It was a blonde. A blonde to make a bishop kick a hole in a stained-glass window"), Raymond's detective has a droll way with words: a psychopathic serial killer is "a wild card hidden in the social pack", an elderly murder victim has the "smile of a lunatic criticizing bad theater," a murderer's lips "bent sharply downward in the shape of a sickle." At times, Raymond's language slides into a bizarre surrealism: we see a "pretty little girl with murderer's ears"—a woman with "legs like crumpled car bumpers and . . . a brightly poisoned hat." At other times, a startling frankness: "Do you know I cry in my sleep? Do you think a man can't cry in his sleep?" Political and moral corruption are ubiquitous in Chandler's quasi-glamorous Los Angeles of the 1940s but something far deeper than corruption, a kind of mad biological rot, pervades the Thatcher-era London, erupting in crazed killings far beyond anything the temperamentally puritanical Raymond Chandler would have wished to dramatize in prose.

"Most people live with their eyes shut, but I mean to die with my eyes open"—this statement by one of the victims Raymond investigates is surely meant to reflect the detective's attitude as well. As in a novel of philosophical investigation, like Sartre's *Nausea*, the meaning of existence is scrutinized in terms of paradox, mystery, and existential horror. The detective is a practiced interrogator in the "Factory"—so named "because of its reputation for doing suspects over in the interrogation room"; to his fellow cops he's an "insolent bastard" whom they grudgingly admire, and whom they bring back to the Department after he's been fired, to take over the most difficult murder cases. Here is the existential pilgrim as detective, the object of his inquiry nothing less than the meaning of life itself; but the pilgrim is also an avenging angel.

Both *He Died with His Eyes Open* and *I Was Dora Suarez* are composed of alternating voices: that of the detective, and that of the murder victim. The first voice is laconic and brusque, the second "poetic," two sides of a divided self. *He Died with His Eyes Open* is the more self-consciously lyric novel, containing excerpts from the taped journal of the badly battered "Charles Locksley Alwin Staniland," aged fifty-one, whose brutal fate seems at odds with the complexity of his character, and whose memories (chronic alcoholism, failed marriages, a "lost" daughter, manual labor in rural Italy, an aborted writing career) closely parallel those of Robin Cook's biography. Far from being a nonentity, as he'd initially appeared, Staniland strikes the detective as "too sane"—"intelligent and direct." After listening to the murdered Staniland's voice over a period of days, as Staniland speaks eloquently of philosophical riddles as well as painfully intimate matters, the detective broods: "Where I identified with Staniland, what I had inherited from him, was the question why." Staniland is revealed as both a debased and an elevated individual; held in contempt as an impotent drunk by the busty *femme fatale* Barbara Spark with whom he'd become riskily involved, yet admired by a BBC producer for whom he'd written brilliant but unproducible TV scripts—"A lovely man." His former wife Margo is devastated by his death, though their marriage had been sabotaged by Staniland's alcoholism and his inability to support his family: "I loved him. . . . The trouble with Charles is that he shot past everyone; he went like a meteor. . . . It's like the tragedy of the world in a little glass. . . . Great things are all smashed to pulp, and none of us who are left have the spirit to carry on."

Staniland's tapes appear to be passages in a journal—(one might

speculate that the journal is Robin Cook's)—interludes in a problematic life illuminated by sudden insights and epiphanies. The
life, revealed piecemeal in the cassettes, as the detective pursues
his investigation among a London netherworld of pubs, drinkers,
petty crooks and probable psychopaths, is a chaotic mixture of the
profane, the pitiful, the bankrupt, the aesthetic, the romantic, and
the philosophical; unrelentingly self-critical, Staniland concludes
that he is a sort of "vomitorium"—an individual who draws out the
very worst, the moral vomit, of others. (This curious insight is a
theme in Derek Raymond's "black" fiction: that murder victims are
in some way complicit with their killers, deserving of punishment,
like Staniland and the hapless young Dora Suarez.) One of the most
vivid passages in *He Died with His Eyes Open* is a description of
pig slaughter on a French farm, a prose poem that, the reader sees
in retrospect, ironically mimics Staniland's brutal murder to come.
Another interlude, hallucinatory in the precision of its images, like
something by Baudelaire or Rimbaud, describes the death-by-fire of
German pilots trapped in a plane that has crashed in the English
countryside:

> I went back and snatched a piece of tailplane that had been
> blown off and kept it for a souvenir. It was exciting, a really
> adventurous day. But the strange part was that, over the years,
> the passing of time altered the meaning of those two figures
> in their leather helmets, relaxed yet intent, shimmering in the
> fumes—time placed a different and deeper meaning on the
> experience.

Ever more deeply involved with the deceased man, the detective
"begins to suffer from the delusion that Staniland is alive." He feels
himself "twisted into a new, more complex self." In the novel's least
probable plot turn, the detective's immersion in Staniland leads him
to fall in love—in a manner of speaking—with Staniland's busty

blond *femme fatale*, a sexually frigid woman who has used her sexuality to make her way in a man's world, carelessly and cruelly: "I don't like things that go on too long." We learn that Barbara Spark with her "big shoulders, heavy arms" has herself been brutalized and wounded; as a girl she'd been incarcerated on a charge of having committed "grievous bodily harm" for having killed an assailant. Despite his shrewdness in recognizing murderers, and Staniland's warning about Barbara—("a frigid iceberg with gross psychic problems and the mind of a petty criminal")—the detective doesn't realize how irremediably scarred the woman is, how she has internalized extremes of sadomasochism violence, and how naïve he has been to imagine that he can subdue her and her partner-in-crime without the assistance of fellow police officers.

I Was Dora Suarez is a yet more intensely imagined work of fiction, generally considered the "black" masterpiece of the Factory series, and not for the fainthearted. The opening scene is a tour de force of choreographed violence imagined by an unnamed narrator—(who will be revealed as the Detective Sergeant, now forty-five years old)— a reenactment of the killings of a sexual psychopath as he wields an ax against the gravely ill, thirty-year-old Dora Suarez, and stumbles on to kill the eighty-six-year-old woman with whom Dora Suarez has been living.

Even more than Staniland, the viciously mutilated Dora Suarez exerts a powerful posthumous spell upon the detective. He is stunned by the sight of her at the crime scene:

> And yet I found, far from being afraid when I did look in her face, that I was in tears. The good side of it, except for one blood smear down her cheek, was intact. The ax had struck her across, and then down the face, the bad side. Her eyes were not damaged; they were black, ironic, and three-quarters open. . . . She was still a very beautiful girl for a few more hours yet.

The lovestruck detective feels a desire to bend over Suarez and whisper, "It's all right, darling, don't worry, everything will be all right, I'm here now."

. . . the feeling was so strong in me that I knelt and kissed her short black hair which still smelled of the apple- scented shampoo she had washed it with just last night; only the hair was rank, matted with blood, stiff and cold. Reading Suarez's diary, as he'd once listened avidly to Staniland's cassettes, the detective acquires intimate information about the murder victim, who calls herself a "Spanish Jewess"; he learns that Suarez was mysteriously, terminally ill, and had in fact planned to kill herself on the very night of her murder.

Once I was Dora Suarez, but even before I die I am not her any more; I have just become something appalling. Looking at myself naked in the mirror, I see that I have lost the right to call myself a person; what's left of me is barely human. . . . I accept that at thirty I am going to die.

Ghastly as the murder enactment has been at the opening of the novel, a subsequent scene in the police morgue in which the mutilated body is examined is yet more lurid, as it's revealed that Dora Suarez was infected with AIDS, her lower body hideously deformed by Karposi's sarcoma. Far from being repulsed by Suarez's affliction, the detective feels more intensely his identification with her: "her death had affected me so deeply that by her defiled face I felt defiled myself." In the interstices of a protracted and blackly comic interrogation in the Factory, in which petty-criminal witnesses are encouraged to provide information by being beaten by police, the detective becomes increasingly obsessed with finding the killer and avenging the young woman's death. Was there ever a police officer so emotionally bound up with his work?—so psychologically fraught?

"Every death I've ever seen in my work . . . are all for me casualties on a single front."

[F]or me the front is the street, and I am forced to see it every day.

I see it, eat it, sleep and dream the street, am the street. I groan in its violent dreams, see it under the rain and in the sun, the hurrying people on it, killers as well as victims, flying past absorbed as if they were praying. The way I am, I sense tears as well as hear them. . . . Where's the justice in it? That's what I want to know.

As in *He Died with His Eyes Open, I Was Dora Suarez* concludes with the identification of a particularly sick, sadomasochistic killer, himself afflicted with AIDS, for whom the detective expresses a perverse sympathy: "Pain is inflicted by those who have no idea what it means . . . because they inflict pain on themselves." The novel ends in an outburst of retributive gunfire and the detective's terse notation: "I felt nothing." Of this curious hybrid of a novel the author notes in his autobiography *The Hidden Files* [1992] that he was attempting here something of "the same message as Christ. . . . It was my atonement for fifty years' indifference to the miserable state of this world; it was a terrible journey through my own guilt, and through the guilt of others."

OF LITERARY GENRES, the mystery-detective novel is the most addictive, as it is the genre that dramatizes the obsessive, monomaniacal quest for the "solution" to a puzzle. (Crime fiction is as likely to be addictive for the writer as for the reader, with the result that virtually all mystery writers are highly prolific. See, for instance, such practitioners as Agatha Christie, Ellery Queen, John Dickson Carr, Rex Stout, P. D. James, Ruth Rendell, Ed McBain, Michael Connelly, et al., and most notably the hyper-prolific Simenon with an estimated two hundred titles.) When Edmund Wilson asked irritably, "Who Cares Who Killed Roger Ackroyd?" (*New Yorker*, 1944), he was bringing to bear the expectations of serious literature in an examination of mystery novels by Christie, Stout, Dorothy Sayers, among others, and finding them wanting; particularly, Wilson objected to the formulaic nature of mystery plots, the flatness of character, the general contrivance and mediocrity of the writer's vision and the banality of the "denouement." (A. Conan Doyle's *Adventures of Sherlock Holmes* Wilson excluded from his censure, for their "wit and fairytale poetry" and for the originality of the character of the detective Holmes.) An additional damning point is that mystery fans don't seem to read mystery novels very carefully; interest fades with the final chapter, and the reader-addict turns to the next mystery. Wilson complained of a reading experience analogous to having to unpack large crates by "swallowing the excelsior in order to find at the bottom a few bent and rusty nails." In his more illuminating analytical and appreciative essay on the detective novel, "The Guilty Vicarage," (1948) W. H. Auden argues that the detective novel offers readers a kind of magic by which "grace" is restored to a social setting and guilt is dispelled; even as Auden identifies himself as a detective-novel addict, he admits that he forgets a mystery novel as soon as he finishes it, and has no interest in reading it again. Auden differentiates between the novel of detection and the novel that is "art"—the latter category including fiction by Raymond Chandler as well as Dostoyevsky's *Crime and Punishment*. With references to Christian tradition, Auden perceives in crime fiction the underlying archetype of sin, salvation, and redemption, of which the secular-minded Wilson seems oblivious. In crime fiction evil is isolated by being identified, pursued, brought under control and rendered harmless; at least temporarily, evil is eradicated. As no religious ritual is absolute and for all time, so the eradication of evil is only temporary, and has to be repeated, and repeated. It's the perennial cycle of crime/sin, investigation, revelation and "justice" that provides the template for works of mystery/detection from Sophocles's *Oedipus Rex* to Dostoyevsky's *The Brothers Karamazov*: the restoration of "grace" in the social community, often at enormous cost to a sacrificial figure. The detective is this figure, frequently an outlaw-savior who must commit crimes and suffer punishment in order to achieve justice. Or, like Sophocles's Oedipus, he must identify himself as the loathed criminal, the violator of taboo; he must exorcise himself, to achieve a bitter and ironic justice. And often this is vigilante justice, as in much of contemporary crime fiction, for the law is notoriously compromised. (The corruption of high police officials and courts is taken for granted in Raymond's bleakly realist *"Factory"* novels as in Raymond Chandler's more romantic L.A.-*noir* novels. Virtually anyone who works in the public sector is synonymous with duplicity and graft while only the "private detective" or the outlaw police detective, is left to pursue justice.) The allegiance of the crime novel isn't to maintaining the stability of law, but achieving, if but piecemeal, and surreptitiously, something like the blessing of justice. Few detectives go so far as Raymond's Detective Sergeant, who falls in love with murder victims *because they have been wrongfully killed,* and there is no one but the Detective Sergeant to avenge them. Edmund Wilson could not have dismissed Derek Raymond's *"Factory"* novels as below the radar of serious literary consideration, and W. H. Auden would surely have been impressed with their stark originality, though Raymond's vision is wholly secular and fatalist and there is little sense of redemption in these blood-drenched pages.

> I said out into the night: "We'll get our dignity back; whether alive or dead, we shall all be as we used to be." I found I absolutely had to state those words out loud because, through the deaths of [the murder victims] I found myself suddenly in a state of great doubt, despair, and in a testing time, not only because of the way the two women had left us but because of the fury I felt on account of it. I found my own life set on the scales as though it were theirs. . . . I only know that [the murder

victims] must, by our forces, be put to rest; because until that is done, the new future will never come, and so none of us can ever be at rest.

Here is the detective as sacrificial visionary. He has literally lost his own, personal life in the service of the impersonal quest for justice, that may seem to us, readers at a distance, a kind of madness. For certainly there is something deranged in so vast and so passionate a quest, in such debased circumstances—this faith in a "new future." It isn't a coincidence that Derek Raymond's knightly detective is also, in temperament, an artist, a poet, and a philosopher for whom "words sometimes take the place of tears."

He Died with His Eyes Open
By Derek Raymond

I Was Dora Suarez
By Derek Raymond

"CATASTROPHE INTO ART": JULIAN BARNES

"How do you turn catastrophe into art?"—this bold question, posed by Julian Barnes in a fabulist exegesis of Gericault's great painting *The Raft of the Medusa,* in one of the chapters of Barnes's *A History of the World in 10½ Chapters* (1989), might be said to be answered by Barnes's new book, *Levels of Life,* a memoir written in the aftermath of the death of Barnes's wife of thirty years, Pat Kavanagh, who died of a brain tumor in 2008. With few of the playful stratagems and indirections of style typical in Barnes's fiction, but something of the baffled elegiac tone of Barnes's Booker Award-winning short novel *The Sense of an Ending* (2011), *Levels of Life* conveys an air of stunned candor: "I was thirty-two when we met, sixty-two when she died. The heart of my life; the life of my heart." The end came swiftly and terribly: "Thirty-seven days from diagnosis to death."

The resulting memoir, a precisely composed, often deeply moving hybrid of nonfiction, "fabulation," and straightforward reminiscence and contemplation, is a gifted writer's response to the incomprehensible in a secular culture in which "we are bad at dealing with death, that banal, unique thing; we can no longer make it part of a wider pattern." With approval Barnes quotes E. M. Forster: "One death may explain itself, but it throws no light upon another"—yet, *Levels of Life* suggests that a singular death, if examined from a singular perspective, may throw a good deal of light upon the universal experiences of loss, grief, mourning, and what Barnes calls "the question of loneliness."

Levels of Life is a not quite adequate title for this highly personal and at times richly detailed book, implying an air of lofty and cerebral contemplation from which the vividness of actual life has departed. For here it would seem that "catastrophe" does result in "art"—the death of Barnes's wife is the genesis for the book, which would not have been written otherwise. "I already know that only the old words would do: death, grief, sorrow, sadness, heartbreak. Nothing modernly evasive or medicalising. Grief is a human, not a medical, condition." The epiphany—or rather one of the epiphanies, for *Levels of Life* is comprised of striking, insightful aphorisms, far too many to note—toward which the memoir moves is the remark of a bereaved friend: "Nature is so exact, it hurts as exactly as much as it is worth, so in a way one relishes the pain. . . . If it didn't matter, it wouldn't matter." In the more intimate passages of *Levels of Life* Barnes would seem to be making the tacit point that the creation of art itself is inadequate to compensate such loss, for it is a virtually ontological, near-physical loss experienced by the survivor in an intensely felt emotional relationship, not unlike a bodily wound. How better to articulate this ineffable loss as a loss of "depth" (or altitude):

> You put together two people who have not been put together before. . . . Then, at some point, sooner or later, for this reason or that, one of them is taken away. And what is taken away is greater than the sum of what was there. This may not be mathematically possible; but it is emotionally possible.

Like Barnes's characteristic works of fiction, in which postmodernist experimentation is a prism through which ethically provocative narratives can be adroitly told, *Levels of Life* is unorthodox in structure and perspective. That it is a widower's memoir is not even evident until page 68 of 118 pages, in a section titled "Loss of Depth" in which the author speaks for the first time of his grief for his deceased wife, which has scarcely abated in the several years since her death. Preceding this section are two shorter, self-contained prose pieces evoking the ebullient era of hot-air ballooning that suggest, in retrospect, something of the airy elation, transcendence and terrible risk that falling in love entails for the survivor of such an adventure.

The first section, titled "The Sin of Height," might be subtitled "A Very Brief History of Hot-Air Ballooning," presented in a sequence of sparkily wrought vignettes about such nineteenth-century ballooning enthusiasts as Colonel Fred Burnaby (circa 1882), Felix Tournacho /"Nadar" (circa 1863), the Godard brothers (circa 1863), and the renowned actress Sarah Bernhardt (circa 1882) whose connection with ballooning is relatively slight and opportunist. Barnes writes of these extravagantly fearless balloonists with the panache of the affably omniscient narrator of *Flaubert's Parrot* and of the quasi-historian of *A History of the World in 10½ Chapters*, condensing what is surely a complex, heterogeneous history into fewer than seventy pages. "Aeronauts were the new Argonauts, their adventures instantly chronicled" in this dazzling new era in which ballooning represented "freedom" as well as danger, and an unexpected sort of "universal brotherhood" as, it was believed, at least at the time, "a balloon brought no evil." Naturally, there is a reverse sentiment, that flying violates a natural law and is therefore a sin: "To mess with flight was to mess with God. It was to prove a long struggle, full of instructive lessons"—most notably the legend of Icarus.

Barnes has researched the history of hot-air ballooning, with an eye for the poetic and the exemplary, and it is only upon a second reading of *Levels of Life* that much in the early sections acquires a symbolic significance. There are beautifully appropriate passages taken from balloonists' memoirs, for instance the remarks of the physicist Dr. J.A.C. Charles (the first person to ascend in a hydrogen balloon, 1783): "When I felt myself escaping from the earth, my reaction was not pleasure but *happiness* . . . I could *hear myself living*, so to speak." The flamboyant Colonel Burnaby is moved to a "moral feeling." The Divine Sarah sees ballooning as a natural equivalent to her "dreamy nature"; she discovers that above the clouds there is "not silence, but the shadow of silence . . . (The balloon) is the emblem of uttermost freedom." Nadar, one of the great photographers of his time, as well as a pioneering balloonist, describes "the silent immensities of welcoming and beneficent space, where man cannot be reached by any human force or by any power of evil, and where he feels himself alive as if for the first time." Yet there is always the possibility—if one persists, the probability—of catastrophe and sudden death: one young balloonist (1786) dies in a fall to earth so powerful that "the impact drove his legs into a flower bed as far as his knees, and ruptured his internal organs, which burst out on to the ground." So horrific is this vision, the memoirist Julian Barnes appropriates it for himself, as an expression of the pain that is "exactly what it is worth."

The second section of *Levels of Life* is aptly titled "On the Level": "We live on the flat, on the level, and yet—and so—we aspire. . . . Some soar with art, others with religion; most with love. But when we soar, we can also crash. . . . Every love story is a potential grief story."

Here is an imagined three-month romance between two radically unlike individuals: Colonel Burnaby and the Divine Sarah. Though begun in innocent fascination on both sides, it's a cruelly uneven romance between a celebrated actress notorious for sleeping with her leading men and a physically awkward, heavyset man. Burnaby falls in love with the petite, ethereal Sarah "hook, line and sinker." A conventional Brit of his class, Burnaby proposes marriage, and Sarah responds languidly, "I am made for sensation, for pleasure, for the moment. I am constantly in search of new sensations, new emotions. . . . My heart desires more excitement than anyone—any one person—can give." Burnaby is devastated, but survives; quasi-suicidal, he enters into a short-lived marriage with another, presumably less enchanting woman, returns to ballooning, and is killed in an illicit expedition at Khartoum in 1885. The reader comes to see belatedly that the fictitious romance between Burnaby and Sarah Bernhardt is analogous to the romance of Julian Barnes and his wife Pat Kavanagh; Burnaby doesn't outlive Sarah Bernhardt, but his loss of her is traumatic as a widower's loss: "The pain was to last several years. He eased it by traveling and skirmishing. He never talked about it. If someone inquired into his black mood, he would reply that the melancholy of the padge-owl was afflicting him."

It would seem to be with some relief, and a good deal of feeling, that Julian Barnes finally speaks in his own voice in the third section of the memoir. Here, the puppet-master/ventriloquist throws aside his stratagems and speaks plainly, as if helplessly; it's as if a master stylist like Nabokov had finally decided yes, let's speak openly, just for once.

Grief is the great human leveler: "You have suddenly come down in the freezing German Ocean, equipped with only an absurd cork overjacket that is supposed to keep you alive."

The remainder of *Levels of Love* is a journal of a kind, not so much of the events of a life as of its interior contours. Barnes identifies himself as a former lexicographer, a "descriptivist rather than a prescriptivist" whose subject in this case is himself. (*Levels of Love* is notable as a memoir of loss in which there is no portrait of the deceased.) Barnes is relentless in self-analysis, exacting to the point of obsession in exposing the raw nature of his grief. "We grieve in character. That . . . seems obvious, but this is a time when nothing seems or feels obvious." The reader senses a conflict between the memoirist's passion to speak and a stoic reticence in the effort of what he calls "grief-work." "There is the question of anger.

Some (of the widowed) are angry with the person who has died, who has abandoned them, betrayed them by losing life. . . . Few die willingly, not even most suicides." Well-intentioned friends suggest to the grief-stricken Barnes that he acquire a dog—"I would reply sarcastically that this did not seem much of a substitute for a wife." A couple suggests that Barnes rent a flat in Paris for six months, or a beach cabin in Guadeloupe; conveniently, the couple could look after Barnes's house in his absence, and "We'd have a garden for Freddie." (Freddie is the couple's dog.) Barnes is eloquent on the myopia of grief—the "solipsism of grief"—noting his anger at the reactions of others: "Since the griefstruck rarely know what they need or want, only what they don't, offence-giving and offence-taking are common. Some friends are as scared of grief as they are of death; they avoid you as if they fear infection. Some, without knowing it, half expect you to do their mourning for them." There is the bright, asinine query, a scant week after the funeral: "So, what are you up to? Are you going on walking holidays?" Others shy away from even speaking of Pat Kavanagh, though they had been friends of hers for years. The Silent Ones he calls them: "I remember a dinner conversation in a restaurant with three married friends. . . . Each had known her for many years. . . . I mentioned her name; no one picked it up. I did it again, and again nothing. Perhaps the third time I was deliberately trying to provoke. . . . Afraid to touch her name, they denied her thrice, and I thought the worst of them for it." Barnes imagines that these individuals might be wanting to say: "Your grief is an embarrassment. We're just waiting for it to pass. And, by the way, you're less interesting without her." Another widower infuriates Barnes by remarking infelicitously that he'd "lost his wife to cancer"—("another phrase that jarred: compare '"We lost our dog to gypsies'")—and reassuring Barnes that one does survive grief and emerge as a "'stronger,' and in some ways a 'better,' person. . . . This struck me as outrageous and self-praising." Naturally, after a while well-intentioned individuals begin to suggest that Barnes find another woman com-panion, remarry: "Have you found someone?" Barnes notes that, statistically, "those who have been happy in marriage remarry much sooner than those who have not: often within six months"—a fact, if it is a fact, that "shocks" the widower with its perfect synthesis of logic and illogic. "Perhaps [this] only applies in the States, where emotional optimism is a constitutional duty." It may be one of the smaller satisfactions of "art" to repay petty hurts with petty hurts, but it is a satisfaction nonetheless, and good to note here that, even in the eloquence of grief, Julian Barnes doesn't present himself as refined of such fully human predilections.

Suicide is pondered by the widower, not impulsively but ratio-nally, even dutifully, over a period of years: "If I cannot live with-out her, if my life is reduced to mere passive continuance, I shall become active. I knew soon my preferred method—a hot bath, a glass of wine next to the taps, and an exceptionally sharp Japanese carving knife." Yet, sensibly, the widower realizes that if he were to die, the most intimate recollections of the loved one will die with him, irremediably: "I could not kill myself because then I would be killing her."

The question is then, for the survivor, how to live? As if one were a balloonist high in the air, imperiled by the whims of the wind-currents, at times becalmed, perplexed. Barnes discovers in himself a sudden love of opera, where previously he hadn't cared for this "least comprehensible" of art forms; but now, in the rawness of grief, he sees how "opera cuts to the chase—as death does." Here is an art not fearful of grandiloquence and overstatement: "an art in which violent, overwhelming, hysterical and destructive emotion was the norm; an art which seeks, more obviously than any other form, to break your heart. Here was my new social realism." *Levels of Life* might have been amplified by more of these unexpectedly uplifting passages, like those in which Barnes remarks that he talks "con-stantly" to his deceased wife, years after her death, as Ivy Compton-

Burnett reputedly talked to her long-deceased companion, even in the presence of others:

"Outsiders might find this an eccentric, or 'morbid,' or self-deceiving, habit; but outsiders are by definition those who have not known grief. . . . The paradox of grief: if I have survived what is now four years of her absence, it is because I have had four years of her presence." Another paradox is that "grief is the negative image of love; and if there can be accumulation of love over the years, then why not of grief?" Barnes quotes with approval Marianne Moore's gnomic remark: "The cure for loneliness is solitude."

Barnes says little in these pages about the roles of others, family, relatives, friends and acquaintances, to help alleviate grief. Perhaps, in his case, these have been of minimal help. The Silent Ones are the more reprehensible in his eyes for not aiding in the recall of the deceased wife as they are precious to the survivor as means for "corroboration": "You need them to tell you that what you once were—the two of you—was seen. Not just known from within." Barnes has little faith in the power of one's will to guide, if not control, the waywardness of emotion. In less secular, more traditional cultures, the grieving after death is ritualized; no individual has to invent for himself a way of mourning, at least externally. Death is an occasion—frequent, if still shocking—in the social fabric, not an aberration in personal, private life. As he lives in a secular, urban, intellectual milieu, Julian Barnes presents himself as essentially adrift and unmoored, and stoically so; his grieving is passionate but narrow, as in the "solipsism of grief" he defines himself proudly beyond the range of understanding that a widow or widower might wish to make others happy, granted their own, inward unhappiness; that one might find a temporary way out of the "solipsism of grief" by taking on the grief of another or even, ludicrous as it might seem, acquiring a dog or a cat not for the sake of actually alleviating one's own grief, but for the animal's sake. Providing companionship for another, a safe home, some sort of sanctuary amid the buffeting of treacherous wind-currents is not equivalent to retrieving the lost loved one, but it is a gesture of modest charity that might have pleased the lost loved one, if she or he could but know.

Levels of Life ends on a tentatively hopeful note—not optimistic, but rather rueful. "There is a German word, *Sehnsucht*, which has no English equivalent; it means 'the longing for something.'" This is one kind of loneliness, the obverse of the widower's more particularized loneliness, which is the "absence of a very specific someone." The final, perfectly honed lines of the memoir suggest the balloonist's quasi-mystic, Romantic expectation: "All that has happened is that from somewhere—or nowhere—an unexpected breeze has sprung up, and we are in movement again. But where are we being taken?"

Levels of Life
By Julian Barnes

"WHEN THE LEGEND BECOMES FACT":
LARRY McMURTRY

When the legend becomes fact,
print the legend.
John Ford

Already in the 1880s a cannily vulgar mythologizing of the Old West has begun. Here are Wyatt Earp and Doc Holliday awkwardly impersonating themselves in *Buffalo Bill's Wild West Show* in Denver, as reported in Larry McMurtry's radically distilled new novel *The Last Kind Words Saloon*:

> The gunfighter skit involving Wyatt and Doc did not, at first, go well at all. For one thing the pair had not bothered to practice—both despised practice, on the whole. "Pull a pistol out of a holster and shoot it—why would that require practice?" Wyatt wondered. . . . Sure enough, on the very first draw, Wyatt yanked his gun out so vigorously that it somehow flew out of his hand and landed twenty feet in front of him with the barrel in the dirt. Doc, meanwhile, had the opposite problem: he had jammed his pistol in its holster so tight that it wouldn't' come out. This behavior annoyed Doc so much that he ripped off the holster and threw it at a bronc, that happened to be loose in the arena. The crowd was largely silent: this was not what they

had expected; many members of the audience were eager to get on to the dramatic reenactment of Custer's Last Stand. . . . "They've made it into a comedy routine," [Bill Cody] said. . . . The second night went little better. Some prop man filled Doc's gun with blanks but forgot to do the same with Wyatt's. Doc then shot Wyatt six times while Wyatt snapped his useless pistol six times.

If the fabled gunslingers had been skilled actors playing "Wyatt Earp" and "Doc Holliday"—quasi-historic Wild West figures—the audience, eager to be entertained, would have applauded; unfortunately, the men are the actual Wyatt Earp and Doc Holliday, thus at a disadvantage. By the time they finally get their routine right, the crowd has lost interest; by the sixth night of performing, the show is shut down by its owner Harry Tammen, "the magnate who owned the show and most of Colorado." The disappointed gunslingers are told that there are other shows: "Texas Jack might hire you, and there's plenty of gambling dens in Denver."[1]

Drawing upon the particular sort of bittersweet/sardonic nostalgia for the Texas past that pervades McMurtry's grand epic *Lonesome Dove* (1985), the most acclaimed and best-loved of McMurtry's many novels, *The Last Kind Words Saloon* is a deftly narrated, often comically subversive work of fiction described by its author as a "ballad in prose whose characters are afloat in time; their legends and their lives in history rarely match." If *Lonesome Dove* is a chronicle of the cattle-driving West that contains within its vast, broad ranges a small but heartrending intimate tragedy of paternal neglect, *The Last Kind Words Saloon* is a dark postmodernist comedy in which intimacy is flattened to cartoon thinness, and human personality is a matter of the most fleeting mortality. Much of McMurtry's fiction, from the early, perfectly rendered *Horseman, Pass By* (1961) and *The Last Picture Show* (1966) through *Lonesome Dove* (1985), *Texasville* (1987), *Streets of Laredo*

(1993), *Duane's' Depressed* (1999), and *By Sorrow's River* (2003) has been richly elegiac,[2] but in *The Last Kind Words Saloon* the author has replaced elegy with a merciless sort of irony. It's as if Vladimir and Estragon of Beckett's *Waiting for Godot* have been transformed into two aging gunslingers trading wisecracks and platitudes in an existentially barren Western landscape, waiting for a redemption that never comes.

Though the author admiringly alludes to John Ford's famous remark about life and legend as a preface to *The Last Kind Words Saloon,* the novel seems to subvert the director's dictum: it isn't the inflated legends of Western gunslingers with which the novel is concerned but the less-than-heroic lives behind the legends; the lives of men like Wyatt Earp, Doc Holliday, Kit Carson, Johnny Ringo, Buffalo Bill Cody, and the participants of the notorious 1881 gunfight at the O.K. Corral, among others, who have figured in the history of the Old West largely by chance, having been in the right place at the right time.

Appropriately, *The Last Kind Words Saloon* derives its title from a portable sign which one of Wyatt Earp's brothers carries with him to affix to a number of saloons in Texas and Arizona. ("Warren Earp drug it around all over the place. We never did know what he meant by it," Wyatt Earp's wife, Jessie, comments years later.) The novel is divided into four sections determined by their settings: *Long Grass, Denver, Mobetie, Tombstone.* As in a classic western film characters seem to arise out of the landscape and to be contained within it; though many things will happen to Wyatt, Doc, their wives, companions, and adversaries, human agents seem curiously passive here in the West, like puppets in the service of history. Less distinctive even than the small Texas brush town Lonesome Dove, Long Grass is "nearly in Kansas, but not quite. It's nearly in New Mexico, too, but not quite. Some have even suggested that we might be in Texas." (As Wyatt observes: "The one thing that's certain is that Long Grass has no newspaper office. . . . For that matter it has no news.") It is in Long Grass that the novel begins, with a cinematic flourish of a scene that swiftly introduces most of the main characters of the novel; it is in Tombstone (Arizona) that the novel's climactic scene is placed, with the legendary gunfight at the O.K. Corral. For pages the novelist has been foreshadowing this dramatic spectacle and yet, when the gunfight at last erupts, it is rendered so offhandedly that the incident feels anticlimactic, unreal. (Note that "offhandedly" is a gun-term, meaning shooting a gun without aiming it and without premeditation.) Narration has shrunk to film-script brevity as Wyatt, Doc, and Wyatt's brothers walk armed up the "dusty street" toward the Clantons' corral:

> *"This is a damn waste of time," Wyatt said.*
>
> *"Now didn't I predict that very thing?" Doc said. "I told you to let it be."*
>
> *But just as he said it gunfire erupted and Morgan went down.*
>
> *"No, no . . . I don't want this," Virgil said. "I'm the sheriff."*
>
> *Then he went down too.*
>
> *Ike Clanton quickly ran into the photographer's shop and was not shot. Both McLaureys fired and Wyatt killed them both. Somebody hit young Clanton, who died after a brief agony.*
>
> *Doc was nicked, Wyatt untouched . . .*
>
> *When Wyatt walked in on Jessie she grabbed him and held him tight and kissed him passionately.*
>
> *"You fool, you could have been killed," Jessie said, crying.*
>
> *"Yes, but I wasn't, let go," Wyatt said.*

So much for legend.

READERS OF *THE LAST* Kind Words Saloon are likely to think of a film script more readily than a ballad, for the novel unfolds with the dreamlike fluidity and lightness of touch of film with its quick cuts, flashbacks and ever-moving, restless camera; there are fifty-nine short chapters divided into paragraphs that are frequently single sentences, and these sentences simple declarative sentences. Landscape is purely visual, atmospheric: "beyond the tiny town there was the vastness of the plains: colorless, gloomy, vast: the sea of grass." The sketchily drawn figures of *The Last Kind Words Saloon* do indeed seem to float about freely in time; often they are hardly more than fleeting images on a screen, uttering gnomic remarks to one another:

> *"Do you ever wonder what it will be like to die?" Doc asked.*
> *"No, I don't spend very little time in idle speculation," Wyatt said.*

Like former Texas Rangers Captain Woodrow Call and Augustus McCrea of *Lonesome Dove,* Wyatt Earp and Doc Holliday are contrasting personalities: Earp is taciturn, Holliday loquacious. Earp has a "big reputation as a gunfighter, which puzzled Jessie, because as far as she knew he had never actually killed anybody." Doc is affable, "rarely sober." Earp has been a pimp, a law enforcement officer for hire, and a saloon-keeper; Doc shuns work, but is a capable gambler. The men appear to be friends by default, as if they have no choice. Their conversations have the ring of repartee. As both are poor at impersonating themselves, both are poor shots at target practice when they are alone and unobserved:

> Wyatt fired three times, shattering no bottles. Annoyed, he threw his pistol at the line of bottles, knocking over three. Then he took a derringer out of an inner pocket and shattered two, to his surprise.
> Doc was still struggling with the difficult prone position. He shot but no bottles shattered. He drew back his arm to throw the gun but then caught himself at the last second. "Throwing

guns is a bad habit," he said. "You might throw your gun away just as some loose Indians come charging down upon you."

"There ain't no loose Indians, Doc," Wyatt said. "But if there were, throwing your gun wouldn't help you." He fired once more with the derringer and shattered a bottle.

"Good lord, I hit one," he said. "Luck ain't to be despised."

"Who said I despised it?" Doc said, dusting off his vest.

The Last Kind Words Saloon begins with a clandestine meeting in a "royal purple" railway car between the Texas rancher Charlie Goodnight and the "tallest man in England, and also the richest" Lord Benny Ernle; their plan is to be partners in "the largest ranch in the world." Ernle has made himself a "legend" in the West "by ordering the construction of a vast castle on a bluff overlooking the Canadian River." But in several swift chapters the wealthy English-man is dead in a riding accident in rough terrain, and the deal with Goodnight is thwarted. Like a sardonic chorus Wyatt Earp and Doc Holliday are observers of this folly at a distance.

In the interstices of the white men's blundering stratagems, Kiowa Indians behave badly under the leadership of the demonic Satank and Satanta the Red Bear. Their atrocities are the stock-in-trade of westerns, though their motive would bear scrutiny in another, more traditional novel of the sociology of the West:

> The teamsters played a heavy price for blundering into the People's country. The leader, a stout man who yelled the loudest, was chained facedown from a wagon tongue and slowly burned alive—his screams could be heard for a long time, along with those of a tall boy who had his genitals cooked over a small fire. . . . The other two teamsters were disemboweled, their guts pulled out so some hot coals could be stuffed into their stomach cavity. Satank also cut off their noses and forced them to eat some of their own offal.

Afterward the members of the little war party felt fine. Torturing whites was a splendid way to spend the afternoon. Seeing to it that your enemies died as painfully as possible was the
best revenge for what the whites had taken from them.

The women of *The Last Kind Words Saloon* are familiar Mc-
Murtry types, sharp-tongued wives and "whores" who appear to be,
however improbably in this rough environment, more than matches
for the men. Wyatt Earp has an uneasy relationship with his wife,
Jessie, who frequently goads him into hitting her; when Doc Holliday asks Jessie why she behaves in this way she says, "To see if
he's alive. To see if he cares." (Earp does, enough to knock Jessie
violently across a room and split her lip. "Oh, Jessie, why will you
provoke me? I don't mean to hit you—it just wells over.") About the
inquisitive reporter Nellie Courtright it is said that annoying as she
could be, "there was no denying she was pretty. Bearing children
had not spoiled her figure. If anything she was higher-breasted
than Jessie." The rancher Charlie Goodnight's sexually aggressive
schoolteacher wife Mary tells her husband that she is giving him
ten years "to make this into a proper county, with judges and courts
and all that goes with a county. And after the courthouse I want a
college, where people can learn their algebra. Do those two things
in a timely fashion and maybe I won't leave you for brighter climes."
The consort of the wealthy, doomed Englishman is the exotic San
Saba, "the most beautiful whore on the plains"; San Saba has a
unique background, having been born in a Turkish seraglio and
raised by eunuchs until she'd managed to be purchased and rescued by Lord Ernle. ("Rather filthy specimen, that sultan," Lord
Ernle said. "Hamid something. I couldn't see wasting such beauty
on Orientals.") Casually it is revealed that Lord Ernle, with an
English wife and an exotic American consort, nonetheless prefers
"enjoying his many boys" though McMurtry doesn't chronicle any
of these dalliances.

With the gunfight at the O.K. Corral, the saga of *The Last Kind Words Saloon* comes to a rudely abrupt end. As a kind of epilogue is a final chapter titled "Nellie's Visits by Nellie Courtright," a chattily nostalgic look back to the 1880s:

> Once I got bitten by the journalism bug there was nothing to stop me from going wherever the stories took me, which was pretty much all over our Old West as it was waning. . . . I had long forgotten Wyatt Earp and his violent brothers when he was brought to my attention by a story in an Oakland newspaper about a riot that took place in Oakland. There had been a big prizefight and Wyatt Earp had been the referee.

Nellie Courtright has been winding her way through *The Last Kind Words Saloon,* writing up tales of the Old West for such papers as the *New York Sun;* of the novel's brave, plucky, reckless and undaunted women, Nellie is perhaps the most admirable: "She was needing money just then—she had six girls to educate and clothe so she immediately took the job."

Suddenly then, at the very end of *The Last Kind Words Saloon* which has been a chronicle of the follies of men, it appears that a woman, Nellie Courtright, has been the chronicler. Very few men of the era have survived, but Nellie has survived, and is living now in Santa Monica. She travels down the coast to San Pedro to interview Wyatt Earp for a final time, discovering to her horror that he and Jessie are living in squalor: "the famous hero of the O.K. Corral was now a rheumy-eyed old man who spent his days spitting into a coffee can." Jessie "had always been a large woman, but now she had spread, while Wyatt seemed to have shrunk." Wyatt doesn't remember Nellie Courtright, or much of the past, but he does recall that his old friend Doc Holliday has died—"of the T.B., up in Colorado." Amid the trash in the Earps' front yard Nellie discovers Warren Earp's old sign THE LAST KIND WORDS SALOON, which she offers to buy, and which Jessie hands over without wanting payment: "So I took the sign, not sure why I wanted it, put it in the back of my convertible, and drove away."

When the celebrated gunslingers have died, or have lapsed into the oblivion of age and senility, Larry McMurtry tells us in this coruscating anti-heroic work of fiction, the "legend" may yet endure—a battered sign haphazardly rescued from a dump heap by a tabloid journalist.

The Last Kind Words Saloon
By Larry McMurtry

NOTES

1. McMurtry has explored the phenomenon of the making of Old West mythology previously, in *The Colonel and Little Missie: Buffalo Bill, Annie Oakley, and the Beginning of Superstardom in America* (2005). In *The Last Kind Words Saloon* the narrator mentions offhandedly how after Wyatt Earp's intervention with the Clanton herd of cattle and the subsequent stampede, the subject of chapter fifty, a popular "dime novelist" wrote about the incident in a "dime novel" *Ghost Herd of the Animas*:

   It sold a million copies. Forty years later tourists thought they saw ghost cattle racing through the sage at dawn. Wyatt and Doc were mentioned, and yet neither of them had fired a shot.

2. In his early essay collection *In a Narrow Grave: Essays on Texas* (1968) Larry McMurtry notes that, for the Texas writer, the passing of the Old West—"the passing of the cowboy"—is an "inescapable subject." Driving the legendary beef herds to slaughter across the Great Plains, however dangerous, impractical, and short-lived in the history of the American frontier, nonetheless lives on in the literature of heroic nos-

talgia, and in popular song, as if what is being lamented isn't just the passing of a way of commercial life but also the romance of life itself:

> I'm going to leave
> Old Texas now,
> They've got no use
> For the longhorn cow.
>
> They've plowed and fenced
> My cattle range,
> And the people there
> Are all so strange.

PAPER LOSSES:
LORRIE MOORE

I shall still be here . . . growing my bark
around the wire fence like a grin.
—Caroline Squire, "An Apple Tree Spouts Philosophy in
   an Office Car Park"

(EPIGRAPH TO *Bark*)

Who could have guessed that the terse, rather rude-sounding mono-
syllable *bark* might have such resonance? There is the harsh, heart-
tripping *bark* of an excited or angry dog, and there is the equally
harsh and heart-tripping *bark* of a human being speaking in anger;
there is the *bark* of a tree, a sort of tough, calcified skin from which
tenderness has vanished; there is the ominous, archaic *bark*—a fragile vessel to transport us on a river journey, just possibly on the River
Styx. There is the embarrassment of *barking up the wrong tree*—like
the self-deluded, aging pop singer of Lorrie Moore's "Wings": "She'd
spent a decade barking up the wrong tree—as a mouse!" There is
the "outer bark of the brain—and it does look like bark"—see Lorrie Moore's "Thank You for Having Me." Less obviously, there are
disembark and *debark* with their suggestion of departure tinged with
repudiation, as in the mid-life/post-divorce crises of "Debarking,"
the first story in Lorrie Moore's mordantly funny and heartbreaking
new collection.

In the frequently anthologized "How to Become a Writer" from *Self-Help* (1985), a favorite among creative writing students, writer and reader are forcibly yoked together in the ambiguous pronoun "you." The young, hopeful writer is urged to first "try to be something, anything else. A movie star/astronaut. A movie star/missionary. A movie star/kindergarten teacher. President of the world. Fail miserably." The writer is urged to major in child psychology; she takes writing seminars that give her no hope; she is said to be "self-mutilating and losing weight" but she continues to write, living for those "untested moments of exhilaration when you know that you are a genius." A tour de force of low-keyed irony, "How to Become a Writer" progresses in brief, ironic vignettes that comprise a number of years in the quasi-writer's life, but it is only in the interstices of her comical self-absorption that we learn that she has an older brother fighting in Vietnam, and that her father is evidently an adulterer; later, we learn offhandedly that the brother has returned from Vietnam a "cripple" and that her parents' marriage has ended in divorce. The fledgling writer has a gift for sardonic observations if for little else. The humor of "How to Become a Writer" is this very myopia: the writer looks in vain for inspiration, concocts absurdly melodramatic stories about subjects of which she has not a clue, while her true subject is in front of her, unheeded: the tragically disabled brother, the broken marriage and its effect upon her mother. Asked by a boyfriend "with a face as blank as a sheet of paper" if writers become discouraged, she is compelled to give a snappy reply: "Sometimes they do, and sometimes they do. Say it's a lot like having polio." Self-pity conjoined with a lack of self-awareness suggests a portrait of the non-artist: the young Lorrie Moore imagining a worst-case scenario of the failed writing life. (The wounded soldier-brother reappears in Moore's novel *A Gate at the Stairs* [2009], as the object of the benumbed narrator's long-deflected grief; what is deflected in "How to Become a Writer" is poignantly evoked in *A Gate at the Stairs,* as if the writer has grown up and is strong enough now to confront her painful subject matter.)

As Coleridge famously remarked of Wordsworth that one might recognize his poetry anywhere, so readers of Lorrie Moore are likely to recognize her prose instantaneously: a unique combination of wit, caustic insight, sympathy for the pathos of her characters' lives, and that peculiar sort of melancholy attributable to time too long spent in the northern Midwest where late-afternoon snow acquires a spectral blue tinge. Over the years Lorrie Moore's characters appear to be keeping pace with her: as the women and men of *Self-Help* were appealingly young and naïve, in their twenties, the women and men of *Bark* have become middle-aged, burnt-out and disillusioned, yet retaining some measure of feckless naïveté; they are likely to be divorced and in ambiguous relationships with individuals of the opposite sex, in awkward relationships with children, and in guilt-wracked relationships with the foreign, abstract victims of American bellicosity: "And then he said the name [of the American prison in Baghdad], but it sounded like nonsense to her, and perhaps it was, though her terrible ear for languages made everything that was not English sound very, well, *mimsy,* as if plucked from 'Jabberwocky.'" ("Subject to Search"). Of the eight stories of *Bark,* the longest, aptly titled "Wings," takes us on a rare flight of self-transcendence; the others are rueful journeys of self-discovery in which epiphanies bring jolts like electric shocks.

THE HAPLESS PROTAGONIST of "Debarking" is a recently divorced man named Ira who, unhinged by the breakup of his fifteen-year marriage, becomes infatuated with a divorcée yet more unhinged than he is: "[Zora] howled with laughter, and when her face wasn't blasted apart with it or her jaw snapping mutely open and shut like a scissors (in which Ira recognized as postdivorce hysteria; "How long have you been divorced?" Ira asked her. "Eleven years," she replied), Ira could see that she was very beautiful." Zora is, somewhat

improbably, a pediatrician; she is eccentric, flamboyant, vulgar, lu-
dicrously infatuated with her adolescent son Bruno. She says of divorce: "It's like a trick. It's like somebody puts a rug over a trapdoor
and says, 'Stand there.' And so you do. Then boom."

As their relationship develops erratically Ira thinks of Zora that she
was "either stupid or crazy," yet can't seem to resist her sexually; he
complains to a friend "she might not be all that mentally *well*." Ira is
humiliated by Zora's tactlessness as by her obsession with her son yet

> I can't let go of hope, of the illusion of something coming out
> of this romance, I'm sorry. Divorce is a trauma. . . . Its pain is a
> national secret! But that's not it. I can't let go of love. I can't live
> without love in my life.

In the foreground of "Debarking" is Ira's unraveling post-marital
life; in the background is the onset of the Iraqi War ("He turned
on the TV news and watched the bombing. Night bombing, so you
could not really see"). Ira's closest friend Mike—(though Moore's
characters are dying of loneliness they seem not to lack the sort
of exemplary wise, caring, and witty friends more often found in
literature than in life)—tells him, "Sanity's conjectural." After Zora
confides in Ira about her nervous breakdown and her prescription
antidepressants, she goes on to tell him much—too much—about
her morbid dependence upon her adolescent son, in effect rejecting
him even as, perversely, she has become at last emotionally intimate
with him. Ira yearns for love—but not at such a humiliating cost:
"He had his limitations."

As its title suggests, "The Juniper Tree" is a fairy tale of a distinctly contemporary sort, set in a Midwestern purgatory for women:

> That was how dating among straight middle-aged women
> seemed to go in this college town: one available man every year
> or so just made the rounds of us all. . . .

Every woman I knew here drank—daily. In rejecting the
lives of our mothers, we found ourselves looking for stray volts
of mother love in the very places they could never be found.

The narrator, a musician, is distressed to have failed to visit a
friend named Robin Ross, who has died of cancer in the local hospital, and in a vividly rendered dream she and two other women
friends make a pilgrimage to Robin's house to offer the deceased
gifts. We learn that the narrator has been jealous of Robin, who has
"dated" a man with whom the narrator is currently involved; she re-
sents "sharing" a man with anyone—"I'm not good at it in the least."
She is the only one of her friends, all of them "academic transplants,
all soldiers of art stationed on a far-off base," to whom "something
terrible" hasn't yet happened: a dancer, Isabel, has lost her arm in
a car crash; an artist, Pat, has had a massive stroke and has only
intermittently recovered.

In death Robin Ross looks as she'd looked in life except for a
white scarf tied around her neck, "the only thing holding my head
on." Robin has the "imperial standoffishness I realized only then
that I had always associated with the dead." At the story's end the
narrator recalls the last time she'd seen Robin Ross before her illness, when an innocently devastating remark of Robin's forces the
narrator to confront the sexual debasement she has been enduring
in sharing a man with another woman. Robin tries to beg forgiveness: but the narrator will not forgive.

The most painful story in *Bark* is "Paper Losses," an intimate
account of the deterioration of a twenty-year marriage. Narrated
from the stunned wife's perspective, the story moves jaggedly; its
structure suggests the rawness of experience before it is fully comprehended and assimilated, like "People Like That Are the Only
People Here: Canonical Babblings in Peed Onk" (1997), Moore's
harrowing account of the cancer diagnosis of an infant from the
perspective of the infant's desperate mother. The wronged wife of

"Paper Losses" is a clinical study in denial: she wants to think that her husband is suffering from a brain tumor or "space alien" genes he has inherited from his parents; his crude, cruel behavior to her is utterly inexplicable, as it is inexplicable that their "old, lusty love mutated to rage." (Of course, the husband is involved with another woman, and it is his guilt that has made him barely civil to the wife; but the wife won't learn this until much later.) With no preparation the wife is served divorce papers in their home; the husband tactlessly suggests their upcoming wedding anniversary as the divorce date: "*Why not complete the symmetry?* he wrote, which didn't even sound like him." Stricken with sexual humiliation, the wife anticipates a post-marital life when she will go on "chaste geriatric dates with other people whose clothes would, like hers, remain glued to the body." A final family trip to the Caribbean fails to mend the "irretrievably broken" marriage as the wife had naïvely hoped it might, and ends with further humiliation for the spurned wife who has only the consolation, if that is what it is, of contriving a "story" out of the experience.

In "Foes," one of Moore's rare stories in which a husband and wife appear to be evenly, companionably matched, a politically liberal biographer has a confrontation with a conservative "evil lobbyist" at a fund-raiser for a pretentious literary journal in Washington, D.C. After they have exchanged political barbs and thinly veiled insults, the biographer discovers to his horror that the lobbyist, a woman he'd misidentified as Asian, is actually disfigured: "the face that had seemed intriguingly exotic had actually been scarred by fire and only partly repaired." He feels pity, sympathy, and yet: "How could someone have come so close to death . . . and how could he still want to strangle them?"

Two stories in *Bark* spring from canonical works of fiction by Henry James and Vladimir Nabokov, though each has been entirely retooled as a Lorrie Moore story. James's *The Wings of the Dove*, with its labyrinthine plot of conspiring lovers hoping to acquire a fortune from a naïve young heiress, is the model for "Wings," the longest story in *Bark*; in Moore's story, a couple of failed musicians—instrumentalist, singer—befriend a lonely elderly man named Milt with the vague hope of inheriting his money when he dies. KC is an aging girl singer perplexed by the failure of her talent, that had been promising at the outset: "its terribleness eluded her." How pitiless Moore is, yet how sympathetic, in delineating the bafflement an individual like KC would feel:

> The gardenia in KC's throat, the flower that was her singing voice—its brown wilt must be painstakingly slowed through the years—had begun its rapid degeneration into simple crocus, then scraggly weed. She'd been given something perfect—youth!—and done imperfect things with it. . . . Sometimes she just chased roughly after a melody—like someone kicking a can down a road.

There is a fairy-tale element in "Wings" also, in its unexpected denouement, that both mimics and repudiates the starker conclusion of *The Wings of the Dove*. The reader is catapulted into a future time in which KC is no longer an aging girl but a solitary middle-aged woman whose "tears had thickened her skin the way brine knitted and hardened the rind of a cheese." Courtesy of the elderly Milt, KC's life has taken an unexpected turn—she lives now in the service of others, the proprietor of a bed-and-breakfast hotel near a children's hospital.

The pathos of "Referential" is evoked clearly at the outset: "Mania. For the third time in three years they talked of what would be a suitable birthday present to bring for her deranged son." (See Nabokov's "Signs and Symbols" which begins: "For the fourth time in as many years they were confronted with the problem of what birthday present to bring a young man who was incurably deranged in his mind.") Both stories recount a visit to a mental institution that ends unhappily; both stories involve an impetuous decision, clearly ill-advised, to bring the deranged boy home; both stories conclude with a mysteriously ringing telephone, somehow terrifying in Nabokov, as it is perplexing and ironic in Moore. Both stories focus upon an adolescent boy whose paranoid schizophrenia forces him to see meaning in all things: "veiled references to his existence" ("Referential") are everywhere. And, "Life was full of spies and preoccupying espionage." Moore's story, more emotionally engaging than Nabokov's, delineates a triangle among mother, deranged son, and mother's lover Pete, who has been, or has seemed, a kind of "stepfather" to the son, though Pete has never lived with the mother and son, and has ceased to show much interest in doing so. Nabokov's coolly detached story evokes a surreal poetry to suggest the delusions of paranoid schizophrenia while Moore's poignant story allows the reader intimate entry to a life with a hopelessly deranged boy:

> A maternal vertigo beset her, the room circled, and the cutting scars on her son's arms sometimes seemed to spell out Pete's name in the thin lines there, the loss of fathers etched primitively there in an algebra of skin. . . . Mutilation was a language.

But the language of derangement isn't finally intelligible, and isn't shareable—brought to visit the paranoid boy, Pete is reticent, and clearly ill at ease. The boy, who has loved Pete, senses his distance, and begins to speak excitedly:

> "You have to look for us! We are sort of hidden but sort of not. We can be found. If you look in the obvious places, we can be found. We haven't disappeared, even if you want us to, we are there to—"

But the mother interrupts the chattering boy, for the boy is coming too close to making sense. And driving home, the mother sees that Pete, like her, is deeply unhappy, "though the desperations were separate, not joined" and she sees that Pete will not stay the night with her, though she comes very close to asking him. But she has lost Pete, as she has lost her son; she has lost Pete because of her son, whose unhappy life is inextricably bound up with her own, as if identical with her own. A Lorrie Moore heroine is a stoic, and in this case not a wisecracking stoic: "Living did not mean one joy piled upon another. It was merely the hope for less pain, hope played like a playing card upon another hope."

Like "Referential," "Subject to Search" is an elegy for a lost, in this case unconsummated love between a woman and a man she has known for many years, who seems to be a covert CIA agent; the woman has lunch with him just as news of American soldiers torturing Iraqi prisoners in Baghdad prison is about to break globally: "It's going to be a scandal big as My Lai." Like the elusive Pete, but far more playful and articulate than Pete, Tom is another lost love for whom a woman might grieve; of Moore's cast of male characters, Tom is the one most a match for Moore's droll, witty women: "'If you're suicidal,' he said slowly, 'and you *don't actually kill yourself,* you become known as 'wry.'" In a dismaying flash-forward the story takes us to a time when Tom is incapacitated with a neurological affliction that resembles Parkinson's, and refuses to see the old friend who has driven a considerable distance to see him; but then, in a magical reversal, we are taken into the past, to a Christmas party where the woman and Tom confirm their sense of a deep rapport ("Do you ever feel that no one knows what you're talking about, that everyone is just pretending—except for me?"). Which is the ending of the story? The tragic ending, or the earlier, happy ending? As Tom says: "We're all suckers for a happy ending."

The concluding story of *Bark* is "Thank You for Having Me"—a sweetly ironic title for an elegy of an era in a woman's life, as in the life of a culture. The first line suggests a singular and yet eccentric loss: "The day following Michael Jackson's death, I was constructing my own memorial." The mourner also laments the death of an old, lost love, which is a way of lamenting her own youth: "Every minute that ticks by contains too little information, until it contains too much." Not unlike other characters in *Bark*, the middle-aged protagonist broods on mortality with a striking lyricism:

Without weddings there would be only funerals. I had seen a soccer mom become a rhododendron with a plaque, next to the soccer field parking lot. . . . I had seen a brilliant young student become a creative writing contest. . . . And I had seen a public defender become a justice fund. . . . I had seen a dozen people become hunks of rocks with their names engraved so perfectly upon them it looked indeed as if they had turned to stone.

"Thank You for Having Me" contains within it the germ of a mother-daughter story, an examination of the fraught relationship between a woman who'd imagined herself doomed to "being a lonely old spinster" and her fifteen-year-old "gorgeous giantess" daughter Nickie, though on its surface it's an amusing account of an outdoor New Age wedding in Midwestern farm country in which the bridesmaids wear pastel of the hues of pharmaceuticals: "one the light peach of baby aspirin; one the seafoam green of low-dose clonazepam; the other the pale daffodil of the next lowest dose of clonazepam." The divorced mother feels a kind of guilt for having brought up her daughter in so abbreviated a household: "Mothers and their only children of divorce were a skewed kind of family dynamic, if they were families at all. . . . [The dialogue between them] contained more sibling banter than it should have." Like the rejected wife of "Paper Losses," this divorcée recalls the rude abruptness with which her husband left her, with no warning: "He had said, 'You can raise Nickie by yourself. You'll be good at it.'" Aloneness is the middle-aged divorcée's most obsessive concern, a kind of compulsive mantra:

If you were alone when you were born, along when you were dying, *really absolutely alone* when you were dead, why "learn to be alone" in between? If you'd forgotten, it would quickly come back to you. Aloneness was like riding a bike. By gunpoint. With the gun in your own hand.

A story about grim events, "Thank You for Having Me" manages not to be a grim story, ending with an antic dance between a middle-aged man whose ex-wife has just married another man and the neighbor whose husband left her to raise their daughter alone. It's a dance of pure pointless joy, a dance to celebrate a wedding, a dance to celebrate the sheer fact of being alive, for now: "I needed my breath for dancing, so I tried not to laugh. I fixed my face into a grin instead, and, ah, for a second the sun came out to light up the side of the red and spinning barn." At such illuminated moments even the consolation of the most eloquent irony can be set aside.

Bark: Stories
by Lorrie Moore

EMOTIONS OF MAN AND ANIMALS:
KAREN JOY FOWLER

He who understands baboons
would do more toward
metaphysics than Locke.

Charles Darwin

In *The Expression of the Emotions in Man and Animals* (1872), Charles Darwin breeches the presumed gap between species by matter-of-factly conflating, in passages fascinating and rich in detail, close examinations of human beings and "lower animals" (by which Darwin meant "non-human animals"); his subject is "the principle of direct action of the excited nervous system on the body, independently of the will and in part of habit." Not what might be self-described by individuals possessing language but rather what is displayed—"behavior"—is the object of the scientist's inquiry.

While most of Darwin's text deals with the phenomenon of emotions in man, in a number of chapters in *The Expression of Emotions* he takes pains not to distinguish between "man" and "lower animals" by commingling species under such headings as "Serviceable Associated Habits," "The Principle of Antithesis," and "Action of the Nervous System." Darwin's implicit thesis is the likeness of man and "lower animals," not their unlikeness. (Darwin's great work *Origin of Species* appeared in 1859; *Descent of Man* in

1871.) As man has a "voice," so do animals have "voices": "Cats use their voices much as a means of expression, and they utter, under various emotions and desires, at least six or seven sounds." The cat's "purr of satisfaction . . . is one of the most curious." A dog will make sounds resembling laughter, and a "bark of joy often follows a grin." A consideration of man in agony or pain is naturally extended to other species in kindred situations: "There is said to be 'gnashing of teeth' in hell; and I have plainly heard the grinding of the molar teeth of a cow which was suffering acutely from inflammation of the bowels. The female hippopotamus in the Zoological Gardens, when she produced her young, suffered greatly; she incessantly walked about, or rolled on her sides, opening and closing her jaws, and clattering her teeth together" and so back to man again, whose eyes "stare wildly as in horrified astonishment" and whose body is covered in perspiration: "Hence the nostrils are generally dilated and often quiver; or the breath may be held until the blood stagnates in the purple face."

Cattle, horses, dogs, cats, monkeys, birds—and man: all are subject to emotions, thus the "expression" of emotions of an involuntary, visceral nature. "With all or almost all animals, even with birds, Terror causes the body to tremble." Wrinkling the face, furrowing the forehead, mating- and fighting-cries, cries of fury, erection of the hair, dilation of nostrils and of pupils of the eye, muscular contortions of the body—all cross species boundaries. Chapter sub-headings include "Sneering, Defiance: Uncovering the canine tooth on one side"; "Depressed Corners of the Mouth"; "Oblique Eyebrows" "Weeping." (Darwin presents a good deal of firsthand observation on the infants in his household of whom there were, over the years, at least ten of his own.)

"Joy and affection" are attributed to monkeys no less than to human beings. Monkeys are seen to blush and redden as a man might do, and a young female chimpanzee is seen to throw a temper tantrum very like that of "a child in the same state." Darwin

notes having felt "through the saddle" the beating heart of a terrified horse as he has, with astonishing acuity, noted the symptoms
of a terrified canary as it turns "white about the base of the bill." A
(human) mother who loses her child may be "frantic with grief . . .
walks wildly about, tears her hair or clothes, and wrings her hands."
Dogs can be "downcast," cats "express affection," monkeys can be
"insulted." Primates display almost as many emotions as human beings, and some of these are nuanced; one of numerous illustrations
in the book is a line drawing of a "disappointed and sulky" chimpanzee. (Woodcuts, photographs, and drawings of the faces of animals
and humans add to the particularly Victorian flavor of this book,
in which the banal and the extraordinary, the average and the grotesque, are brought together as "illustrations" of the text. Physiog-
nomy, largely faded in our time, was explored with great seriousness
in the nineteenth century.)

A secondary work of Darwin, the 390-page *Expression of the
Emotions in Man and Animals* would likely have been a major work
by another nineteenth-century scientist, and in its highly persuasive,
resolutely unpolemical juxtaposing of "man" and "lower animals" it
would surely have aroused controversy. All that is so cogently argued
in *Descent of Man* is taken for granted here. The author's natural
empathy for his heterogeneous subjects crosses species-boundaries
with the conversational air of an individual making points to an
audience of his peers so self-evident that they need scarcely be de-
fended: who could doubt that the grief, terror, and suffering of human beings is different not in kind but merely in degree from the
response to "horrid tortures inflicted in foreign lands on exhausted
animals"? Ever the Victorian gentleman, Darwin is careful always
to designate "lower animals" even as, by this usage, he is suggesting
that there exists a "higher"' being that is in fact an "animal": man.

It isn't surprising that Darwin exerted a considerable influence
on the provisions of the Cruelty to Animals Act passed into law by
the British parliament in 1876, which governed the (licensed) ani-

mal experimentation of scientists. Before this, grotesque and sadistic "experiments" were sometimes committed on helpless animals, often for demonstrative and educational purposes rather than for scientific research; after this, animals used in experiments had to be anesthetized whenever possible, and only experiments required for scientific research were qualified to be licensed. (Though Darwin believe that vivisection was essential for scientific research he felt strongly that it should not be performed "for mere damnable and detestable curiosity. It is a subject that makes me sick with horror, so I will not say another word about it, else I shall not sleep tonight."

In the late twentieth century, highly influential major works of philosophy and ethics began to be published in the field loosely described as "animal rights," notably Peter Singer's *Animal Liberation* (1975) and Tom Regan's *The Case for Animal Rights* (1983), both of which have become classics. The argument for animal rights is fundamentally a moral and epistemological argument for a restructuring of the conception of "consciousness"—is it uniquely human?—and of the very concept of "animal." Singer has been particularly eloquent on the issue of "speciesism"—the belief that the human species is not only superior to all other species, but can use (or misuse) these species as they wish, an injunction that seems to have a Biblical, i.e., Godly, imprimatur. Traditionally, moral philosophers calibrate degrees of moral behavior with the fastidiousness of Thomists arguing how many angels might dance on the head of a pin, yet have seemed, on the whole, unequipped philosophically to extend a principle of morality to those beings Darwin called "lower animals," now called, in some enlightened quarters, "non-human animals." (A philosopher-friend estimates that less than 2 percent of books on moral philosophy include the word *"animal"* in their indexes.) Both Singer and Regan have challenged this as a highly limited conception of morality; Regan argues that animals have "certain basic moral rights" and that "recognition of their rights requires fundamental changes in our treatment of them." Both philosophers reason from hedonistic-Utilitarian principles of the greatest good for the greatest number—which is to say, the least pain for the greatest number of "sentient beings." Singer argues that animals need not be acknowledged as having "rights" for us to wish to alleviate their suffering—that they are capable of feeling pain, and that pain is a negative experience, should be enough for us to have a moral obligation to refrain from inflicting needless pain upon them. Though "animal rights" and "animal liberation" ethics tend to be overwhelmingly vegetarian, and opposed to the eating of animals, yet the argument can be made, as Singer has done, that there is nothing inherently evil in eating animals if they are not raised and slaughtered inhumanely—which is the case, unfortunately, for the vast majority of animals at the present time. For further discussions of "animal rights" see J. M. Coetzee's *The Lives of Animals* (1999), Jeff McMahan's *The Ethics of Killing: Problems at the Margins of Life* (2002), Cass Sunstein's "The Rights of Animals: A Very Short Primer" (2002). For a richly polemical discussion of the relationships among patriarchal culture, the exploitation of women and of animals, and the politics of meat-eating, see Carol Adams's *The Sexual Politics of Meat* (1990).

In children's literature as in fables, fairy tales, and Disney fantasies, talking animals abound; these usually affable "animals" are human beings in disguise, sheerly anthropomorphic concoctions rarely betraying any genuine or alarming animal nature. Yet, the fantasies tend to be benign, and sympathy for animals is the rule, with no acknowledgment of the adult caste system of "species" that would automatically render them inferior beings, if not food. In literature for adults, imaginative evocations of animal consciousness are rarities. A relatively little-known novel by the Canadian writer Barbara Gowdy, *The White Bone* (1999), a kind of tragic epic of African elephants narrated from the perspective of the elephants, undertakes to cross the boundary between species in an extraordinarily visceral, sensuous, and poetic rendering of language unparalleled in contemporary literature. You need not believe that elephants can think in language—(in this case, a highly lyric English language)—to be enthralled by the author's imaginative immersion in her subject, a brilliantly inspired melding of research into the lives of African elephants and the creation of a distinctly original, indeed *sui generis* alternative world. Inevitably, in a time in which African elephants are being ravaged by poachers, and their species endangered by incursions into their natural habitat, *The White Bone* is not a casual reading experience. It will linger long in the memory, like an intensely unnerving yet wonderfully strange dream.

Less stylistically inventive than *The White Bone,* and less ambitious in scope and vision, Karen Joy Fowler's *We Are All Completely Beside Ourselves* is nonetheless a boldly exploratory evocation of a cross-species relationship that begins as a somewhat naïve but well-intentioned scientific experiment and ends as something like domestic tragedy, with consequences that destroy a family and permanently traumatize a sister and brother—and a "non-human animal" named Fern. Like the documentary film by James Marsh, *Project Nim* (2011), which depicts a similar ill-considered and eventually doomed experiment involving an infant chimpanzee brought to live in close contact with human beings, *We Are All Completely Beside Ourselves* is less about the scientific background and rationale for such experimentation than it is about an intensely emotional, nonverbal, and visceral relationship between "sisters" of whom one happens to be a "human" and the other "non-human." In both the film and the novel, immediate sympathy is evoked for the innocent young primate, brought into a domestic household rife with its own, secret undercurrents of emotion and power struggles; in both, the innocent young primate is smotheringly loved, refashioned into a quasi-child, eventually erupts in violence and is feared, and expelled from the human household. In both documentary and novel, an initially reasonable yet finally tyrannical and unfeeling professorial father-figure exerts his terrible, irrevocable power: in

Project Nim, this villainous figure is Columbia University Professor of Psychology Herbert S. Terrace, chief investigator in a now-notorious experiment of the 1970s undertaking to determine if a chimpanzee ("Nim Chimpsky": punning on "Noam Chomsky") raised in close contact with human beings could develop communication skills akin to "language"; in *We Are All Completely Beside Ourselves,* the villainous figure is University of Indiana Professor of Psychology Cooke, father of Rosemary Cooke and "stepfather" of chimpanzee Fern, who undertakes a near-identical experiment into the possibilities of cross-species communication, involving a young female chimp instead of a male, with identical results—expulsion for the chimp-subject, remorse and regret for the human participants, a failed and discredited experiment. Terrace's punishment was his exposure in *Project Nim* as the very embodiment of the coldhearted, manipulative and irresponsible scientist, exploiting not only the lovable chimp Nim but also an indeterminate number of young woman assistants: beyond ridicule of his science was disdain for his very appearance (hairstyle, Burt Reynolds mustache) and the type of car (BMW) he drove. That Terrace maintained the unpopular stance that chimps can't be taught to use "language" as human beings use it was held against him, as if scientific integrity were a matter of special pleading, and a research scientist should be swayed by political or sentimental pressures; it was seen as particularly reprehensible that Terrace ended his experiment, and his relationship with Nim, with shocking abruptness as soon as he saw that the experiment had failed, and shipped Nim away to a research facility in Oklahoma.

Unlike the notable Terrace, who has published much important work in the behavior of animals, Fowler's Professor Cooke is an undistinguished academic so shortsighted he fails to consider that bringing a young chimpanzee into his household as a month-old infant to grow up alongside his infant daughter might have disastrous consequences. Cooke seems not to know that a wild, congenitally undomesticable animal would eventually be impossible to control and dangerous in any household. Nor does Cooke do anything to mitigate the harm to both his daughter and son precipitated by the abrupt expulsion of their "sister" Fern of whom the son Lowell says bitterly: "She deserved to be missed and we missed her terribly." We know early on that Cooke will not be an ideal caregiver to a young animal when he deliberately and stupidly runs over a cat with his car, his young daughter Rosemary as a witness. (Rosemary naïvely wonders: "Was my father kind to animals?")

Belatedly, after the father's death from alcoholism and diabetes, when Rosemary and her mother have been reconciled, Rosemary learns from her mother of her parents' initial, misguided idealism regarding the experiment with Fern:

> We thought . . . your father and I . . . that Fern would be with us forever. Your part of the study would end when you went off to school, but we'd keep working with Fern. Eventually you'd go to college . . . and she'd stay home with us.

It is difficult to believe that any behavioral psychologist at a reputable university could be so naïve, but not difficult to believe that the nefarious Cooke has manipulated and exploited his trusting family as well as poor Fern and his eager and ardent cadre of graduate student assistants.

Fowler seems to have thoroughly researched her fascinating subject. Some of the most engaging passages in *We Are All Completely Beside Ourselves* involve historical information provided by Rosemary who has researched the subject obsessively herself. (She discovers papers written by her father online, in which she is the behavioral psychologist's child-subject.) Among the earliest experimenters in the United States were a couple named Kellogg who, in the 1930s, brought a chimpanzee home to live with them: "The stated purpose was to compare and contrast developing abilities, linguistic and otherwise. This was the stated premise of our study as well." (The Kellogg experiment ended ignominiously with the "clever, docile little Gua" dying soon after being shipped back to a research lab.) With the exception of the most famous of research chimps Washoe, whose alleged ability to sign in American Sign Language was the stimulus for Herbert Terrace's experiment, most of the chimpanzee stories have tragic endings. Taken into human families, "loved" and fussed over, then abruptly sent back to research labs or farms, the young chimps soon sickened and died. Ebullient and irrepressible Nim Chimpsky, dropped by his researcher, was himself shipped to medical labs until one of his former graduate students launched a public fund that released him to an animal sanctuary in Texas where he died at the young age of twenty-six.

Fowler suggests that the chimpanzee experiments might have been misdirected. Instead of studying how well Fern could communicate with her human family, Professor Cooke might have studied how well Rosemary could communicate with Fern. "Here is the question our father refused to admit he was asking: can Rosemary learn to speak to chimpanzees?" While very young, Fern and Rosemary engage in preverbal idioglossia, "a secret language of grunts and gestures" which Professor Cooke chooses not to report.

From the time she is one month old to the time of Fern's expulsion, when Rosemary is five, Rosemary never knows a day when she isn't the "twin" of a chimpanzee.

> I'd scarcely known a moment alone. She was my twin, my fun-house mirror, my whirlwind other self. . . . I loved her like a sister, but she was the only sister I ever had.

After Fern's departure, she senses herself a "counterfeit human"; she is cast adrift amid human children in grade school, who perceive her as "monkey girl." She will always stir ambivalent responses in others because she doesn't seem quite human. It's the "uncanny-valley" response: "the human aversion to things that look almost but not quite like people."

While Fowler's earlier novels *Sarah Canary* (1991) and *Sister Noon* (2001) are populated with strikingly rendered, serio-comic-grotesque characters, the hapless protagonist of *We Are All Completely Beside Ourselves* is numbed and inexpressive as one who has lost the most intense love of her life, and has been afflicted with amnesia regarding the loss; it is her "chimp nature" she has lost, as well as the actual Fern. Both she and her older brother Lowell, who runs away from home as a teenager, are presented as "traumatized" siblings—"Lowell appeared unstable in the most literal sense, like someone who's been pushed off his balance." Where Rosemary is a kind of cipher, drained of personality, Lowell is a militant, reckless animal rights zealot, wanted by the FBI for his participation in "domestic terrorism" as a member of the Animal Liberation Front. Lowell is nearly caught by authorities, but manages to escape, and his whereabouts are unknown at the conclusion of *We Are All Completely Beside Ourselves.*

Given the almost entirely retrospective nature of Rosemary Cooke's story, in which all that is significant in her life has happened before she was five, Fowler is challenged to make Rosemary's present-day life as an undergraduate at UC-Davis engaging. There is a disadvantage in telling a story so obliquely—nothing really interesting happens to Rosemary until page seventy-seven, when she finally reveals that her lost sister Fern is a chimpanzee: "Some of you will have figured that out already. Others may feel it was irritatingly coy of me to have withheld Fern's essential simian-ness for so long." The prospect of a "premature and calamitous end" is dangled before the reader.

We Are Completely Beside Ourselves provides an intimate, child's-eye look at a Midwestern academic household of the 1980s. Before Fern is brought into their lives, the Cookes are presumably an ordinarily happy family; thereafter, they are revealed as dysfunctional, inhabiting a domestic limbo somewhere between satire and sorrow. Rosemary's recollections come in fragments, a relentless dirge of loss; it may be difficult for the reader to fully sympathize with such trauma, as even Rosemary admits that she understood that her simian sister was "getting out of control" after Fern kills and disembowels a kitten in front of her. The stunned child is forced to think:

> That there was something inside Fern I didn't know. That I didn't know her in the way I'd always thought I did. That Fern had secrets and not the good kind.

Rosemary will learn years later that there are other, equally alarming incidents involving Fern which she witnessed—but claimed not to recall: bitings, a savage and unprovoked attack against a graduate student, a lawsuit against the university.

Once a loquacious little girl, like her simian twin a whirligig of energy, by the time we meet Rosemary Cooke she has become a stunted and suppressed young woman of college age, whose "monkey-girlishness" is in such denial that she has a panic attack while watching *"The Man in the Iron Mask,"* a parable of twins—- "Something was rising from the crypt, and what I did know was that I didn't want to see what it was."

By limiting her narration to Rosemary's perspective, Fowler has sacrificed the myriad possibilities of alternative points of view that might have made of the story something more than a domestic catastrophe not unlike any exploration of a childhood trauma— death, loss, betrayal, abuse, incomprehension—that has crippled the survivor for life; the more considerable achievements of *The White Bone* and *Project Nim* arise in part from their wider range of viewpoints, which amplify and deepen their subjects. But Fowler's decision allows for the emotional intensity of narrowness, as in the quintessential contemporary memoir in which crisis, collapse, and resolution are the point, not an amplitude of experience or illumination, even as the novel's trajectory suggests the coming-of-age ritual of the young adult novel in which, in the end, there is uplift, and hope: Rosemary is reconciled with her mother, with whom she has written a children's book about Fern; she has become a kindergarten teacher ("as close to living with a chimp troop as I've been able to get so far"); she and her mother live near Fern, now kept at an animal sanctuary in —. The novel ends with a poignant image, the more precious as it is transient, of sister-sister affirmation, when Rosemary visits Fern after an interval of twenty-two years, bearing a poker-chip talisman of their childhood:

> Fern stood heavily and came to me. She placed her own large hand opposite mine, fingers curling slightly, scratching, as if she could reach through and take the poker chip. I signed my name again with my free hand, and she signed it back with hers. . . . Then she rested her forehead on the glass. I did the same and we stood there for a very long time, face-to-face. . . .
>
> I didn't know what she was thinking or feeling. Her body had become unfamiliar to me. And yet, at the very same time, I recognized everything about her. My sister, Fern. In the whole wide world, my only red poker chip. As if I were looking in a mirror.

Life may be meandering and irresolute, but an experiment must come to an end.

We Are All Completely Beside Ourselves
By Karen Joy Fowler

WIINDIGOO JUSTICE:
LOUISE ERDRICH

The loss of their land was lodged deep inside them forever.
Louise Erdrich, The Plague of Doves

Dense with meaning, both symbolic and literal, the first scene of Louise Erdrich's fourteenth novel, *The Round House,* involves an arduous attempt at the pruning of small trees that have "attacked my parents' house at the foundation." Only just seedlings with very few leaves, these small predators have nonetheless managed to squeeze through cracks in shingles and into a wall: "I thought it was a wonder the treelets had persisted through a North Dakota winter." The foundations of the Coutts household are under assault from without; father and son will unite to protect it, but belatedly, and incompletely. The narrator Joe, thirteen years old at this time, in 1988, continues to "pry at the hidden rootlings" even after his father, a tribal judge, has given up the difficult task; so too will Joe, despite his youth, persevere in a desperate quest for justice in the wake of a brutal assault against his mother, even as Bazil Coutts, his father, finds himself powerless and humiliated.

The setting of *The Round House* is a Native American reservation in North Dakota, near the fictitious small town of Hoopdance, in which "no one didn't have a clan"; one of those lovingly annotated communities familiar to readers of Louise Erdrich's fiction in which

Native American and mixed-blood inhabitants "knew place in the world and [their] relationship to all other beings" and "Nothing that happens, *nothing,* is not connected here by blood." Less idiosyncratically populated than Erdrich's more characteristic novels *Love Medicine* (1984), *The Beet Queen* (1986), *Tracks* (1988), *The Plague of Doves* (2008), *The Round House* is a chronicle of individuals whose identities are inexorably bound up with their families, clans, tribal and interlocking histories—"an impenetrable undergrowth of names and liaisons"; it's a mixture of lyrical narration, regional history, and digressive tall tales narrated by tribal elders that allow the author to establish the contemporary in the ancestral/mythic past. The novel resembles previous works of multigenerational fiction by Erdrich in which a crime, usually committed by a non-native against Native Americans, is the catalyst of a sequence of events involving decades and generations, but its tone is gravely analytical; a work of confessional summation, a looking-back over years, not unlike a legal brief. Instead of Erdrich's multiple, colorfully unreliable narrators, *The Round House* is narrated by a single, reliable individual, Joe Coutts, speaking of a crucial period in his life and in the lives of his parents. Joe addresses the reader from an indeterminate present tense in which we know only of his adult self that he is married, and has become a lawyer like his father, with a law degree from the University of Minnesota; we understand that, whatever horror has been perpetrated at the start of *The Round House,* whatever violation of the soul of the Native American community, this Native American witness has survived intact.

"WHERE IS YOUR MOTHER?"—this abrupt question, put to Joe by his father on a Sunday afternoon, is the first indication that something is wrong in the Coutts household. Joe's mother, Geraldine, who works in the Bureau of Indian Affairs of their reservation as a tribal enrollment specialist, has been at the office just a little too long:

"Her absence stopped time." Immediately Joe becomes anxious:

> I was aware that what was happening was in the nature of
> something unusual. A missing mother. A thing that didn't hap-
> pen to the son of a judge, even one who lived on a reservation.

Added to the sense of urgency is the knowledge that Geraldine Coutts's job is "to know everybody's secrets." Not unlike the
novelist-proprietor of a fictional landscape who is privy to interrela-
tions and facts about individuals about which the individuals themselves might be ignorant:

> Children of incest, molestation, rape, adultery, fornication
> beyond reservation boundaries or within, children of white
> farmers, bankers, nuns, BIA [Bureau of Indian Affairs] super-
> intendents, police, and priests. My mother kept her files locked
> in a safe. No one else knew the combination of the safe.

Father and son drive hurriedly to the reservation to look for Joe's
mother, who unaccountably speeds past them in her car, on her way
home; when they discover her in the garage of their house, still in
her car, it's immediately obvious that something has happened to
her: "I could see it in the set of her body—something fixed, rigid,
wrong." Erdrich skillfully dramatizes the slow-dawning horror of
the thirteen-year-old Joe as he's forced to confront the fact that his
beloved, beautiful, so-capable mother has been unspeakably violated, and that their lives as a family—a relatively privileged Native
American family—have been irrevocably changed.

It is not giving away too much of *The Round House* to note that
Geraldine has been the victim of a particularly brutal rape and beating by an individual in the community whom she knows, and could
identify to authorities, if she were not terrified of the consequences
for herself and for her family of such an identification. (Yet more

horribly, the rapist sprinkled gasoline on her with the intention of
setting her afire, except the desperate woman managed to escape
from him. The smell of gasoline on his mother's clothing seems
mysterious to Joe but not to the reader who understands immediately its meaning.) In any case, the situation is exacerbated by the
traumatized victim's inability to precisely recall where the assault
took place: on tribal or North Dakota land.

This ambiguity, this uncertainty, precipitates another sort of
nightmare, a legal one: for it isn't clear if the assault against Geraldine Coutts should be investigated by the State of North Dakota,
the small town of Hoopdance, N.D., or by tribal police; initially, it
isn't even clear who'd committed it, an Indian or a non-Indian. Joe
thinks:

> I already knew . . . that these questions would swirl around
> the facts. I already knew, too, that these questions would not
> change the facts. But they would inevitably change the way we
> sought justice.

One of the (minor) problems with *The Round House* is the seeming precocity of the thirteen-year-old Joe who isn't regarded, within
the world of the novel, as exceptional or prodigious. Even less believable is his good friend Cappy who speaks, as surely no thirteen-
year-old North Dakota boy has ever spoken, of loving a girl his age
with a "true love": "The Creator made us for each other. Me here.
Zelia there. Space was put between us by human error. . . . Every
bit of what we did was made in heaven." (Cappy's language would
be difficult to take seriously no matter his age.) Interludes in which
the boys behave with self-conscious "boyishness" are particularly
forced, and feel like filler amid the serious narrative. The reader
is advised to suspend disbelief when Joe seems to shift character,
for Joe is our only witness in *The Round House*, the bearer of the
author's outrage, like those sharp-eyed child-witnesses in Erdrich's

Shadow Tag (2010) who see into the sick, festering heart of their parents' marriage as neither of their parents can see and take on some of the omniscience of the author. Since the opening pages of Erdrich's debut novel *Love Medicine*, Erdrich's vision has been suffused with "magical realism"; *The Round House* is not so suffused, but its language is often highly charged and metaphorical, and not merely, or primarily, literal. Joe is the author's instrument for seeing with a poet's eye:

> The sun fell onto the kitchen floor in golden pools, but it was an ominous radiance, like the piercing light behind a western cloud. A trance of dread came over me, a taste of death like sour milk. . . . Her serene reserve was gone—a nervous horror welled across her face. The bruises had come out and her eyes were darkly rimmed like a raccoon's. A sick green pulsed around her temples. Her jaw was indigo. Her eyebrows . . . were held tight by anguish. Two vertical lines, black as if drawn by a marker, creased her forehead.

And, as Joe approaches the "round house," the likely scene of the assault:

> A low moan of air passed through the cracks in the silvery logs of the round house. I started with emotion. The grieving cry seemed emitted by the structure itself. The sound filled and flooded me. Finally, it ceased. I decided to go forward. . . . I caught the faint odor of gasoline. . . .
>
> . . . He had attacked her here. The old ceremonial place had told me—cried out to me in my mother's anguished voice, I now thought, and tears started into my eyes. I let them flood down my cheeks. Nobody was here to see me so I did not even wipe them away. I stood there in the shadowed doorway thinking with my tears. Yes, tears can be thoughts, why not?

Of course, the very act of reading fiction is after all a willing, or willed, "suspension of disbelief."

The "round house" is a derelict tribal building, used, pre-1978, for religious ceremonies at a time when Indians were forbidden to practice their religion by white authorities. Surreptitiously, Indians would gather at the round house and if white authorities raided the building, "water drums and eagle feathers and medicine bags and birchbark scrolls and sacred pipes were in a couple of motorboats halfway across the lake. The Bible was out and people were reading from Ecclesiastes." That Geraldine Coutts is raped and beaten in a "sacred space" is the more bitterly ironic, like the (legal) statute that protects a non-native from being prosecuted in a tribal court.

DESCRIBED BY ITS AUTHOR as "a suspense novel masking a crusade" (*Time*, January 14, 2013), *The Round House* is a painstakingly narrated account of memory, and of guilt bound up with memory; if the novel is a sort of crusade, galvanized by the author's outrage against the incursion of federal criminal law into tribal law and custom, it is also an elaborately structured literary work in which polemics are subordinate to the author's sympathy for her (troubled, imperfect) characters and "suspense" is rather more theoretical than evident. Certainly no one would confuse *The Round House,* or its yet more minimally structured predecessor *Shadow Tag* (2010), with a generic suspense novel. Like earlier works of fiction by Erdrich, it is indebted to those novels of William Faulkner in which a brooding and eloquent narrator obsesses over an event, criminal or taboo, that comes to acquire a powerful symbolic significance; in Faulkner, the crimes of unrepentant slave owners like Thomas Sutpen (*Absalom, Absalom!,* 1936) constitute the "original sin" of an entire slave-owning society, the inhumanity of privileged whites against helpless blacks, and the tragic consequences that follow for both races. Recall the radiantly mad vision of Johanna Burden of *Light in August,* whose impassioned and torturous speech is very likely Faulkner's own, as she evokes the violent deaths of her "carpetbagger" Burden relatives who'd been devoted to the cause of freed Negroes in Mississippi:

> I had seen and known Negroes since I could remember. I just looked at them, as I did at rain, or furniture, or food or sleep. But after [the deaths] I seemed to see [Negroes] for the first time not as a people, but as a thing, a shadow in which I lived, we lived, all white people, all other people. I thought of all the children coming forever and ever into the world, white, with the black shadow already falling upon them before they drew breath. And I seemed to see the black shadow in the shape of a cross. And it seemed like the white babies were struggling, even before they drew breath, to escape from the shadow that was not only upon them but beneath them too, flung out like their arms were flung out, as if they were nailed to the cross. . . . The curse of the white race is the black man who will be forever God's chosen own, because He once cursed Him.

Speaking like this to her lover Joe Christmas, Johanna Burden assures her doom at Christmas's hands, for surely the last thing the "mulatto" Christmas wants to be told is that his existence has meaning only in relation to the guilt of the white oppressor.

In Erdrich's cycle of North Dakota novels, her equivalent of Faulkner's cycle of Yoknapatawpha County, the perspective that is dramatized is that of the violated, and not, as in Faulkner, the violator; not guilt but rage is the appropriate emotion. (Indeed, the guilt of Faulkner's privileged whites may strike our twenty-first-century ears as condescendingly racist.) For Erdrich, the original and irrevocable crime of marauding European invaders is the theft of Native American lands and the displacement of Native American tribes onto "reservations"—(inevitably in regions in which whites had no commercial interest); this is the primordial theft that lodges deep inside all her Native American characters, not an original sin but the outrage of sin perpetrated upon them. The quotation that begins this review is, more fully:

> I saw that the loss of their land was lodged deep inside them forever. This loss would enter me, too. Over time, I came to know that the sorrow was a thing each of them covered up according to their character—my old uncle through his passionate discipline, my mother through strict kindness and cleanly order. As for my grandfather ("Mooshum"), he used the patient art of ridicule.

These words are spoken by a girl named Evelina, one of the principal narrators of *The Plague of Doves,* whose relationship with her parents suggests the closeness, respect, and mutual love of Joe Coutts and his parents, as her role as clear-sighted observer within a maelstrom of adult confusion resembles his:

> [My mother's] face, and my father's face, were naked with love. It wasn't something we talked about—love—and I was terrified of its expression from the lips of my parents. But they allowed me this one clear look at it. Their love blazed from them.

The risk for the culturally displaced is that family life, the core of their existence, will be undermined by the malevolent, rapacious, larger society—beyond the reservation.

Displacement presages more specific crimes, like the lynching of (blameless) Ojibwes in *The Plague of Doves* by white men intent upon revenging a vicious crime that had been committed, in fact, as we eventually learn, by a white man and not by Ojibwes; this second, vicious crime echoes through decades and generations, even as natives, mixed-bloods, and non-natives intermarry beneath a North

Dakota sky that constitutes "one gigantic memory for us all."

In *The Round House,* immediately following the rape, Geraldine Coutts sinks into clinical depression and refuses to leave her bed. It isn't so much the assault itself, terrible as it is, that precipitates this reaction as the victim's sense of helplessness and passivity: she doesn't want to tell even her husband the identity of her rapist, for fear that the psychopath-rapist will murder her family, as well as her. The exasperation Joe begins to feel for his mother in this inert state is entirely believable: "It was as though I had been locked up with a raging corpse." Perhaps less believable is the absence in the text of an acknowledgment of a community of rape victims, so to speak. Both Bazil Coutts (one of the multiple narrators of *The Plague of Doves*) and his wife would be acquainted with numerous rape cases, hardly a rarity on Native American reservations, as it is hardly a rarity in the United States generally. But Geraldine Coutts appears to be unnaturally isolated—like someone suffering from a rare disease of which no one else has heard.[1]

Not all whites are "skins of evil" (*RH*, p. 242), but an unforgiveable majority of whites are indifferent to the sins of other whites, perpetrated against native peoples; or, they shield such whites, like the villainous psychopath of *The Round House,* who would go unpunished by "white" law. Evoked in both *The Round House* and in *The Plague of Doves* is a tale of a cannibal white man, Liver-Eating Johnson:

> [Mooshum] related the horrifying tale of Liver-Eating Johnson's hatred of the Indian and how in lawless days this evil trapper and coward jumped his prey and was said to cut the liver from his living victim and devour that organ right before their eyes. He liked to run them down, too, over great distances.
>
> [Mooshum] said, I ever tell you boys about the time I outran Liver-Eating Johnson? How that old rascal used to track down Indians and kill us and eat our livers? That was a white wiin-

digoo, but when I was young and fleet, I run him down and
whittled him away bite by bite and paid him back. I snapped
off his ear with my teeth, and then his nose. Want to see his
thumb?

Liver-Eating Johnson is but one example in Erdrich's Indian lore
of a white "wiindigoo"—a soulless creature who must be killed in
self-defense. But there is a technique to successfully killing a wiindigoo: "You couldn't do it alone." (*RH*, p. 180) In *The Round House*,
the acts of the psychopath rapist (who is revealed as a murderer
as well as a rapist) "cry out to Heaven for Vengeance." Interlarded
through *The Round House* are references to law books—("the law
book my father called The Bible. Felix S. Cohen's *Handbook of
Federal Indian Law*")—and court cases in which Joe's father has
ruled—(in very few of which the Native American judge is able to
claim "limited jurisdiction over a non-Indian" subject). Clearly it's
the case, Erdrich suggests, that Native American criminal justice
should not be subordinate to state or federal U.S. law; in an interview she has said that the "survival" of Native Americans depends
upon their young people becoming lawyers. But there are instances
in which even tribal law is irrelevant, for the killing of a "wiindigoo"
has precedence, as Joe's father tells him, in a "very old law," that
supersedes and nullifies merely human law.

Rendered impotent by federal law, which forbids arresting, in-
dicting, and trying U.S. citizens in tribal courts when they've committed crimes on Native American reservations against Native
Americans, Bazil Coutts explains his moral position to his son:

I ask myself in this situation, as one sworn to uphold the law
in every case, what would I do if I had any information that would
lead to the identity of the killer. . . . [of the rapist] I've decided that
I would do nothing. Any judge knows that there are many kinds of
justice—for instance, ideal justice as opposed to the best-that-we-
can-do justice. . . . There was no question of [the rapist's] guilt. He

may even have wanted to get caught and punished. We can't know his mind. [The rapist's] killing is a wrong thing which serves an ideal justice. It settles a legal enigma. It threads that unfair maze of land title law by which [the rapist] could not be prosecuted. His death was the exit. . . .

> It could be argued that [the rapist] met the definition of a wiindigoo, and that with no other recourse, his killing fulfilled the requirements of a very old law.

Thousands of years after Aeschylus's *The Oresteia*, in which the impersonality and durability of law is shown to supersede the ferocity of blood-vengeance, it would be a rare work of literary fiction that shrank from condoning some sort of vigilante law in the face of the failure of impersonal law; popular wisdom concurs that these are not base motives for revenge, but the stirrings of a higher morality, a "higher law," to which one has the right to appeal if the law ordained by governments fails or is corrupt. (*Hamlet* is the great "revenge" play—young Hamlet's reluctance to exact vengeance is felt by him, and by the spectator, as a moral failing and not a lofty, Kantian virtue.) Except for the young age of the individual who exacts the vigilante justice, *The Round House* is not revolutionary or original in this regard, and does not appear to have aroused controversy since its publication in 2012. Certainly the execution of the rapist/"wiindigoo" is not an easy task for the boy, and is not carried out alone but with at least two collaborators of whom one is the (female) twin of the rapist; and the aftermath of the killing is fraught with wholly credible guilt and unease, as well as the accidental death of one of the collaborators. Joe is made to think: "There was in me . . . a disconnect so profound I could think of nothing but obliteration. I would somehow find the means to get drunk. The world would take on that amber tone. Things would soften to brown as if in old photographs."

The Round House is not, like time-shifting *The Plague of Doves,* a "whodunit"—we soon learn the identity of the perpetrator of the despicable rape; what is indeterminate is the punishment—if there will be punishment, and what its nature will be, and its aftermath, arguably the most interesting phase of any act of violence. As usual in works of fiction by Louise Erdrich *The Round House* contains passages of Catholic theology, morality, and reasoning—the author was brought up Catholic and attended a reservation Catholic school: "I'm so full of fury that it doesn't even register anymore"— which confronts Joe's anguish only abstractly, as in this exchange with the (white) Catholic priest Father Travis:

> We've got to address the problem of evil in order to understand your soul or any other human soul. . . . There are types of evil, did you know that? There is material evil, which causes suffering without reference to humans but gravely affecting humans. Disease and poverty, calamities of any natural sort . . . These we can't do anything about. . . . Moral evil is different. It is caused by human beings. . . . Now you came up here, Joe, to investigate your soul hoping to get closer to God because God is all good, all powerful, all healing, all merciful. . . . So you have to wonder why a being of this immensity and power would allow this outrage—that one human being should be allowed by God to directly harm another human being. . . . The only answer to this, and it isn't an entire answer . . . is that God made human beings free agents. . . . And in order to protect our human freedom, God doesn't often, very often at least, intervene. God can't do that without taking away our moral freedom. Do you see?

Joe half-sees, but clearly the answer isn't satisfactory in the face of his mother's suffering, his father's humiliation and his own misery. More ambiguously, Father Travis tells him, "We are never so poor that we cannot bless another human being, are we? So it is that every evil, whether moral or material, results in good. You'll see." The priest seems to know what Joe is planning to do but makes no urgent attempt to dissuade him. As his parents, who realize after the fact what he has done, do not speak to him about it at all: "There was nothing to be said. . . . Nobody shed tears and there was no anger." One has the sense of a tragic condition made worse by an obtuse and seemingly irremediable criminal justice system in which individuals must follow their own consciences and hope to survive. For Joe and his family, "The sentence was to endure."

The Round House
By Louise Erdrich

NOTE

1. In fact it is estimated that one in three Native American women living on tribal lands are raped, or sexually assaulted, in their lifetimes, more than twice the number of non-native women. A high percentage of these rapes are committed by non-native men, and are rarely prosecuted. In 2011, the Justice Department failed to prosecute 65 percent of all reported rape cases on tribal lands, and it is estimated that a low percentage of rapes are actually reported. The Indian Health Service is tragically underfunded. Crimes of various types on tribal land—domestic violence, child abuse, drug use (especially methamphetamine), robbery and murder, as well as rape—are so frequent, the Justice Department seems to have virtually given up prosecuting them, as tribal police frequently make no arrests when crimes are reported. A Native American woman advocate for victims of sexual violence (herself a rape victim) is quoted saying that sexual assault was "virtually routine" in her community. See "For Native American Women, Scourge of Rape, Rare Justice" in the *New York Times*, May 22, 2012.

IN OTHER WORLDS:
MARGARET ATWOOD

Science fiction is a mode of romance with a strong inherent tendency towards myth.

—Northrop Frye

Margaret Atwood's eclectic and engaging miscellany of essays, reviews, introductions, and "tributes" is a literary memoir tracing the myriad links between science fiction and literature, and relating both to those archetypal forms and structures so famously anatomized by her University of Toronto professor Northrop Frye in *The Anatomy of Criticism* (1957). It is simultaneously a self-portrait of the artist as an inquisitive, questing, impressionable and avid reader since childhood of a remarkable variety of popular and esoteric entertainments—from comic strips and comic books to classics of the genre by Jonathan Swift, H. G. Wells, Aldous Huxley, George Orwell. Atwood's intention is to break down the artificial distinctions between science fiction and "serious" literature by close readings of works by these writers as well as H. Rider Haggard's *She* (1887), enormously popular in its time, Bryher's *Visa for Avalon* (1965), Kazuo Ishiguro's *Never Let Me Go* (2005), and Ursula K. Le Guin's *The Left Hand of Darkness* (1969) and *The Birthday of the World and Other Stories* (2002).

The primary impetus behind *In Other Worlds* seems to have

been a public debate between Margaret Atwood and Ursula K. Le Guin on the subject of science fiction, initiated by remarks made by Le Guin in the *Guardian* in a review of Atwood's *The Year of the Flood* (2009):

> To my mind, *The Handmaid's Tale, Oryx and Crake,* and now *The Year of the Flood* all exemplify one of the things that science fiction does, which is to extrapolate imaginatively from current trends and events to a near-future that's half prediction, half satire. But Margaret Atwood doesn't want any of her books to be called science fiction. . . . She doesn't want the literary bigots to shove her into the literary ghetto.

In her admiring essay on Le Guin—"The Queen of Quinkdom"—Atwood notes that Le Guin speaks of science fiction as a genre that "should not be merely extrapolative" and should not attempt "prophetic truth"—"Science fiction cannot predict, nor can any fiction, the variables being too many." Atwood concurs with Le Guin that "the moral complexity proper to the modern novel need not be sacrificed . . . thought and intuition can move freely within bounds set only by the terms of the experiment, which may be very large indeed." (Certainly this is true of both Atwood and Le Guin, as very fine writers who have undertaken to explore the imaginative possibilities of "science fiction" and in the process have added inestimably to the riches of the genre in twentieth-century American fiction; but it is probably not true of most practitioners of the genre.) Both writers would describe their fictions as "thought-experiments"—ways of describing "reality, the present world" by way of original metaphors. Both writers would argue that "a novelist's business is lying"—as a "devious method of truth-telling."

With the good-natured patience of a teacher who has made a point repeatedly, yet is still being misunderstood in some quarters, Atwood sets forth her particular set of beliefs regarding science fiction in the introduction, stating her aversion to misleading readers who might be drawn to her speculative novels with the expectation of reading more typical genre work, and being disappointed—"I would like to have space creatures inside [my] books. . . . But, being unable to produce them, I don't want to lead the reader on, thus generating a frantic search within the pages—*Where are the Lizard Men of Xenor?*" Atwood draws a distinction between the more typical genre work and her own predilection for "thought-experiment" fiction:

> What I mean by "science fiction" is those books that descend from H. G. Wells's *The War of the Worlds,* which treats of an invasion by tentacled, blood-sucking Martians shot to earth in metal canisters—things that could not possibly happen— whereas, for me, "speculative fiction" means plots that descend from Jules Vernes's books about submarines and balloon travel and such—things that really could happen but just hadn't completely happened when the authors wrote the books. I would place my books in this second category: no Martians.

The daughter of a prominent forest entomologist at the University of Toronto, and an undergraduate at that university in the heady era of Northrop Frye, Atwood is more concerned with taxonomy than most writers, ever-elucidating definitions and sub-classifications:

> What Le Guin means by "science fiction" is what I mean by "speculative fiction," and what she means by "fantasy" would include some of what I mean by "science fiction."

As Atwood notes, "bendiness of terminology, literary geneswapping and inter-genre visiting has been going on in the SF world . . . for some time." She quotes the veteran SF writer Bruce Sterling, who coined the term "slipstream" in the influential essay "Slipstream" (1989):

A category . . . [is distinct from a] genre . . . a spectrum of work united by an inner identity, a coherent aesthetic, a set of conceptual guidelines, an ideology if you will. . . . I want to describe what seems to me to be a new, emergent "genre," which has not yet become a "category." This genre is not "category" SF; it is not even "genre" SF. Instead, it is a contemporary kind of writing which has set its face against consensus reality. It is fantastic, surreal sometimes, speculative upon occasion, but not rigorously so. . . . Instead, this is a kind of writing which simply makes you feel strange; the way that living in the late twentieth century makes you feel, if you are a person of a certain sensibility.

Apart from this scrupulousness about definitions, which may be of relatively less interest to her readers than to Atwood, *In Other Worlds* is a wonderfully warm, intimate excursion through Atwood's life as a reader and as a writer. There is much overlap between Atwood's memoirist recollections in the first section of the book and the remainder of the book, for Atwood is foremost an avid and enthusiastic reader of any and all texts that were available to her in a childhood of social deprivation but intellectual richness that suggests, to a degree, the legendary childhood of the Brontë children in remote Haworth bordering on the English moors:

I grew up largely in the north woods of Canada, where our family spent the springs, summers, and falls. My access to cultural institutions and artifacts was limited: not only were there no electrical appliances, furnaces, flush toilets, schools, or grocery stores, there was no TV, no radio shows. . . . no movies, no theatre, and no libraries. But there were a lot of books. These ranged from scientific textbooks to detective novels, with everything in between. I was never told I couldn't read any of them, however unsuitable some of them may have been.

Atwood's reading is, as one might expect, heterogeneous; her earliest efforts at writing are fantasies ("superhero rabbits in *Mischiefland*") of a sort common to imaginative children. Looking back at her childhood predilection for comic book superheroes, Atwood notes that, for instance, Captain Marvel "descends to us, in part, through ancient mythology"; Wonder Woman has "links with the goddess Diana the Huntress", and Batman "is born of technology alone . . . entirely human and therefore touchingly mortal, but he does have a lot of bat-machinery and bat-gizmos to help him in his fight against crime." Atwood asks: Where do other worlds and alien beings come from? Is the "under-bed monster" an archetype of "prehistory"? Could it be that the tendency to produce "other worlds" is an essential property of the human imagination, "via the limbic system and the neocortex, just as empathy is?"

In an essay titled "Burning Bushes; or, Why Heaven and Hell Went to Planet X," Atwood argues persuasively that myths have become detached from traditional religion, thus from traditional religious imagery; the mythmaking imagination is now attuned to the "supernatural"—"Planet X." Atwood's many questions spring from the analytical-critical-scholarly imagination that once sent her, as a Woodrow Wilson fellow, to Radcliffe for an M.A. degree in English, in 1962, and from there to Harvard, where she enrolled in the English Ph.D. program, dropping out before she completed a dissertation on "The English Metaphysical Romance":

Do stories free the human imagination or tie it up in chains by prescribing "right behavior," like so many Victorian Christian-pop novels about the virtues of virtuous women? Are narratives a means to enforce social control or a means of escape from it? Is the use of "story" as a synonym for "lie" justified, and if so, are some lies necessary? Are we the slaves of our own stories— our family narratives and dramas, for instance—which compel us to re-enact them? Do stories optimistically help us shape our lives for the better or pessimistically doom us to tragic failure? Do they embody ancient tropes and act out atavistic rituals?

This essay also traces the influence of Northrop Frye upon Atwood, and her fascination with the viability of "myth" in everyday life, as in classic works of literature: "Thus it was a grave matter to be told as a Canadian—as one constantly was told, in the late 1950s—that one lacked a mythology."

Atwood is very funny about the "old theologies and old rituals" of the past, but she is very funny about new theologies as well: she sees science as a new-myth system not so very different from the old, though expressed in a new vocabulary:

> Science, too, has generated new myth systems. . . . Here, for instance, is a new creation myth: the universe began with a Big Bang. Then the Earth was formed of cosmic dust. What came before the Big Bang? A singularity. What is a singularity? We don't know.
>
> Here is a new origin-of-people myth: people emerged via something called evolution forces from pre-human life forms that also so emerged. Who created the rules for evolution? Life did. Where did life come from? We're not sure, but we're working on it. Why are we on Earth? No particular reason.

Atwood notes that in "proper" novels characters are placed for us securely in social space by being provided, usually, with a family, and a background; such characters experience "inner problems, or conflicts," in contrast to less realistic, more fabulist works of fiction—by Kafka and Gogol, for instance—in which characters appear virtually out of nowhere, in unrecognizable or radically altered settings. In addition, SF stories can take us where no one has ever gone—in spaceships, or on cyberspace trips that are analogues to ancient quests:

I'm far from the first commentator to note that science fiction is
where theologically linked phenomena and reasonable facsimiles
of them went after *Paradise Lost.* The form has often been used
as a way of acting out a theological doctrine, as— for instance—
Dante's *Divine Comedy* was once used. . . . The religious reso-
nances in such films as *Star Wars* are more than obvious.

Atwood is particularly illuminating in her discussion of utopias,
dystopias, and "ustopias"—(an Atwood-invented word made by
combining *utopia* and *dystopia*). Here, texts including *She,* James
Hilton's *Lost Horizons*, H. G. Wells's "Country of the Blind," Ursula K. Le Guin's *Earthsea Trilogy* and J. R. R. Tolkien's ubiquitous
The Lord of the Rings are discussed in terms of "cartographies"—
"mappable locations and states of mind." Atwood reconsiders her
own "metaphysical romance" thesis of four decades previous as a
possible answer to the self-query: "Why did I jump the tracks, as
it were, from realistic novels to dystopias?" The most immediate
literary catalyst for Atwood's first "ustopia," *The Handmaid's Tale,* is
Orwell's *Nineteen Eighty-Four* (1949): "I grew up with George Orwell. I was born in 1939, and *Animal Farm* was published in 1945."
Nineteen Eighty-Four, read by Atwood when she was in high school,
made an even stronger impression upon her than the beast fable
Animal Farm, for the novel dwelt in excruciating detail on what it
was like to live "entirely within a [totalitarian] system." Yet, Atwood
doesn't see Orwell's great novel as unremittingly pessimistic, since
it contains a final chapter, an essay on "Newspeak," that seems to
suggest that the nightmare totalitarian government has been abol-
ished, and that some measure of sanity has been restored, signaled
by a return to standard English; so too, as if in homage to Orwell,
Atwood concludes *A Handmaid's Tale* with an appendix reporting a
symposium held several centuries in the future, in which the totalitarian right-wing-Christian regime has become, like so much else in
tragic human history, "a subject for academic analysis."

The hedonistic counterpart to Orwell's nightmare state is, of course, Aldous Huxley's *Brave New World*: "In the latter half of the twentieth century, two visionary books cast their shadows over our futures." Set beside *Nineteen Eighty-Four,* Huxley's satirical utopia proposes "a different and softer form of totalitarianism—one of conformity achieved through engineered, bottle-grown babies and hypnotic persuasion rather than through brutality." *Brave New World* posits an essentially infantilized society in which "free will" has been surrendered to the state in exchange for an unflagging, fatuous soma-produced "happiness"—"a world in which everything is available, [and] nothing has any meaning." As a work of prose fiction *Brave New World* is itself, Atwood notes, lacking in depth— "All is surface"—"an effect not unlike a controlled hallucination." Yet Huxley's mock-utopia holds up very well seventy-five years after publication: "It was Huxley's genius to present us to ourselves in all our ambiguity."

Commenting on her own mock-utopia *Oryx and Crake,* Atwood notes that the "utopia-facilitating" element in this future society isn't a new kind of social organization, mass brainwashing, or a "soul-engineering program," but a transformation inside the human body: "This seems to be where ustopia is moving in real life as well: through genetic engineering." Atwood's trilogy of speculative fictions—concluding with *The Year of the Flood*—is characterized by a kind of historical realism, or plausibility: the author has taken care not to include in the novels anything that human beings have not already done, or are not likely to do, given certain circumstances; there is no reliance upon "other worlds" in the conventional SF sense of alien infiltration. If there is species-destruction, it will be intra-species.

In other, less formally focused chapters in *In Other Worlds,* Atwood discusses prevailing SF themes in individual works of fiction—from the "rip-roaring" *She* of Rider Haggard and the brilliant "scientific romance" of H. G. Wells, *The Island of Dr. Moreau,* to Atwood's contemporaries Kazuo Ishiguro and Marge Piercy's *Woman on the Edge of Time* (1976). Atwood interprets Piercy's novel as not a seriously flawed realist novel as reviewers had believed it to be at the time of publication but rather as an attempt at presenting a "utopia"—though for all her enthusiasm Atwood isn't able to summon much convincing evidence that this novel, seemingly in thrall to the quasi-visionary novels of Doris Lessing, is anything other than a mismatch of utopian/feminist notions attached to an improbable and sometimes "whimsical" plot.

One of the seminal texts in Atwood's life as a reader and writer is the pop-classic *She,* an adventure-quest saga in which intrepid Englishmen set out for Africa to hunt the beautiful "Queen of the Amahaggar, 'She-who-must-be-obeyed.'" Atwood's Harvard doctoral dissertation was to have been on nineteenth-century Victorian "quasi-goddesses"; the "she" of Haggard's novel is squarely in this tradition, albeit "she" is the suffocatingly good Victorian woman in reverse. Atwood convincingly interprets Haggard's demonic heroine as a reaction to the "rise of 'Woman' in the nineteenth century, and with the hotly debated issues of her 'true nature' and her 'rights,' and also with the anxieties and fantasies these controversies generated." If women were to acquire political power, what horrors would ensue? If *she* is revealed as not aligned with nature in the benign Wordsworthian sense of that term, is the goddess Darwinian? And what does this mean for men? Atwood ponders: "Would it be out of the question to connect the destructive Female Will, so feared by D. H. Lawrence and others, with the malign aspect of She?"

The most fastidiously decoded dystopias in *In Other Worlds* are the third voyage of Gulliver in Jonathan Swift's *Gulliver's Travels* (1726)—"Of the Madness of Mad Scientists: Jonathan Swift's Grand Academy"— and H. G. Wells's *The Island of Dr. Moreau* (1896)— "Ten Ways of Looking at *The Island of Dr. Moreau*." Atwood posits the eccentric scientists of Swift's Laputa and the Grand Academy of Lagado as precursors of the more malevolent-minded "mad scientists" of popular culture; they are precursors of Mary Shelley's ideal-istic young Dr. Frankenstein (1818) as of Robert Lewis Stevenson's Dr. Jekyll (1886) and of any number of deranged men of science in B-movie science fictions with titles like *The Brain That Wouldn't Die*. Of all of these, Wells's Dr. Moreau is the most demonic, as his trans-species experiments involve hideous physical suffering in helpless animal subjects; in fact, Moreau is the "god" of his island, very like the Old Testament Jehovah, the Creator who "makes" liv-ing things in His image. Is Wells suggesting that "Moreau is to his animals as God is to man"?—then God himself is accused of "cru-elty and indifference." In retrospect, Wells said of this early sci-entific romance of his, perhaps with some degree of boastfulness, that it was "a youthful piece of blasphemy." Clearly *The Island of Dr. Moreau* is one of Atwood's favorite dystopias, a touchstone of sorts for her private, post–*Paradise Lost* mythology.

Bryher's novella-length *Visa for Avalon* is "an odd duck of a book. . . . *Everyman* meets *The Pilgrim's Progress* crossed with 'The Passing of Arthur' with undertones of *The Seventh Seal*. . . . it would be stretching matters to call it an entirely successful work of art," while Ishiguro's heartrending parable *Never Let Me Go* is "a brilliantly executed book by a master craftsman who has chosen a difficult subject: ourselves, seen through a glass, darkly." Atwood concludes *In Other Worlds* with several enigmatic sci-fi parables of her own, and as if to suggest the casual, non-scholarly nature of the undertaking, appendices comprised of "An Open Letter from Mar-garet Atwood to the Judson Independent School District" (who'd banned *A Handmaid's Tale* in 2006) and "*Weird Tales* Covers of the 1930s" ("The 'low art' of one age often cribs from the 'high art' of the preceding one; and 'high art' just as frequently borrows from the most vulgar elements of its own times.")

In Other Worlds is not, as Atwood acknowledges in her intro-duction, "a catalogue of science fiction, a grand theory about it, or a literary history." It is "not a treatise, it is not definitive, it is not exhaustive, it is not canonical." Still, one would have expected some consideration of an exemplary film like Stanley Kubrick's *2001: A Space Odyssey* (1968), which dramatizes many of the themes with which Atwood is concerned, as well as discussions of representative fictions by Arthur C. Clarke, Isaac Asimov, and Ray Bradbury (who is mentioned only in passing); conspicuous too is an omission of the feminist-SF work of Atwood's older contemporary Doris Lessing, who speaks of her "space fiction" sequence *Canopus in Argos* as her most important work

Though this affable collection does not aspire to the kind of bravely original cultural overview that made Atwood's *Survival: A Thematic Guide to Canadian Literature* (1972) such a valuable anatomy of Canadian literature, yet *In Other Worlds* is an excellent introduction to science fiction as a genre as well as an entertainingly written memoir of the author's "lifelong relationship with a literary form, or forms, or subforms, both as reader and as writer."

In Other Worlds:
SF and the Human Imagination
By Margaret Atwood

THE STORYTELLER OF THE "SHATTERED PERSONALITY": PATRICK McGRATH

"A psychiatrist introduced me to ideas of madness when I was eight years old. He was my father."

So begins "Writing Madness," Patrick McGrath's wonderfully intimate memoir of his childhood spent on the grounds of Broadmoor Lunatic Asylum in rural Berkshire, England. In the top-security facility, formerly known as the Broadmoor Criminal Lunatic Asylum, McGrath's distinguished psychiatrist-father Pat McGrath was the tenth (and last) medical superintendent of what had become, since Victorian times, an "obsolete, overcrowded" and "decrepit" asylum housing eight hundred mentally ill women and men. (Broadmoor was originally designed to hold no more than five hundred inmates.) Yet, McGrath's childhood seems to have been idyllic in unexpected ways, as he explains in this essay and in its companion, "A Boy's Own Broadmoor." For it was on the grounds of Broadmoor (comprising 170 acres including a farm) that the young writer-to-be first learned of such illnesses as schizophrenia—not a "split personality" (a popular misconception) but a "shattered personality." Like Edgar Allan Poe, whom McGrath avidly read as a boy, he became fascinated by the "disintegrating mind"—"a vein of black gold."

The elder McGrath appears to have been an admirable father, as he was an unusually liberal, reform-minded and generous psychiatric administrator who made every effort to involve his family in the routines of the asylum, like attending church services with inmates and making the acquaintance of the less seriously ill. Dr. McGrath "wanted the outside world inside the Wall, and the patients outside it, as often as possible"; the hope was to "break down institutional isolation"—with the result that the young McGrath seems to have experienced the utter naturalness of what the world labels "madness" and the fluidity of such definitions as "madness" and "mental health." It is touching to learn that, at Broadmoor, theatrical productions performed by the asylum's drama society the "Broadhumoorists" included, by tradition, the figure of an escaped lunatic "regardless of the plot."

Not surprisingly, Dr. McGrath had hoped that his son might become a doctor, a psychiatrist like himself, and we see how, in his remarkably knowledgeable and sympathetic fiction, Patrick McGrath has internalized the psychiatric analyst with his predilection for the revelatory sign or image and the instinct to provide a narrative—a "case history"—to dramatize what might otherwise be too obscure and private to comprehend. McGrath brings to his wildly inventive, often luridly "gothic" fiction a talent for storytelling that looks back to our great nineteenth-century predecessors (Poe, Mary Shelley, Algernon Blackwood, M. R. James, Robert Louis Stevenson, Bram Stoker, Joseph Sheridan Le Fanu, Charlotte Perkins Gilman, and Ambrose Bierce among others) even as it is wholly contemporary in its wry, dark humor.

The storytelling of McGrath is masterful and seductive. Simply to read the opening of a typical McGrath story is to be drawn into devouring it in one sitting. ("Devouring" is a not inappropriate term considering the extreme subject matter of many of McGrath's short fictions.) For example:

"All very tranquil, all very pastoral, hearts at peace under an English heaven and so on; why then did I have such an awful feeling of *dread*?" ["Not Cricket"]

Have you ever eaten monkey? The Cajuns have long considered Louisiana spider monkey a great delicacy. ["Marmilion"]

One of the most memorable events of my long journalistic career was the series of interviews I conducted with Arnold Crombeck, the infamous "death gardener" of Wimbleton, England, shortly before he was hanged in the summer of 1954. ["The Arnold Crombeck Story"]

I am, it is true, a mere boot, and no longer young. My leather is wrinkled now. ["The Boot's Tale"]

I am a fly named Gilbert and I live by a pond, a stagnant pond in a bird sanctuary. ["The E(rot)ic Potato"]

There is a room in my house that for reasons of my own I have always kept locked. ["The Smell"]

One fresh and gusty day in the damp autumn of her twelfth year Evelyn found a lost explorer in the garden of her parents' London home. ["The Lost Explorer"]

I have been in the town, a disquieting experience, for New York has become a place not so much of death as of the terror of death. . . . It is the Fourth of July 1832, fifty-five years after my mama died, and I have no doubt but that I will follow her before the week is out. ["The Year of the Gibbet"'

It is no place for a woman, the Barbary Rock. ["The Wreck of the Aurora"]

These bold, original, and disquieting tales are told by narrators who are themselves bizarre (a boot, a fly—to name just two) and are in most cases omniscient. Deftly, slyly, with eerie grace, they leap about from one character to another, like a film made surreal by frequent vertiginous cuts; see the very short, brilliantly rendered "Down the Rift," which gives us a perspective of a colonial mansion (in the Great Rift Valley, Kenya) whose outer wall has been removed so that we can see the individuals inside, imagining themselves unobserved as they behave very badly. In "Ambrose Syme" a cruel, doomed man of God and "superb classicist" acts out a particularly lurid scenario of repressed erotic desire, which we view with the detachment of medical students observing a dissection; in the novella-length "Julius," we brood upon a quasi-accursed family as its fortunes evolve, or devolve, over a period of decades following a secret betrayal: "do they not all clamor the same sad warning? That love denied will make us mad? I think so." In another novella-length tale, "Ground Zero," the stark horror of 9/11 and its devastating aftermath are rendered with the restraint of realism, evoking madness that isn't otherworldly and "gothic" but altogether real—the bleak atmosphere of New York City in the months following the terrorist attack, to which Patrick McGrath bears witness with unsparing care and sympathy. "The Other Psychiatrist" is narrated by a resident psychiatrist in a private mental home in upstate New York who may, or may not, be "reliable"—a worthy kinsman of the eloquent, and untrustworthy, psychiatrist-narrator of McGrath's powerful novel *Asylum*.

Bizarre, lurid, and startling images emerge in these tales: a disembodied stump of a hand ("Hand of a Wanker") that terrifies observers; a tiny black hand "growing out of Cecil's head" ("The Black Hand of the Raj"); a pitiless Grand Guignol bloodletting in the gothic *tour de force* "Blood Desire." In the ominously titled "The Smell," a stiffly formal gentleman is made to realize that he is the source of the smell that has contaminated his household—"I the smell, I the thing that dripped and stank. Behind the locked door I could hear [a woman] laughing, while I slowly suffocated, stuffed up my chimney like a dirty cork in a bottle of rancid milk."

In the least paraphrasable of tales, "The E(rot)ic Potato," a human corpse is eviscerated by scavengers in a "Triumph of the Insectile Will," and in the post-nuclear parable "The Boot's Tale" cannibalism is suitably punished by—more cannibalism. An idiosyncratic vampire named Cleave is identified in "Not Cricket":

> I was surprised, at first, at how small he was—just an inch over five feet. . . . He was very thin, with a disproportionately long face dominated by a huge, cadaverous jaw, deeply sunken eyes, and a fierce shock of jet-black hair, thickly oiled, that was brushed straight back from a sharp leak dead in the center of a low cliff of overhanging forehead. He was very elegantly turned out, little and horrible though he was. . . . In mid-stride [on the cricket field] the creature seemed suddenly to freeze, and hung there, suspended in the air, as though he were a photograph, with his little legs rearing off the ground and his head thrown back, hair wild, eyes blazing redly.

(Has any vampire ever been more viscerally *alive* on the page, even as "Cleave" radiates chaos and death?) These zestfully imagined nightmare images suggest V. S. Pritchett's commentary on the horror tales of Le Fanu (which McGrath includes in his essay on Le Fanu, "In a Glass Darkly"): "blobs of the unconscious that have floated up to the surface of the mind."

The stories, memoirist essays, and introductions to classic texts (*Dracula, Frankenstein, Moby-Dick, The Monk* among others) gathered in this collection suggest the range of Patrick Mc-Grath's imagination and erudition. As a rightful heir of the great nineteenth-century gothic writers, and the most celebrated practitioner of contemporary literary-gothic, McGrath knows what it is to be haunted, and how most persuasively to transcribe nightmares of the "shattered personality" that resonate within us all.

WHY BE HAPPY WHEN YOU COULD BE NORMAL?: JEANETTE WINTERSON

The one who breaks the silence is never forgiven.

Jeanette Winterson,
Why Be Happy When You Could Be Normal?

Surprises abound in Jeanette Winterson's painfully candid and often very funny memoir of her girlhood in a North England household ruled by an adoptive Pentecostal mother—the "flamboyant depressive" Mrs. Constance Winterson. ("Mrs. Winterson" is the name by which the memoirist speaks of her adoptive mother: a way of distancing herself from the monstrous woman even as the younger woman confirms by reiteration their shared last name.) Virtually every sentence in this impassioned document doubles back upon itself, carrying complex and often contradictory meanings, as the memoir itself is a *cri de coeur* of doubleness: a story of terribly unrequited love from "the wrong crib"; a lament not so much for a wretched childhood as for the adopted daughter's failure to have rescued both herself and her mother from the wretchedness of life not lived.

Why Be Happy When You Could Be Normal? collapses time in the way of a recurring nightmare in which a single traumatic incident is envisioned from a variety of perspectives that come to the same (compulsively reiterated) conclusion: "I never felt safe in [Mrs. Winterson's house] and when she made me leave [at the age of sixteen] I felt betrayed." And: "I walked around for most of the night that I left home. . . . I was in a night that was lengthening into my life. I walked away and I was trying to walk away from the dark orbit of [Mrs. Winterson's] depression. I was trying to walk out of the shadow she cast. I wasn't really going anywhere." The adult Jeanette Winterson, born in Manchester in 1959, and best known in the U.K. for her first, autobiographical novel *Oranges Are Not the Only Fruit* (1985), writes still with the vehement reproach and hurt love of adolescence. This is not a memoir of the acquiring of maturity but a memoir lamenting the inaccessibility of maturity. So fiery—so unabashedly *adolescent*—a document inevitably burns itself out, and may seem to the sympathetic reader abruptly terminated rather than concluded. The memoirist remains in thrall to her early, contentious life set beside which her present life, that of a middle-aged writer of reputation and controversy, seems to lack direction and coherence. The memoir's final terse paragraph is: "I have no idea what happens next."

The quirky title of Jeanette Winterson's memoir, like so many brilliantly bizarre turns of phrase in the book, is a replication of Mrs. Winterson's question to her daughter, when Jeanette reveals to her that she is a lesbian:

> "Mum . . . I love Janey."
>
> "So you're all over her. . . . hot bodies, hands everywhere. . . ."
>
> "I love her."
>
> "I gave you a chance. You're back with the Devil. So I tell you now, either you get out of this house and you don't come back or you stop seeing that girl. . . . It's a sin. You'll be in Hell. Soft bodies all the way to Hell."
>
> I went upstairs and started packing my things. I had no idea what I was going to do.
>
> When I came down my mother was sitting stock-still staring into space.
>
> "I'll go then. . . ." I said. . . .

"Jeanette, will you tell me why?"

"What why?"

"You know what why. . . ."

"When I am with her I am happy. Just happy."

She nodded. She seemed to understand and I thought, really, for that second, that she would change her mind, that we would talk, that we would be on the same side of the glass wall. I waited.

She said, "Why be happy when you could be normal?"

The wonder of the question is that it is utterly sincere and not ironic. *Why* seek happiness when, despite a lifetime of misery, and the creation of misery in the lives of others in your family, you might be perceived by your narrow-minded neighbors as "normal"?—in the case of Mrs. Winterson, nominally heterosexual, though in fact deeply repelled by the very thought of sex, even within "sanctified" marriage.

Winterson's memoir has the unsettling air of the most disturbing fairy tales—those in which there would seem to have been a happy ending, after much fearful struggle; yet, the happy ending turns out to be a delusion, and the old malevolence returns redoubled. Mrs. Winterson is an ogre of a woman to set beside any mythical devouring stepmother: "She was a big woman, tallish and weighing around twenty stone [280 pounds]. Surgical stockings, flat sandals, a Crimplene dress and a nylon headscarf. . . . She filled the phone box. She was out of scale, larger than life. She was like a fairy story where size is approximate and unstable. She loomed up. She expanded." When we are first introduced to Mrs. Winterson she seems to us a Dickensian comic character:

A woman who kept a revolver in the duster drawer, and the bullets in a tin of Pledge. A woman who stayed up all nights baking cakes to avoid sleeping in the same bed as my [adoptive] father. A woman with a prolapse, a thyroid condition, an enlarged heart, an ulcerated leg that never healed, and two sets of false teeth—matt for everyday, a pearlised set for "best."

Mrs. Winterson is beset by problems with the body—her own, her husband's, their bodies together, and the adopted child's:

> She had muffled her own body in flesh and clothes, suppressed its appetites with a fearful mix of nicotine and Jesus, dosed it with purgatives to make her vomit, submitted it to doctors who administered enemas and pelvic rings, subdued its desires for ordinary touch and comfort, and suddenly [as a new, adoptive mother], she had a thing that was all body. . . . A burping, spraying, sprawling faecal thing blasting the house with rude life.

Mrs. Winterson is tyrannical, suffocating, willfully obtuse and self-righteous; a messianic anti-intellectual who is, in the Winterson household, in which books are forbidden, "in charge of language." Every night she reads the Bible aloud to her husband and her daughter, always standing up before them:

> She read . . . for half an hour, starting at the beginning, and making her way through all sixty-six books of the Old and New Testaments. When she got to her favorite bit, the Book of Revelation, and the Apocalypse, and everyone being exploded and the Devil in the bottomless pit, she gave us a week off to think about things. Then she started again, Genesis Chapter One.

(Yet Jeanette Winterson notes in an aside that her familiarity with the 1611 King James Bible has been immensely valuable to

her, like the plays of William Shakespeare; that such a rich language was readily available to the English working class was a great
resource, in the later decades of the twentieth century, "destroyed
by the well-meaning, well-educated types who didn't think of the
consequences for the wider culture to have modern Bibles with the
language stripped out. The consequence was that uneducated men
and women . . . had no more easy everyday connection to four hundred years of the English language.")

Winterson discovers belatedly that her mother had deceived her
in the matter of the ending of *Jane Eyre,* which she'd read to Winterson when she was seven: "This was deemed suitable because it
has a minister in it—St. John Rivers—who is keen on missionary
work." In Mrs. Winterson's bowdlerized version of the Brontë novel,
Jane Eyre doesn't marry Rochester but marries St. John Rivers and
accompanies him into the missionary field: "It was only when I finally read *Jane Eyre* for myself that I found out what my mother had
done. And she did it so well, turning the pages and inventing the
text extempore in the style of Charlotte Brontë"

As Winterson presents her formidable stepmother, in a succession of vividly delineated scenarios, we are led to wonder if
Mrs. Winterson isn't merely an eccentric bully who uses the threat
of eternal damnation to frighten her willful young daughter, but a
mentally ill woman beset by physical ailments, a seemingly chronic
insomnia, and a raging paranoia. Here is a "humor" character out of
Dickens—

> We went past Woolworth's—"A Den of Vice." Past Marks and
> Spencer's—"The Jews Killed Christ." Past the funeral parlor
> and the pie shop—"They share an oven." Past the biscuit stall
> and its moon-faced owners—"Incest." Past the pet parlor—
> "Bestiality." Past the bank—"Usury." Past the Citizens Advice
> Bureau—"Communists." Past the day nursery—"Unmarried
> mothers." Past the hairdresser's— "Vanity"

—yet there is really nothing funny about a parent who is quite literally "waiting for the Apocalypse" and for whom life is "a burden to be carried as far as the grave and then dumped . . . a pre-death experience."

Every day Mrs. Winterson prayed, "Lord, let me die." This was hard on me and my dad.

Mrs. Winterson tells her young daughter that the universe is a "cosmic dustbin" from which no one escapes except in Armageddon— "the last battle when heaven and earth will be rolled up like a scroll, and the saved get to spend eternity with Jesus."

Everywhere in the house Mrs. Winterston has posted pious exhortations:

Under my coat peg a sign said THINK OF GOD NOT THE DOG.

Over the gas oven, on a loaf wrapper, it said MAN SHALL NOT LIVE BY BREAD ALONE.

But in the outside loo, directly in front of you as you went through the door was a placard. Those who stood up read LINGER NOT AT THE LORD'S BUSINESS.' Those who sat down read HE SHALL MELT THEY BOWELS LIKE WAX.

When her stepdaughter goes to school, Mrs. Winterson inserts Scripture quotes in her hockey boots. At mealtimes she places little scrolls beside plates: THE SINS OF THE FATHERS SHALL BE VISITED UPON THE CHILDREN." Her comprehension of the physical world is so uninformed, Mrs. Winterson explains mice activity in the kitchen as "ectoplasm." She locks her young daughter outside the house, or in the coal-hole; there, Jeanette "made up stories and forgot about the cold and the dark." ("The one good thing about being shut in a coal-hole is that it prompts reflection.")

Speaking obsessively of the Devil, and the "wrong crib"

(Mrs. Winterson and her husband had apparently planned to adopt an infant boy, and not the infant girl who turns out to be Jeanette Winterson), Mrs. Winterson isn't speaking in any way other than literal; if she's in charge of language in the Winterson household, it's a grim, grinding language against which the young Jeanette has to establish a defiant if shaky identity. Lacking friends, Mrs. Winterson had hoped naïvely to achieve a "friend" in her adopted daughter; but the daughter instinctively rejects the sick mother's negativity, in favor of "the pursuit of happiness"—a "salmon-like determination to swim upstream."

It's why I am a writer—I don't say "decided" to be, or "became." It was not an act of will or even a conscious choice. To avoid the narrow mesh of Mrs. Winterson's story I had to be able to tell my own.

And:

> It took me a long time to realize that there are two kinds of writing: the one you write and the one that writes you. The one that writes you is dangerous. You go where you don't want to go. You look where you don't want to look.

Writing *Why Be Happy When You Could Be Normal?* is clearly an act of exorcism on the part of the writer, a way of assuaging her "radioactive anger" as well as a blackly comic valentine of sorts in commemoration of the upbringing that, after all, has resulted in Jeanette Winterson.

IN PARTICULAR, the story of an adopted child is a special sort of story, for adoption "drops you into the story after it has started. . . . The feeling that something is missing never, ever leaves you—and it can't, it shouldn't, because something *is* missing." Mrs. Winterson is perceived, by the adult Jeanette Winterson, as herself a wounded person, who had had to "sever some part of herself to let me go"—"I've felt the wound ever since." A late chapter of *Why Be Happy When You Could Be Normal?* is a quick, cursory summary of wound-and-quest stories, of Odysseus, the centaur Chiron, the fire-stealer Prometheus, the Fisher King: "The wound is symbolic and cannot be reduced to a single interpretation. But wounding seems to be a clue or a key to being human. There is value here as well as agony." These are brave platitudes to pit against the prevailing horror of the blighted childhood.

It is not surprising that Jeanette Winterson's salvation is books:

Books, for me, are a home. Books don't make home—they are one, in the sense that just as you do with a door, you open a book, and you go inside. Inside there is a different kind of time and a different kind of space.

Winterson is a fierce and eloquent supporter of the literary arts, having lived through Thatcher's England as a university student at Oxford, and beyond:

So when people say that poetry is a luxury, or an option, or for the educated middle classes, or that it shouldn't be read in school because it is irrelevant, or any of the strange and stupid things that are said about poetry and its place in our lives, I suspect that the people doing the saying have had things pretty easy. A tough life needs a tough language—and that's what poetry is. That is what literature offers—a language powerful enough to say how it is. It isn't a hiding place. It's a finding place.

Books quite literally result in a major crisis in the Winterson household, when Jeanette is caught with dozens of contraband books hidden beneath her mattress:

Anybody with a single bed, standard size, and a collection of paperbacks, standard size, will know that seventy-two per layer can be accommodated under the the mattress. By degrees my bed began to rise visibly, like the Princess and the Pea, so that I was soon sleeping closer to the ceiling than to the floor.

Mrs. Winterson discovers a copy of D. H. Lawrence's *Women in Love* and knowing that Lawrence was a "Satanist" and a "pornographer," throws the books out into the yard and burns them. Determined to outwit the monster-mother, Jeanette begins to memorize her favorite texts.

Of course the most severe crises in the adolescent Jeanette's life are those involving her affections for other girls, which were not, as Winterson says, primarily sexual but emotional; looking at women's bodies "was a way of looking at myself, and, I suppose, a way of loving myself." The great trauma of Jeanette's stepdaughter life with the Wintersons is an exorcism to which she has to submit in the Elim Pentecostal Church in Accrington, which had been "the center of my life for sixteen years"; the exorcism follows a sermon by the minister in which it is announced to the congregation that "two of the flock were guilty of abominable sin." (See *Romans* 1:26: "The women did change their natural use into that which is against nature"). Jeanette's girlfriend Helen, with whom she has been intimate, runs out of the church, but Jeanette can't escape, presumably because Mrs. Winterson has captured her. The circumstances of the exorcism are not clearly described by the author but don't seem to have involved the more lurid rites associated with exorcisms in the Roman Catholic Church:

> When I was locked in the parlor with the curtains closed and no food or heat for three days, I was pretty sure I had no demon. After being prayed over in shifts and not allowed to sleep

for more than a few hours at a time, I was beginning to feel that I had all Hell in my heart.

At the end of this ordeal, because I was still stubborn, I was beaten repeatedly by one of the elders. . . . He shoved me onto my knees to repent those words and I felt the bulge in his suit trousers. He tried to kiss me. He said it would be better than with a girl. A lot better. He put his tongue in my mouth. I bit it. Blood. A lot of blood. Blackout.

That the exorcism in the Elim Pentecostal Church doesn't provide a comical episode for Jeanette to transform into prose seems to suggest it was too damaging. Following it, the sixteen-year-old "went into a kind of mute state of misery." Soon she is expelled from the Winterson household and never returns.

Yet, Jeanette Winterson cautions the reader not to judge the church as a crude and primitive religious sect, but a place of contradictions:

The camaraderie, the simple happiness, the kindness, the sharing, the pleasure of something to do every night in a town where there was nothing to do—set this beside the cruelty of dogma, the miserable rigidity of no drink, no fags, no sex (or if you were married, as little sex as possible), no going to the movies . . . no reading anything except devotional literature, no fancy clothes . . . no dancing . . . no pop music, no card games, no pubs—even for orange juice.

Winterson asserts that the principle of this extreme form of Protestantism, which draws its congregation together no less than six evenings a week, is a valid one, overall:

I saw a lot of working-class men and women—myself included— living a deeper, more thoughtful life than would have been possible without the Church. These were not educated people; Bible study worked their brains. They met after work in noisy discussion. The sense of belonging to something big, something important, lent unity and meaning. . . . The Western world has done away with religion but not with our religious impulses; we seem to need some higher purpose, some point to our lives. . . . For the members of the Elim Pentecostal Church in Accrington, life was full of miracles, signs, wonders, and practical purpose.

Unfortunately, one of these practical purposes is the casting out of demons from unruly adolescent bodies.

Why Be Happy When You Could Be Normal? is, in a less original and engaging way, a kind of self-help manual. Winterson has obviously been in therapy and would seem to have benefited enormously from it, judging from the fact of this memoir, as much as its literary quality. The subtext of her story is Love—her perpetual quest for love, the perpetual bafflement and disappointment in love, her panic at believing herself incapable of either giving or receiving love. A woman lover tells her that most women are trained to "give" love but "find it hard to receive" and that she, Jeanette, daughter of Mrs. Winterson, is particularly handicapped in receiving love, and she thinks:

No . . . I am the wrong crib . . . this will go wrong like all the rest. In my heart of hearts I believe that. The love-work that I have to do now is to believe that life will be all right for me. I don't have to be alone. I don't have to fight for everything.

Yet, her legacy from Mrs. Winterson is a profound distrust of love from any quarter:

Add to that my own wildness and intensity and love becomes pretty dangerous. I never did drugs, I did love—the crazy reckless kind, more damage than healing, more heartbreak than health. . . . Love is vivid. I never wanted the pale version. Love

is full strength. I never shied away from love's hugeness but I
had no idea that love could be as reliable as the sun. The daily
rising of love.

Winterson's suicide attempt is bluntly recorded, without embel-
lishment and with little of the narrative context of the Mrs. Winterson chapters:

In February 2008 I tried to end my life. My cat was in the garage with me. I did not know that when I sealed the doors and
turned on the engine. My cat was scratching my face, scratching my face, scratching my face.

Yet, with that doubleness that characterizes much of the memoir, Winterson has casually remarked that her mother, who'd loved
"miracle" stories in the Bible, had overlooked a "miracle" in her own
stepdaughter:

I was a miracle in that I could have taken her out of her life and
into a life she would have liked a lot. It never happened, but
that doesn't mean that it wasn't there to happen.

So many years later, after Mrs. Winterson's death, the middle-
aged memoirist is fantasizing, like a rejected lover, the ways in
which she might have made the resolutely unhappy stepmother
happy. Nothing in the memoir is so touching, as it seems to the
reader so utterly improbable.

WHY BE HAPPY WHEN YOU COULD BE NORMAL? concludes with the author's discovery, after much bureaucratic stalling and frustration,
of her birth mother, a former machinist named Ann who'd given
her infant girl ("Janet") away to assure her of a better life, and who

lives in a Manchester suburb twenty miles from Accrington. Their meeting is not overly emotional, though Jeanette's birth mother is "bright-eyed, with an open smile"; the antithesis of the scandalized Mrs. Winterson, Ann is not only unruffled by Jeanette's lesbianism but proud of her books. Ann is from a family of ten children. Ann has had four husbands: "I like men, but I don't rely upon them." Jeanette is relieved and grateful to meet her, but doesn't want to become a part of her birth mother's family: "I don't feel a biological connection. I don't feel, 'Wow, here's my mother.'"

The concluding chapters of Winterson's memoir have an air of the improvised and hastily written as if, after the death of Mrs. Winterson, the intransigent and fundamentally unknowable soul of the text has vanished. The memoir loses its energies of narrative discovery, incredulity, and hurt and shifts to the self-help mode of impersonal benevolent wisdom: "Happy endings are only a pause. There are three kinds of big endings; Revenge. Tragedy. Forgiveness. Revenge and Tragedy often happen together. Forgiveness redeems the past. Forgiveness unblocks the future." One feels that this is the sort of consolatory advice the author has been told rather than something she has discovered herself, as she'd discovered the curious interweaving of love and hatred in her childhood. Winterson sees her biological mother again, and they quarrel: "I am shouting at her, 'At least Mrs. Winterson was there. Where were you?'"

Yet, there is poignancy in Winterson's discovery, from her birth mother, that Ann's mother, too, was emotionally distant:

> When her mother was exceedingly old Ann found the courage
> to ask the question, "Mam, did you love me?" Her mother was
> very clear. "Yes. I love you. Now don't ask me again."

Why Be Happy When You Could Be Normal?
By Jeanette Winterson

DIMINISHED THINGS:
ANNE TYLER

In his beautifully spare poem "The Ovenbird," Robert Frost concludes

> The bird would cease and be as other birds
> But that he knows in singing not to sing.
> The question that he frames in all but words
> Is what to make of a diminished thing.

"What to make of a diminished thing" is a proposition that becomes ever more crucial with the passage of time in our lives, and particularly in the lives of writers who began young, with early successes and early fame. Like her older contemporaries John Updike and Philip Roth, Anne Tyler has addressed this painful subject in recent novels, notably *Noah's Compass, Ladder of Years,* and this new novel, her nineteenth; but she has addressed it in her characteristically minimalist, understated and modest way. Not for Tyler the boldly generic claim of such titles as *Toward the End of Time* (Updike), and *The Dying Animal* and *Everyman* (Roth); hers is *The Beginner's Goodbye*—a title so unprepossessing, so quaintly self-referential, you will have to read the novel to understand its significance.

Where Updike and Roth confront mortality in precisely delineated and, at times, excruciating terms, with an emphasis upon the

humiliating incursions of time upon the (male) body, in a diminution of sexual desire and of a passion for life generally, Tyler presents
her insistently ordinary, seemingly asexual characters with sympathy, but with no claim for our particular attention. These are not
special people, Tyler insists; they are not even "interesting" people
in the sense in which most (fictitious) people are "interesting." (For
why write about them, otherwise? Only the genius of a Samuel
Beckett can transform a mundane subject matter into gold, through
the singularity of style.) In Updike's *Toward the End of Time,* a long-
married and now rather crotchety older couple find themselves, in
a quasi-future United States, in a depleted suburban society both
familiar and unfamiliar to them; so confined, and needing to wear
diapers ("Depends Adult Incontinence Pants") Ben ponders alternative worlds stimulated from reading science books; the grandfather
of eleven children by the novel's end, Ben acknowledges himself
as "impotent"—yet "stirred by perverse fantasy." The quintessential
Updike protagonist has always been a highly sexual being, at times,
in such late novels as *The Village,* with its comically voluptuous (In-
gres) cover, to an obsessive and even preposterous degree; the quintessentially Rothian protagonist is no less sexually driven, though, in
Roth, the sexual component is often complicated by feelings of re-
sentment, revulsion, rage, even sexual politics, as in *The Humbling.*
In Updike, sexual love is the great, all-encompassing experience,
that blinds one—temporarily—to the ubiquitous fear of death; in
the epigraph to *Couples,* from Alexander Blok's "The Scythians," are
the striking lines, "We love the flesh: its taste, its tones, / Its charnel
odor, breathed through Death's jaws. . . ."

In Roth, any sort of genuine love is rare, and sexual desire is
a hook to ensnare us, as in the enigmatic ending of *The Dying
Animal,* when an unnamed (female) companion warns the aging
lecher Professor Kepesh against succumbing to the plaintive sum-
mons of a former lover, "if you go, you're finished." In Roth's more
recent *Everyman,* a grim contemporary allegory that begins with

its protagonist's burial and works through his largely uneventful
life, the unnamed "everyman" becomes obsessed with his health,
or rather with his bodily decrepitude, and a terror of what lies
ahead: "The profusion of stars told him unambiguously that he
was doomed to die." Surrounded by friends and former lovers who
are also aging, and dying, Roth's hapless protagonist feels a sympathy with others that is largely missing in Roth's younger and
brasher protagonists:

> She's embarrassed by what she's become [through illness], he
> thought, embarrassed, humiliated, humbled almost beyond her
> own recognition. But which of them wasn't? They were all em-
> barrassed by what they'd become. Wasn't he? By the physical
> changes. By the diminishment of virility. What lent a horrible
> grandeur to the process of reduction . . . was of course the in-
> tractable pain.

This is the fate of "Everyman" as a species, and no one is spared.
Yet, though a heroic gesture is futile, swallowed up in so impersonal
a fate, Roth's everyman is so overcome with emotion when he sees
his parents' graves in a cemetery—(the very cemetery in which he is
soon to be buried)—he breaks down:

> He couldn't go. The tenderness was out of control. As was the
> longing for everyone to be living. And to have it all over again.

By contrast, Anne Tyler's characters are never subjected to such
purely physical extremes. Their creator is not so cruel: her agenda
isn't to terrify her readers, or to wring from them genuine pity and
sympathy; her more modest intention is to provide an assurance that
what we've always known, or should have known, about family life,
romantic love, and loss is true after all. Her most engaging novels—
Searching for Caleb, Celestial Navigation, Dinner at the Homesick

Restaurant, The Accidental Tourist—are sweetly sentimental valentines to the ordinary, domestic, unambitious life, usually set in Baltimore's oldest suburb Roland Park. In these early novels, written under the inspired influence of Eudora Welty, Tyler's characters are magical without being whimsical or fey; even when down on their luck, they seem to inhabit enchanted realms of the spirit. In more recent novels, however, Tyler's lyricism has largely faded; the amplitude of spirit—magic—for which Tyler was known has diminished nearly to the vanishing point. Her protagonists are older, and detached from their dysfunctional but not terribly charming families; they are cranky eccentrics for whom it's often difficult to feel much more than exasperation. There are few poetic moments in *The Beginner's Goodbye,* perhaps appropriately, given the depressed state of its protagonist, but there is little to shock or discomfort. This is a novel about grief in which the raw visceral experience of *grieving* is not explored except in a cursory way. Experiences, impressions, emotions are blunted, as in a soft-focus movie:

> We were traveling through the blasted wasteland surrounding [Johns Hopkins University], with its boarded-up row houses and trash-littered sidewalks, but what struck me was how healthy everyone was. That woman yanking her toddler by the wrist, those teenagers shoving one another off the curb, that man peering stealthily into a parked car: there was nothing physically wrong with them. A boy standing at an intersection had so much excess energy that he bounced from foot to foot as he waited for us to pass. People looked so robust, so indestructible.

An actual street scene in this part of Baltimore suggests a very different sort of "robustness"—but Tyler's characters are suburban whites prone to see what they want to see, out of the habitude of a lifetime, and Tyler is their tirelessly indulgent chronicler. Though their time is supposed to be the present, it's a sort of time warp into which little of real life intrudes, as in one of those films in which it's always the 1950s or the early 1960s, before Kennedy's assassination—and before Baltimore's homegrown epics *Homicide: Life on the Streets* and *The Wire*. One senses, behind this political timidity, a "liberal" sensibility—but the moral compass of the fiction is determinedly old-fashioned, "traditional" and conservative; it takes no risks, and confirms the wisdom of risklessness. In *The Beginner's Goodbye*, a thirty-six-year-old man named Aaron has lost his wife Dorothy in a sudden, freak accident, when a dead tree falls on their house; Dorothy is crushed, though her body is bloodless— "The mound of her bosom was more of a . . . cave. But that was understandable! She was lying on her back." In a state of affectless shock following his wife's death Aaron is akin to Macon Leary of *The Accidental Tourist,* who'd lost his son in a robbery-shooting in a fast-food restaurant, and soon loses his wife of twenty years to divorce. Aaron walks with a limp and suffers from an intermittent stutter; his sense of himself, in physical terms, is rather more that of a seventy-six-year-old man than one of young middle age, as it's difficult to believe that he ever lived in California or, indeed, had the pluck to approach the older Dorothy, to ask her to dinner. Both novels of regeneration-through-loss present quasi-men who never quite strike us as convincingly "masculine"; their lives are circumscribed by domestic routines of stupefying dullness, of which they seem but dimly aware. Tyler has always been fond of eccentrics, loners, recluses; not "neurotics"—still less "psychotics"; not the passionately God-possessed freaks of Flannery O'Connor's fiction but milder aberrants who live at the periphery of society in near-anonymity, until someone or something comes along to shake them out of their lethargy.

Narrated in the first person by the widower Aaron, *The Beginner's Goodbye* begins with seriocomic urgency: "The strangest thing about my wife's return from the dead was how other people reacted." Aaron's doctor-wife Dorothy, dead for almost a year, suddenly begins to appear to him unpredictably, and in public. Aaron is convinced that Dorothy isn't an apparition or a hallucination but "real":

> People would pretend not to recognize either of us. They would catch sight of us from a distance, and this sort of jolt would alter their expressions and they would all at once dart down a side street, busy-busy. . . . I didn't hold it against them. I knew this was a lot to adjust to.

It isn't clear if Aaron is hallucinating, or very quietly mad; or, in an alternative universe to which fiction alone has the key, he is actually being visited by his wife:

> Maybe the reason I didn't ask Dorothy why she had come back when she did was that I worried it would make her ask herself the same question. If she had just sort of *wandered* back, absentmindedly . . . then once I brought it up she might say, "Oh! My goodness! I should be going!"

At other times, Dorothy's presence is more ambiguous, and may not be public but merely private:

> Then I was walking toward the post office . . . and Dorothy was walking beside me. She didn't "pop up" or anything. She didn't "materialize." She'd just been with me all along, somehow, the way in dreams you'll find yourself with a companion who didn't arrive but is simply there—no explanation given and none needed. . . . Oh, she looked so . . . Dorothy-like! So normal and clumsy and ordinary, her eyes meeting mine directly, a faint sheen of sweat on her upper lip, her stocky forearms crossing her stomach.

And there is the Dorothy who appears to her former husband as a plainly guilty conscience:

> She said, "I *would* have asked more questions."
> "Pardon?"
> "We could have talked all along. But you always pushed me away."
>
> After a year and more, Aaron has begun to think that his grief has been covered over with some kind of blanket. It's still there but the sharpest edges are . . . muffled, sort of. Then, every now and then, I lift a corner of the blanket, just to check, and—whoa! Like a knife! I'm not sure that will ever change.

Though Aaron insists that he loves Dorothy, or had loved her, he rarely recalls her in terms other than those that stress her physical plainness and clumsiness. She was five-feet-one—(he is six-feet-four). Dorothy was "short and plump and serious-looking" with "owlish, round-lensed glasses that mocked the shape of her face. Her clothes made her figure seem squat—wide, straight trousers and man-tailored shirts, chunky crepe-soled shoes. . . . Only I knew her dear, pudgy feet, with the nails like tiny seashells." She was eight years his senior, with the "social skills of a panda bear." Only Aaron knows that beneath her boxy clothes she was "the shape of a little clay urn." Even in their wedding picture Dorothy is ill-dressed, in a "bright-blue knit stretched too tightly across the mound of her stomach." It's difficult to imagine the couple as lovers, as both seem asexual, or prepubescent, incongruously encased in middle-aged bodies. Aaron and Dorothy haven't the impassioned adolescent yearning of Carson McCullers's misfit lovers, which so pervades that writer's work as to make the grotesquely improbable probable, and poignant. Even as he awaits her visitations Aaron continues to find fault with Dorothy:

If she had properly valued *me,* for instance, wouldn't she have taken more care with her appearance? It was true that I had been charmed at first by her lack of vanity, but now and then it struck me that she was looking almost, well, plain, and that this plainness seemed willful. As the months went by I found myself noticing more and more her clumsy clothes, her aggressively plodding walk, her tendency to leave her hair unwashed a day too long.

The possibility strikes Aaron in the imagined words of his older sister *It's too bad his wife had to die, but was she really worth quite this much grief? Does he have to go on and on about it?*

Aaron learns that a carpenter-friend was visited by *his* father after the father's death, and that the carpenter wasn't particularly surprised or upset by the visitations, to check up on his work:

"Must have been a couple of months he did that. . . . He never *said* anything. Me, neither. I'd just stand there watching him, wondering what he was after. See, the two of us had not been close. . . . So I wondered what he was after. Anyhow, he moved on by and by, I can't say exactly when. He just stopped coming around anymore. . . . He came back to make sure I'd turned out okay."

When Dorothy's' unpredictable ghost is on the scene, *The Beginner's Goodbye* quickens, and the reader is drawn into the pathos of Aaron's delusion. Obviously Aaron is being haunted by the unfulfilled nature of his marriage, and by his inadequacy as a husband. Like Macon Leary of *The Accidental Tourist,* who drives his wife from him through his inability to mourn with her the death of their only son, Aaron is meant to be congenitally obtuse, and maddeningly passive. For most of the time Tyler can't seem to think of anything for Aaron to do other than try to avoid well-intentioned friends and neighbors who ply him with unwanted casseroles ("After I recorded each dish, I dumped it in the garbage") or take him out to restaurants where he has to endure relentlessly banal conversations about food. He sees his dull, predictable friends and fellow office-workers; he has supper with his garrulous, possessive older sister Nandina ("born lanky, and ungainly, and lacking all fashion sense. . . . An aging girl, was what she was. . . . Her elbows jutted like coat hangers, and her legs descended as straight as reeds to her Ping-Pong-ball anklebones"); he revisits his demolished house, which is being repaired and renovated. Unlike Leary of *The Accidental Tourist,* who falls in love with an endearingly ditzy dog-trainer who transforms his zombie-bachelor life into something approximating real life, Aaron remains in a stasis of indecision, waiting for his deceased wife to "appear" to him.

Anne Tyler has a special place in her heart for individuals who lack enthusiasm, zeal, spirit—who prefer to stay at home watching favorite television programs rather than venture forth into independent lives. Ezra of *Dinner at the Homesick Restaurant* conceives of a restaurant that is resolutely non-chic, non-glamorous and non-gourmet, where "he'd cook what people felt homesick for," and "what you long for when you're sad and everyone's been wearing you down." No waiters but waitresses who are "cheery, motherly" and might urge upon customers "gizzard soup . . . made with love." Macon Leary of *The Accidental Tourist* makes a living writing moderately profitable self-help books in "chunky, passport-sized paperbacks" with such titles as *Accidental Tourist in America, Accidental Tourist in France, Accidental Tourist in Germany, et al.,* simply written little books for people who find themselves in intimidating situations for which they are not temperamentally or intellectually suited. ("Did Amsterdam have a McDonald's? Did Mexico City have a Taco Bell? Did anyplace in Rome serve Chef Boyardee ravioli? Other travelers hoped to discover distinctive local wines; Macon's readers searched for pasteurized and homogenized milk.") So too in *The Beginner's Goodbye,* Aaron works for a family publishing house known in the trade as The Beginner's Press, part vanity press (typical books are memoirs titled *My War, My Years with the City Council, The Life of an Estate Lawyer,* published for a fee, and virtually unedited) and part self-help press that has published a series with such titles as *The Beginner's Book of Kitchen Remodeling, The Beginner's Book of Birdwatching, The Beginner's Wine Guide, The Beginner's Book of Dog Training*— "These were something like the *Dummies* books, but without the cheerleader tone of voice—more dignified. And far more classily designed." The best seller in this series is *The Beginner's Colicky Baby.* In the depressed state of clarity following his wife's death, Aaron one day feels revulsion for his life's work:

> A set of instruction manuals whose stated goal was to skim the surface. A hodgepodge of war recollections and crackpot personal philosophies that no standard publishing house would have glanced at. This was the purpose of my existence?

Aaron comes to realize that his marriage had been unhappy— "Or it was difficult, at least. Out of sync. Uncoordinated. It seemed we just never quite got the hang of being a couple the way other people did. We should have taken lessons or something, that's what I tell myself." And, more harshly: "What I do remember is that familiar, weary, hopeless feeling, the feeling that we were confined in some kind of rodent cage, wrestling together doggedly, neither of us ever winning." Aaron remains baffled and exasperated by his wife in their posthumous marriage:

> I felt she expected something of me she wouldn't state outright. Her face would fall for no reason sometimes, and I would say, "What? What is it?" but she would say it was nothing. I could sense that I had let her down, but I had no idea how.

By the novel's end, Aaron has worked through his "issues" of miscommunication with Dorothy, and the final vision he has of her, she is "shining all over, and growing shimmery and transparent. . . . And then she was gone altogether." Unsurprisingly, Aaron soon re-marries, a woman from his office of whom we know little other than that she has eyes of a kind "a child might have drawn . . . with the lashes rayed around them like sunbeams" and enjoys cooking, and so will nourish him in a way that Dorothy could not. This a spare, quiet, understated little novel, a slender autumnal tree from which most leaves have fallen. Like the *Beginner's* series from which the title has been taken, it makes no great claim upon our imaginations or our emotions; it "skims the surface" of grief in a trajectory that ends, as if inevitably, in the widower's remarrying his office secre-tary. Tyler's affably bright prose style isn't geared for irony or a deep countermining of emotion, let alone profound emotion; if this is a novel of loss, it's also a novel of the failure to express loss, the failure to have fully lived before loss, as one senses that the protagonists of Updike's and Roth's autumnal novels have indeed lived. Yet there is a singular, curious passage in *The Beginner's Goodbye* like no other I can recall in Tyler's fiction, in which the zombie-like Aaron under-goes a sensuous private experience that verges upon the erotic in its wonderment and intensity:

> The cookie was oatmeal-chocolate chip. It wasn't a flat disk, like the kind you buy in stores; it was a big, humped hillock of a thing, lumpy with whole oats and studded with extra-large bits of chocolate, not chips so much as chunks. I took an ex-perimental nibble. The chocolate lay coolly on my tongue a few seconds before it melted. The dough had been baked exactly the right length of time—some might say underbaked, but not I—and it was chewy inside but crisp outside, with some tiny sharp pieces of something that provided a textural con-trast. Nuts, maybe? No, not nuts. Harder than nuts, more edgy

than nuts. I really didn't know. I seemed to have finished the cookie while I was deliberating, so I pried the lid off the tin and selected another. I needed to pin this thing down. I bit off a mouthful and chewed thoughtfully. The oats had their own distinct identity; I suspected they were the old-fashioned kind, rather than the quick-baking. I would have liked a glass of cold milk but you can't have everything.

On and on the cookie-eating continues in a trance of bliss, as, unwittingly, the widower is falling in love with whoever baked these cookies in which, as she will later reveal to him, the secret ingredient isn't nuts but soy grits—"For the supplemental protein." In a world of diminished things, Tyler seems to be telling us, such cookies, underbaked and lumpy as they may be, are as much as we can hope of romance.

SMILING WOMAN:
MARGARET DRABBLE

A woman who has spent the morning having a broken tooth replaced finds herself in a part of London where, three years before, she'd frequently met a lover for surreptitious lunches during the course of "a long and lovely year." She returns to their restaurant—telling herself it's just expediency, not sentiment—where, within a few minutes, she's unexpectedly joined by her former lover for whom the encounter is just as unexpected. After a flurried exchange the two discover—not surprisingly—that they are still in love with each other, and not with their spouses, and will resume, it's suggested, the love affair that had brought them such anxiety and such happiness. The story ends with the omniscient narrator's droll, detached, yet not unsympathetic observation:

> Like many romantics, they habitually contrived with
> fate by remembering the names of restaurants and the
> streets they had once walked along as lovers. Those who
> forget forget, he said to her later, and those who do not
> forget will meet again.

This deft commingling of the unabashedly sentimental and the ironic matter-of-fact is characteristic of Margaret Drabble. A fastidi-ous, if at times somewhat compulsive, chronicler of the vagaries of women's lives in England since the early 1960s—when Drabble's bright, insouciant debut novel *A Summer Bird-Cage* (1963) was published to critical acclaim—Drabble has conjoined the strengths of "old-fashioned" realism with the playful detachment and blatant myth-making of Postmodernism; the early, slender novels intensely focused upon distinctly female experience—*The Garrick Year, The Millstone, Jerusalem the Golden, The Waterfall*—dramatically evolved into more broadly based, researched novels narrated in the third person, often from multiple perspectives, on subjects of "sociopolitical" and historical significance—*The Needle's Eye, The Ice Age, The Realms of Gold, The Witch of Exmoor, The Seven Sisters, The Red Queen*. Like her boldly original predecessors Iris Murdoch, Muriel Spark, and Doris Lessing, Drabble has cast a cold, analytical eye upon her society; at a relatively young age she came to the conclusion, as she states in her *Paris Review* interview of 1978, that individuals are not isolated but part of a "theme" or "pattern" greater than themselves. Not the narrowness of individual experience was to be her subject but, in the magisterial way of George Eliot and Arnold Bennett, as much of contemporary English society as she could conjure into her fiction.

Drabble, born in 1939 in Sheffield, England, married since 1982 to the distinguished man of letters Michael Holroyd and, since 2008, a Dame of the British Empire, is one of the most versatile, and the most accomplished, writers of a dazzling generation that includes Martin Amis, Julian Barnes, Pat Barker, and Ian McEwan. Not only is Drabble the author of seventeen novels but she has also written biographies of Arnold Bennett and Angus Wilson and literary studies of Wordsworth and Hardy; she is the author of *A Writer's Britain: Landscape in Literature* and the encyclopedic *The Oxford Companion to English Literature*. She is the middle sister of an impressive literary family: her elder sister is the novelist A. S. Byatt and her younger sister the art historian Helen Langdon.

It was with the publication of *The Needle's Eye* (1972) that Drabble shifted the range of her subjects, and in this way the depth of her
prose fiction. Not a single, fixed-perspective female voice animates
The Needle's Eye but voices: one of them the voice of the divorced,
feckless Rose Vassilou whose ex-husband is suing her for custody of
their children, and the other, more startling voice of Simon Camish,
a London barrister who is male, skeptical, mercilessly sharp-eyed
and judgmental. Bringing these voices together, creating out of the
interplay of jarringly different personalities a rich and compelling if
in no way extraordinary narrative, Drabble found a way of exploring her larger, abiding subject—the vicissitudes of contemporary
English culture—not unlike a diviner's rod that would animate the
ambitious succession of densely textured and somewhat dystopian
novels to follow.

By degrees Drabble's Britain became, in the era of Prime Minister Thatcher and beyond, the "mean, cold, ugly, divided, tired,
clapped-out, post-imperial, post-industrial slag-heap covered in
polystrene hamburger cartons" deconstructed in *The Radiant Way*
(1987) and its sequel *A Natural Curiosity* (1989), *The Gates of Ivory*
(1991), *The Witch of Exmoor* (1996) and *The Seven Sisters* (2002).
At times the novelist's issue-oriented agenda suggests a formulaic
structure, as if Drabble were checking off timely issues to explore,
like immigration, or the outrages of Thatcherite capitalism; but
more often, the novels brim with sharply observed life and the author's seemingly infinite sympathy for "ordinary" women who must
remake their lives out of the wreckage of domestic life—very likely
echoing the way in which Margaret Drabble remade herself, after
the breakup of her first marriage to the actor Clive Swift, in 1975,
which left her with three young children and no means of support
other than writing.

Of course, these "ordinary" women turn out to be, like poor
left-behind Candida in *The Seven Sisters*, anything but ordinary.

Candida begins as a diarist of her own life in London, postmarital, accidental and haphazard; as the novel unexpectedly takes flight in an orthogonal move tracking the adventures of seven "sisters" who trace the journey of Virgil's Aeneas from Carthage to Naples, it moves through a sequence of dramatic shifts of perspective that define Drabble as a curious blend of the Postmodern and the storyteller of tradition, and reveal Candida as something of a seer—a female Aeneas of our time. (*The Seven Sisters* is Drabble's *Ulysses*—not Odysseus but Aeneas is the progenitor, and not the male Leopold Bloom but the female Candida is the mythographer.)

If there is any drawback to Drabble's bravura technique it might be that the author has cultivated an Olympian overview that somewhat reduces and flattens the significance of her characters, occasionally, as in *A Natural Curiosity* and the more broadly satiric *The Witch of Exmoor,* cramming too many characters into too conscribed a space.

Despite the detached and ironic tone of much of her fiction, Margaret Drabble is by no means an apolitical or indifferent observer of contemporary times. In May 2003 she published a vehement critique of American foreign policy in *The Telegraph* under the title "I Loathe America and What It Has Done to the Rest of the World": "My anti-Americanism has become almost uncontrollable. It has possessed me like a disease. It rises in my throat like acid reflux." In fact it isn't America or the American people whom Drabbles loathes but the Bush-Rumsfeld Iraqi War with its death-bearing planes painted like grinning cartoons and its Orwellian perversion of language—"friendly fire," "collateral damage."

> I hate feeling this hatred. I have to keep reminding
> myself that if Bush hadn't been [so narrowly]
> elected, we wouldn't be here, and none of this
> would have happened. There is another America.

Long live the other America, and may this one pass
away soon.

With the exception of a skillfully wrought little antiwar story
titled "The Gifts of War" that manages to be (gently) anti-pacifist
as well, there is little that is overtly political in Drabble's first collection of short fiction, ironically titled *A Day in the Life of a Smiling Woman,* but much that suggests an understated and oblique
moral vehemence. These fourteen stories, the earliest published
in 1974 and the most recent in 2000, focus upon the experiences
of women primarily: women as lovers, as wives, as mothers, and
finally as older women free of domestic and erotic entanglements.
Read chronologically, the stories move from youthful, romantic
yearnings ("Les Liaisons Dangereuses," "A Voyage to Cythera")
and adulterous nostalgia ("Faithful Lovers") to middle-aged disil-
lusion with marriage ("A Day in the Life of a Smiling Woman")
and finally to the freedom of the older, independent woman with
a relish for life of an impersonal, Wordsworthian nature ("The
Merry Widow," "The Caves of God," "Stepping Westward: A Topographical Tale"). What is characteristic of Drabble in her short fiction as in the novels that have made her famous is her sympathetic
clear-mindedness: Drabble isn't judgmental of even her most naïve characters, particularly her young, romantic-minded women,
whose delusions are so seductively presented they scarcely seem
delusions:

> She was already in her heart on her way to Mrs. Smithson's,
> already surrendering to the lure of that fraught, romantic, pain-
> ful world, which seemed to call her continually from the sor-
> rows of daily existence to some possible other country where
> she felt she would recognize though strange to it, the scenery
> and the landmarks. She thought often of this place, as of some

place perpetually existing, and yet concealed; and she could describe it to herself only in terms of myth or allegory. . . . A place other than the real world, and it was both more beautiful and more valid.

In the crueler and less forgiving worlds of Murdoch, Spark, and Lessing, such a fanciful "feminine" imagination would be likely devastated by a crushing counter-vision, but in Drabble's variant of a "voyage to Cythera" the naïve young woman is granted a vision commensurate with her romantic yearnings, a (literal) look into the privacy of a happy domestic life in an elegant but homey terrace house in Victoria Place, London, with lovely children—"a vision of something so beautiful that its relevance could not be measured." (Through Drabble's fiction, from the tenderhearted if exhausted young mothers of the early novels to the doting grandmother Frieda of *The Witch of Exmoor,* children, at least young children and infants, are unassailable symbols of The Good.) The more satiric "Hassan's Tower," set in a seemingly inhospitable Morocco where an affluent, ill-matched English couple are honeymooning, ends with a similar vision of our common humanity, realized atop the local landmark Hassan's Tower:

[The English tourist] saw all these foreign people keenly lit with a visionary gleam of meaning, as startling and as breathtaking in its own way as Tangiers had once been. He saw these people, quite suddenly, for what they were, for people, for nothing but or other than people . . . their relations became dazzlingly clear, as though the details of common humanity . . . had become facts before his eyes.

Yet Drabble's most elaborated ecstatic visions arise from spontaneous experiences in the English countryside, or, in the case of the reclusive actress of "The Dower House at Kellynch: A Somerset Romance," an infatuation with an old ruin of an English country house that brings with it, as in the most sentimental of women's romance fiction, the handsome heir Burgo Bridgewater Elliot. He was "in his way translucent. He was worn thin with a lonely pain." Will she marry Burgo, who has proposed to her, or will she merely live with Burgo in his gorgeous ruin of a country estate: "Love of person, love of property." The reclusive actress sounds very like the Drabble of *A Writer's Britain*: "I trod in the footsteps of the Wordsworths and Coleridge and Lorna Doone, I made my way through a thousand pages of [John Cowper Powys's] *A Glastonbury Romance*." One would expect Drabble to end with Charlotte Brontë's triumphant *Reader, I married him*.

In "Stepping Westward: A Topographical Tale," a schoolteacher unmelodiously named Mary Mogg—"You must not imagine me speaking to you in my own person. I speak to you as Mary Mogg, and it is her story I tell"—falls in love, perhaps not entirely consciously, with a woman naturalist whom she meets in the remote countryside of the Lake District on what was to have been a solitary excursion into both nature and her deprived emotional past: "She was about my age, with thick streaked black and grey hair, and a handsome, ruddy, veined, wind-weathered face. . . . 'I read,' she said, 'the messages of the forest. I decode the text of the trees. I read the lichen through my little lens.' And she passed me a small round hand lens." Drabble concludes her story with a forthright declaration:

> I am back in urban Northam now. . . . I am back at work and my excursion seems like a dream, but I am changed, I am fortified. . . . I stepped westward to test my destiny. And I found there Anne Elliot, with a wild gleam in her eyes at sixty. . . . I brought some magic back with me, and it will keep me through the winter.

There's an ironic cast to Drabble's calculatedly "happy" endings that suggests a perspective not unlike that of, for instance, Jane Austen: the narrator of "The Dower House" notes, "It is widely held that Elizabeth [Bennet] was joking when she declared that she fell in love with Darcy when she first saw Pemberly"—but the narrator isn't joking, really; nor does Drabble suggest that Elizabeth, or Jane Austen, were joking, for the point of Elizabeth's "love" for Darcy is that it isn't an easy, melting female sentiment but one that must be wrested from her. Austen knew the not-very-romantic truth that it wasn't individuals who married in the Britain of her time but family fortunes, or their absence; to resist, as Elizabeth Bennet might fantasize, is not, finally, possible.

Nor is Drabble joking in the glibly narrated "A Success Story" when her female protagonist, a famous English playwright, is most thrilled by the aggressive sexual attentions of an American novelist-womanizer, rather than the man's alleged admiration for her work:

> She thought of his face, looking at her, heavy, drunk, sexy, battered, knowing, and wanting her, however idly: and it gave her a permanent satisfaction, that she'd been able to do that to him, that she'd been able to make a man like that look at her in that way. It was better than words, better than friendship.

Kathie Jones isn't so naïve as to succumb to Howard Jago, however: she knows that, as soon as she does, Jago will lose interest in her. Only a woman writer secure in her feminist principles and reputation could write such a story in celebration of female attraction to male chauvinist desire, with the casual disclaimer: "It's an awful thing to say, but some women are like that. Even nice, sensible, fulfilled, happy women like Kathie Jones. . . . Whatever can one do about it?" "A Success Story" reads like a rejoinder to grimmer, humorless stories by Doris Lessing of women who find themselves used and discarded by men resembling Drabble's sexually rapacious Howard Jago (identified, in the chatty introduction to the collection by a Spanish academician, José Francisco Fernandez, with startling abruptness and perhaps not altogether fairly as Saul Bellow). Lessing's stories of the sexual exploitation of women—(see "One Off the Short List," for example)—are more powerful and memorable than Drabble's story, as they are more subtly wrought, and tragic, but Drabble's story glows with an anecdotal authority that lingers, too, in the reader's mind, as a corrective—playful? satirical?—of an older, condemnatory feminism.

The most gripping and suspenseful story in *A Day in the Life of a Smiling Woman* is the title story, an intimate account of a beautiful, accomplished wife and mother whose husband ceases to love her in proportion to her success in broadcast television, and whose vision of the world surrounding her is suddenly recast, after an argument with her husband:

> And now . . . looking around the polished table at their faces—at thin, grey, beaky Maurice, at tiny old James Hanney, at brisk young smoothy Chris Bailey, at two-faced Tom (son of one of the powers), at all the rest of them—she found that she disliked them fairly intensely. This is odd, she said to herself. . . . This is very odd.
>
> And she thought, What has happened to me is that some little bit of mechanism in me has broken. There used to be . . . a little knob that one twisted until these people came into focus as nice, harmless, well-meaning people. And it's broken, it won't twist any more.

It's a gem of a vision that might have been embedded in any of Drabble's dystopian-Britain novels, an entire life's-story writ small.

Only Margaret Drabble could make of this demoralizing anti-epiphany a means of liberating self-realization for the "smiling" woman who perceives it, thereby changing her life from this day onward. Drabble's heroine has even the courage to confront the possibility of uterine cancer, the symptoms of which she'd been trying desperately to ignore for weeks: "Looking back, she was to think of this day as both a joke and a victory, but at whose expense, and over whom, she could not have said."

THE INVENTIONS OF JEROME CHARYN

Of literary sleights of hand none is more exhilarating for the writer, as none is likely to be riskier, than the appropriation of another— classic—writer's voice. In recent years there has emerged a company of remarkably imaginative, sympathetic, and diverse fictional portraits of classic predecessors: Michael Cunningham's *The Hours* (Virginia Woolf); Colm Tóibín's *The Master* (Henry James); Jay Parini's *The Last Station* (Tolstoy); Edmund White's *Hotel de Dream* (Stephen Crane, with writer-friends Henry James and Joseph Conrad); Sheila Kohler's *Becoming Jane Eyre* (Charlotte Brontë, with sisters Emily and Anne). In these exemplary works of biographically fueled fiction it's as if the postmodernist impulse to rewrite and revise the past has been balanced by a more Romantic wish to re-enter, renew, revitalize the past: not to suggest an ironic distance from its inhabitants but to honor them by granting them again life, including always the stumbling hesitations, misfires, and despair of actual life—in contrast with the very notion of "classic." As each generation would seem to require new translations of great texts, so new visions of our great predecessors would seem to exert a powerful attraction for fellow/sister writers.

No conventional biography of Henry James, for instance, could present the Master as tenderly yet unsparingly as Colm Tóibín's' Jamesian portrait, for the novelist is in possession of information about which his subject is in "denial"; no conventional biography of Stephen Crane can bring us so intimately, terribly, and funnily into the hectic private lives of the tuberculosis-stricken Crane, his (former brothel-owner) wife, and their writer-friends, as Edmund White's lyric novel; no conventional biography of the Brontë sisters is likely to present their highly charged family drama—in which Charlotte emerges, as if by chance, as the triumphant survivor among her gifted siblings—more convincingly than Sheila Kohler's impressionistically rendered group portrait.

In this company, Jerome Charyn's *The Secret Life of Emily Dickinson* is something of an anomaly. With an epigraph from Dickinson—"To shut our eyes is Travel"—the novel is best described as a fever-dream picaresque in a slightly less febrile mode than Charyn's previous *faux*-historical novel *Johnny One-Eye: A Tale of the American Revolution* (2008). Clearly, these are bold postmodernist appropriations of the past—playful, subversive, phantasmagoric. Charyn's Emily Dickinson speaks with the appealingly wistful naïveté of Charyn's young hero, or anti-hero, Johnny One-Eye; like this keen-witted observer of vividly rendered eighteenth-century colonial American life, who describes himself as "unremarkable" amid a querulous crew of quasi-historical figures like George Washington, Alexander Hamilton, and Benedict Arnold, Charyn's Dickinson is essentially a marginal figure in her own life, a succession of "wild masks" in thrall to the ever-elusive (male) objects of her desire.

Far from being a faithful or even a plausible portrait of the historical Dickinson, for whom poetry was a kind of sustained guerrilla warfare against the confines of her daughterly life amid a conventional Protestant-Christian small town society, Charyn's portrait makes of Dickinson a defiant adventuress more enamored of prowling "rum resorts" (Amherst College drinking clubs), back alleys, and circuses in search of male companionship than of such bookish pursuits as reading the classics and "scribbling" poetry. In one of her guises as "the ghost of Currer Bell" (Charlotte Brontë) Dickinson is discovered by her older, disapproving brother Austin in a "dark dead-end of Roominghouse-Row" on the wrong side of the college town of Amherst, Massachusetts:

> "Emily, what are you doing in this godforsaken corner?" "The same as you, I imagine. Looking for adventure." "And what sort of adventure could you possibly find in Roominghouse-Row?" asks, his enormous ears suddenly materializing in front of my eyes.
>
> "I am not much traveled, Mr. Gould, being a member of the female sex who is not permitted to venture far without a male. But I had an irresistible urge to see where the maids and house keepers of our finest families live."

At her most audacious this Emily exchanges kisses with shadowy suitors in taverns, risks being treated very roughly—"scalped"—by mobs of surly Union army deserters, and pursues the phantom of a handsome handyman-lover through decades from Mount Holyoke Female Academy (1848) to her bedridden life as Queen Recluse in her father's house the Homestead (1880s). Repeatedly, her delusions of romantic love are rebuffed or vaporize into thin air; yet she persists in imagining herself as having "no more morals than a harem girl." Poor Emily, a poet by default! Her quixotic yearnings persist to her final delirium: "I am wearing a bridal gown with my slippers and yellow gloves, though I'm not certain whose bride I am."

In short, Charyn has invented for Emily Dickinson an active, at times frantic counter-life the poet never had: a "secret" life of unrepressed erotic desire. There is serio-comic pathos here—as well as a brashly subjective vision of our greatest American woman poet. Through years of amorous adventures and misadventures Dickinson flirts with men, maneuvers herself into compromising situations with men, yet seems never to actually lose her virginity—or does she? ("Lord, I did not know who I am or ever was.") Near the end of her life—Dickinson died at the age of fifty-five, in May 1885, of Bright's disease—she was courted by an elderly widower, a friend of her father's, Judge Otis Phillips Lord of the Commonwealth Supreme Court, who did not live long enough to marry her, though he seems truly to have loved her, as Dickinson seems to have loved him; this poignant late-life romance is rendered delicately by Charyn, if ironically:

> Suddenly I was Cleopatra with a plain simple face. . . . I could feel Phil's longing as we lay together, and it emboldened me to think that I could arouse the want of a man. I did not scheme like Cleopatra in my Salem's arms. If I held back, did not allow him into the Moss of my own little garden, it was not to punish or declare my modesty. I had none. It was just that my Salem was not a male witch. Whatever magic he had wasn't enough to slay me into submission.
>
> But our ecstasy did build with all the slow craft of a snail.

Among Charyn's writerly gifts is his seemingly unstoppable energy—a highly inflected rapid-fire prose that pulls us along like a pony cart over rough terrain, blurring author (Charyn) and subject (the "masks" of Emily) in a collage of short, often poignant scenes that generally end with the poet returned to her home deflated, rebuffed, dazed yet still enthralled:

> But I ain't comforted much . . . I could have slept on Zilpah's porch and waited for the sun to rise. I would have learned something about that robber's roost of hers. But what if the robbers had swept me inside and I never saw Pa-pa and Carlo [her dog] again? They wouldn't have bothered ransoming an old maid. And suppose their leader, Richard Midnight, tried to peck at me with his filthy mouth while Zilpah guffawed with delight and savored her own triumph? She'd have Pa-pa

all to herself. She'd inherit my pencils and writing paper, and Pa-pa would consider it a miracle to have a housekeeper who could scratch an occasional Verse. Lord, it was too much to bear.

And again, following a particularly hallucinatory episode:

The mosquitoes were . . . tormenting me. I couldn't move without marching into a whole skirt of them. I must have been near the river. The rot of marshland burned in my nose. And then the first signal of moon blindness struck—the feel of a terrifying stitch at the back of my head. And I plunged into total darkness, as if I'd fallen into Father's well, but it was like a hollow without an end. I spun within its walls, faster and faster, and woke with a stifled scream on the front steps of 86 Austin, wrapped inside the shelter of an old horse blanket.

The "secret life" is narrated by Emily in brief, breathless chapters bracketed by passages of italicized prose in which the subject is viewed from the perspective of family observers. Here, where we might expect to see a different Emily, the portrait is more or less identical to the girlish self-portrait, even when the poet has become middle-aged:

Then, years after all the clandestine deliveries [Dickinson's correspondence with the Reverend Wadsworth], her Master showed up at the door. Emily was in the garden with her pail. And Vinnie knew it was the Master, knew it in an instant, as he clutched the bell pull. He didn't announce himself, but asked for Emily in that deep voice of his, like wind barreling out of a tunnel. . . . And Emily, who'd always fled from intruders and depended upon Vinnie to be her shield, rid herself of the pail and ran to Rev. Wadsworth, her Master, like a child out of breath.

It's after this scene that Vinnie searches out her sister's "Snow"— one of Dickinson's words for her poetry—and discovers it hidden away in Dickinson's bedroom bureau:

> Little sewn booklets in a box, like the magic fans of a courte-san or coquette. And with these fans were scraps of paper and envelopes and fliers with poems scratched onto them in Em-ily's own hand.
>   [Vinnie] began to cry and laugh at this startling treasure, but was too timid to read a line. . . . She couldn't say why, but she started to dance in Emily's room. She wanted to cover herself in Emily's Snow, to feel it against her skin. Perhaps she was the coquette. . . . Vibrations went through her body like the shiver-ing of the Lord.

A *Secret History of Emily Dickinson* is filled with such lumi-nous, fleeting scenes, as if in mimicry of Dickinson's account of her own inspiration: "Lines came like lightning, and left like light-ning, and I had to write each one down with my pencil stub or lose it forever."

IT IS COLM TÓIBÍN'S' INTERPRETATION of Henry James in *The Master*, that James's life as an artist was determined by erotic desire not only unexpressed but unacknowledged by James; in *The Secret Life of Emily Dickinson*, by contrast, Charyn's artist-heroine is defined almost entirely by her erotic-romantic desires, not only expressed but "acted-out"—at least, to a degree highly improbable in a well-born young woman of Amherst, Massachusetts, in the early to mid-1800s. For admirers of Dickinson for whom the biographical facts of her much-scrutinized life are sacrosanct, even as interpretations of these facts might widely vary, the liberties taken by Charyn in *The Secret Life of Emily Dickinson* may be distracting: such purely invented characters as the illiterate tattooed Tom the Handyman and the Amherst College tutor Brainard Rowe, as well as Dickinson's wild-girl alter-ego-poetess Zilpah Marsh, who at one point lives in the root cellar of the Dickinsons' stately house, are principal in the novel, even as historic figures like Thomas Wentworth Higginson, Dickinson's controversial first editor, with whom she corresponded for many years, and the flamboyant young woman Mabel Loomis Todd, with whom Emily's much-revered older brother Austin had an adulterous relationship and who would be Dickinson's controversial posthumous editor, are relatively undeveloped. Even Dickinson's charismatic Vesuvius of a sister-in-law Sue, the aggrieved wife of Austin, makes a belated appearance in Dickinson's life as Charyn recounts it; Dickinson notes in passing, "I fell in love with her when I was but a Boy"—but we see relatively little of the famously volatile sister-in-law. And the much-reiterated appeal of Tom the Handyman—metamorphosed finally as "that blond Assassin in the sunlight" in one of Dickinson's poems—is difficult to comprehend over a period of so many years—so many picaresque experiences—and hundreds of pages.

A fully realized principal character in *The Secret Life of Emily Dickinson,* as he was a principal character in the historic Dickinson's life, is Dickinson's father Edward Dickinson, a Christian pillar of the Amherst community and a U.S. congressman. "Squire" Dickinson exudes an air of benevolent despotism in his household of mostly women:

> It is only Father who can make me tremble. He has the wrath
> of God in his wayward eyebrows. But Father suffers a little
> without me. He swears to Mother that he can only survive on
> the Indian bread that I bake. He loves to have me near.

The distinguished Mr. Dickinson—"Pa-pa"—enters into the poet's fever-dreams like the objects of her erotic fascinations, and seems at times identical with them:

> Swirling in Father's arms, I feel like a broken doll. *Pa-pa,* I want to shout, *I am not your favorite feather but a woman with a ferocious will.* I do not utter a peep, [Father plunks me under the quilt with the same brutal tenderness that has become his signature.]

Dickinson adores her father even as she has no illusions about his estimate of his "womenfolk":

> He took care of us, but in his own heart he must have felt that we were crippled creatures—mermaids who couldn't swim. Daughters don't matter much. I was a cripple to him, in spite of all my Plumage.

Nor does Dickinson's father evince much interest in her literary inclinations: "Pa-pa did talk Poetry, but only with his horse. The rest of the world was pure Prose." In a bitter-comic passage that recalls a similar experience of Charlotte Brontë when she'd given her self-centered minister-father a copy of *Jane Eyre* to read, along with a selection of very good reviews, Dickinson complains:

> It tore at me that Father did not know one damn thing about *my* Treasure. A couple of years ago I gathered up the courage to leave one small booklet of Verses under his door. Lord, I wasn't looking for praise, but the privilege of having a tiny anthill of my own. Months later I found that booklet shoved back under my door like a misused missile. And never a sound from Pa-Pa, never a syllable. . . . It wouldn't even have pleasured Pa-pa had he known that half my songs were to him.

Dickinson is then stunned when her father unexpectedly ser-
enades her with lines from her poetry, explaining that it had taken
him two years to recover from the experience of reading her poems:
"They nearly tore my head off."

Among the many lyrical vignettes in *The Secret Life of Emily
Dickinson* the most memorable have to do with death: the death of
Dickinson's beloved, elderly dog Carlo, and the death of the Squire.
Charyn has never written more powerfully and persuasively than
in these lovely pages in the section titled "Queen Recluse" that
covers the years following 1865 when Dickinson has taken up with
masochistic fervor the mantle of "irascible old maid." Far more significant in Dickinson's life than her string of romantic infatuations
is "The Pup [who] has seen me cry, throw jealous fits, plot against
Pa-pa. . . . I cannot recall being lonely in his presence."

Following Carlo's death, Dickinson is more easily "terrified." The
wild alter-ego Zilpah dies a suicide in 1873 having scribbled "Zilpah
is zero at the bone." Soon after, the great catastrophe of Dickinson's
life occurs, when she's forty-three and her father seventy-one—
Edward Dickinson's death of a stroke in Boston. So deeply bereft
is Dickinson, she can't attend his funeral but hides away—"The
slumber I had was like a tiny groan in a sea of wakefulness." An
"avalanche of dreams" shakes her intermittently for years.

I moan in the middle of the night. A Monster chases me,
with a ruffled, unfamiliar form, yet owning my father's dark
eyes. I cannot bring myself to call him *Pa-Pa* . . . and so I call
him *Dark-Eyed Mister,* and his horrid, unnatural face begins
to smile—or grin, I should confess, since he does not have
a regular mouth, but a lipless hole that serves as a mouth. It
puzzles the mind. Is this Monster my Pa-Pa, the earl of Amherst, transmogrified by some substation between celestial
and terrestrial ground?

The Secret Life of Emily Dickinson gains emotional momentum as it moves from the picaresque romps of Dickinson's youth to the stoicism of her final years. Losses of Carlo, her father, and a beautiful young nephew have the effect of easing Dickinson toward her own death, presaged by the diminution of her "lightning" powers: "My pencil hung on its string at my side like a sick snake, or a pendulum that could sometimes breathe."

IN HIS WINNINGLY WRITTEN AUTHOR'S NOTE to *Johnny One-Eye*, Jerome Charyn speaks of his lifelong interest in George Washington and the Revolutionary War era—"I have been writing *Johnny One-Eye* ever since I was nine, a street kid in the South Bronx." In his author's note to *The Secret Life of Emily Dickinson*, Charyn acknowledges an even deeper kinship with Dickinson—"She was the first poet I had ever read, and I was hooked and hypnotized from the start. . . . It was the old maid of Amherst who lent me a little of her own courage to risk becoming a writer." As Jerome Charyn has been an exuberant chronicler of the mythos of American life from the start of his career in a succession of highly stylized novels—he has written thirty-seven books, including three memoirs—it's likely that he has imagined "Jerome Charyn" in romantic-mythic terms as well, a precocious *naïf*:

> We had so little in common. She was a country girl, and I was a boy from the Bronx. She had a lineage with powerful roots in America, and I was a mongrel whose heritage was like an unsolved riddle out of Eastern Europe. Yet I could hear the tick of her music in my wakefulness and in my sleep. Suddenly that plain little woman with her bolts of red hair was as familiar to me as the little scars on my own face.

Charyn's Dickinson is "terrifying in her variety . . . bitchy, petulant, and seductive, and also a mournful, masochistic mouse in love with a mystery man she called 'Master.'" As biographers and commentators have noted, this "Master" might have been any of a half-dozen men, or no one, as the poetry inspired by "Master" seems to conceal as much as it reveals. Both the historical Dickinson and the poetry she left behind in the little hand-sewn booklets lend themselves to endless speculation, decoding, and mimicry—attempts at appropriation and mimicry, in Charyn's words:

> [A *Secret History of Emily Dickinson*] will be told entirely in Emily's voice, with all its modulations and tropes—tropes I learned from her letters, wherein she wears a hundred masks, playing wounded lover, penitent, and female devil as she delights and often disturbs us, just as I hope *my* Emily will both delight and disturb the reader and take her roaring music right into the twenty-first century.

Yet the voice Charyn has created for Emily Dickinson doesn't truly suggest this range of personalities. This Dickinson is forever defined by—if not trapped in—the breathless yearnings of a (female) adolescent as imagined by a (male) novelist: we are led to wonder of the Emily Dickinson who read widely, and purposefully, in all the great poets she could get her hands on, including Shakespeare, Byron, Keats, and "Mr. and Mrs. Browning"—what of the poet who read with an eye for the craft of poetry? It is surely true that lines came like "lightning" to the poet—as to many poets; but it is also true that Dickinson worked and reworked her poems, often over a period of years, as she worked and reworked her brilliantly teasing letters.

Consider the celebrated last letter of Emily Dickinson's life, written to her Norcross cousins shortly before her death:

> *Little Cousins,*
> *Called back.*
> *Emily.*

Is this a letter, or a poem? Is it—both? One can see by the very spacing of the lines that this seemingly tossed-off farewell isn't just "lightning" but also conscious, considered craft. And among Dickinson's extraordinary 1,775 poems and many hundreds of letters this is just one tiny gem. To have created a portrait of Emily Dickinson that accommodated both the girl-adolescent and the canny poet suffused with a wish to make of her craft something beyond the fleeting moment—a portrait that acknowledged the subject's literary ambition and her not-modest assessment of her own writerly gifts—would have required a different, more spacious vision of Dickinson than Charyn seems to wish to provide here. Could one imagine a portrait of a male poet—Dickinson's contemporary Walt Whitman, for instance—for whom poetry wasn't the very center of his life, far more inextricably bound up with his identity than a succession of mere romantic yearnings? It may even have been that, in the tradition of (male) poetry, Emily Dickinson employed her "Master" as a sort of muse: a scaffolding of sorts for her art. How else to interpret such lines of poetry as Dickinson often wrote, leaping from a private subject to a purely contemplative statement:

> Oh Life, begun in fluent Blood
> And consummated dull!
> Achievement contemplating thee—
> Feels transitive and cool.
> (1130)

There is considerable pathos, however, in Charyn's warmly imagined tracking of his subject's doomed attempt to thwart her destiny—to escape her father's house and, as if incidentally, to escape the very circumstances that made her "Snow"—her brilliant poetry—possible. This is not a portrait of the artist with which we can easily identify, but *The Secret Life of Emily Dickinson* makes of this questionable thesis a poignant, delicately rendered vision. It's as if all art is but a strategy to "invent" a bearable life, as Charyn's Dickinson suggests in this elegiac passage late in the novel:

> I would suffer each time Circus season arrived. . . . The nearness of my blond Assassin intoxicated me, and I wasn't even sure that Tom was a renegade clown in the Circus. But that was the disease of Miss Emily Dickinson. I had to invent what I could not ascertain—no, did not want to ascertain. I was the voluptuary who lived on the thinnest air, who survived *and* conquered through invention alone.

"AFTER AUSCHWITZ":
MARTIN AMIS

When the German cultural critic Theodor Adorno famously said, in 1949, that "poetry after Auschwitz is barbaric," he could hardly have anticipated the sheer quantity of poetry and prose that was to follow in the wake of the Holocaust, still less its astonishing range and depth. Poetry, fiction, memoir, film—from the elliptical, surpassingly beautiful and original fictions of W. G. Sebald (*The Emigrants, Austerlitz*) to the brash meta-filmic fantasy of Tarantino's *The Inglourious Basterds*; from the starkly narrated *The Reader* by Bernhard Schlink to *The Book Thief* by Markus Zusak, flamboyantly narrated by Death; from the densely narrated psychological/historical classic realism of André Schwarz-Bart (*The Last of the Just*) and Imre Kertész (*Fatelessness, The Failure, Kaddish for an Unborn Child*) to the Kafkaesque dream-landscapes of Ahren Appelfeld (*Badenheim 1939, Tzili, Katerina*); from the emotional intensity of Cynthia Ozick's *The Shawl* to the parable-like austerity of the Polish film *Ida* by Pawel Pawlikowski. With the passage of time works of art that confront the phenomenon of Nazi Germany, World War II, and the Holocaust have tended to become more circumspect as the generations that had been firsthand witnesses give way to younger generations: recent novels by Susanna Moore (*The Lives of Objects*) and Ayelet Waldman (*Love and Treasure*) achieve their considerable emotional power by focusing upon characters peripheral to the terrible European history that has nonetheless altered their lives. The conflagration is too blinding to confront directly but rather at a little distance, as in the reflective shield of Athena, which renders the horrific image of Medusa bearable, and the Gorgon to be slain by the hero Perseus.

Such artful circumspection has not been Martin Amis's strategy in approaching the Holocaust. It is the notorious Polish Nazi death camp Auschwitz that is the partial setting for Amis's *tour de force Time's Arrow; or The Nature of the Offense* (1991) in which the lifetime of a Nazi doctor/experimenter is presented in reverse chronological order, from the instant of his death (as the affably American "Tod Friendly") to his conception (as the ominously named German "Odilo Unverdorben"), witnessed by a part of himself that seems to be his conscience, or his soul. Nearly a quarter century later in his new and equally risky Nazi novel, *The Zone of Interest,* Amis has revisited Auschwitz, more specifically the "Zone of Interest," which contains the Polish death camp and the headquarters and domiciles of its Nazi staffers and assistants, a "dumping ground for 2nd-rate blunderers" as its commandant wryly observes. This is a place to which hapless and doomed Jewish "evacuees" are brought by train to be imprisoned as forced labor and/or gassed and their remains dumped in the euphemistically named but virulent-smelling Spring Meadow. (As the commandant wonders, "If what we're doing is so good, why does it smell so bad?") In this hellish place in August 1942 there are several narrators of whom none is quite so eloquent in Nabokovian irony as the unidentified narrator of *Time's Arrow,* but each bears witness to the unspeakable in his own way.

Lieutenant Angelus "Golo" Thomsen is the first of the narrators of the Zone of Interest, a mid-level Nazi officer in charge of the Buna-Werke factory and the favored nephew of the high-ranking Nazi Martin Bormann—"The man who controls the appointment book of the Deliverer." (For some unexplained reason, no one in *The Zone of Interest* calls Adolf Hitler by his name, only by elevated circumlocutions.) Thomsen's commitment to the Nazi war effort is haphazard and expedient: "We were obstruktiv Mitlaufere. We went along. We went along, *we went along with,* doing all we could to drag our feet . . . but we went along. There were hundreds of thousands like us, maybe millions like us." Yet, the lieutenant is a self-described Aryan specimen—"six foot three . . . [with] thighs as solid as hewn masts"; he has cobalt blue "arctic eyes" and "Michelangelan" calves. A compulsive womanizer and a sexual braggart, Thomsen is erotically obsessed with the wife of Commandant Paul Doll, the elusive and haughty Hannah who "conformed to the national ideal of young femininity, stolid, countrified, and built for procreation and heavy work." As the Nazi erotic ideal, Hannah is "huge and goddessy"—yet not so easily categorized, as Thomsen discovers through the course of his (mostly futile) pursuit of her.

Camp Commandant Paul Doll is the second narrator, a vainglorious buffoon-Nazi stricken with self-pity for most of the novel at being ill-treated by his wife (who loathes him) and being overworked by his superiors (who disdain him); it is Commandant Doll who must oversee the frequent arrival of the evacuees and their subsequent fates at Auschwitz, a matter of thousands of individuals. Doll laments being caught between the demands of the Economic Administrative Head Office to help "swell the labor strength (for the munitions industries)" even as the Reich Central Security Department "presses for the disposal of as many evacuees as possible, for obvious reasons of self-defense." He sits through Nazi entertainments calculating "how long it would take to gas the audience." Amis clearly takes pleasure in throwing his satirical voice into Doll, giving the Nazi's rants a savagely comic tone as Doll complains of being stuck in the Zone of Interest "offing old ladies and little boys,

whilst other [Nazis] gave a luminescent display of valor." Here is a
wickedly funny Monty Python figure in Nazi regalia:

> And mind you, disposing of the young and the elderly re-
> quires strengths and virtues—fanaticism, radicalism, sever-
> ity, implacability, hardness, iciness, mercilessness, Und so
> weiter. After all . . . somebody's got to do it—the Jews'd give
> us the same treatment if they had ½ a chance, as everybody
> knows.

The fatuous Doll is an ideal repository for Amis's considerable
historical research into the horrific absurdities of what Amis calls,
in his afterword, "the exceptionalism of the Third Reich":

> [A Nazi colleague] Mobius was originally a penpusher at the
> HQ of the Secret State Police, the Gestapa—not to be con-
> fused with the Gestapo (the actual Secret State Police), or the
> Sipo (the Security Police), or the Cripo (the Criminal Police),
> or the Orpo (the Order Police), or the Schupo (the Protection
> Police), or the Teno (the Auxiliary Police), or the Geheime
> Feldpolizei (the Secret Field Police), or the Gemeindepolizei
> (the Municipal Police), or the Abwehrpolizei (the Counter-
> Espionage Police), or the Bereitschaftpolizei (the Party Police),
> or the Kasernierte Polizei (the Barracks Police), or the Grenz-
> polizei (the Border Police), or the Ortspolizei (the local Police),
> or the Gendarmerie (the Rural Police).

As in a stage comedy routine, at times the buffoon-Nazi mask
falls away and we here another, startled voice break through, as in
this reverie of Doll's:

> She is a personable and knowing young female, albeit too Flach-
> brustig (though her Arsch is perfectly all right, if you hoiked up

that tight skirt you'd. . . . Don't quite see why I write like this.
It isn't my style at all.)

There is little irony, still less humor, in the figure of Amis's
third narrator, Sonderkommandofuhrer Szmul, head of a team of
"Sonders" (Jewish prisoners who assist the Nazis in killing and dis-
posing of their fellow Jews—"vultures of the crematory") who appear to "go about their ghastly tasks with the dumbest indifference."
Szmul perceives himself in very different terms as a "martyr/wit-
ness" to the horror: "I feel that we are dealing with propositions and
alternatives that have never been discussed before. . . . I feel that if
you knew every minute, every hour, every day of human history, you
would find no exemplum, no model, no precedent." Like all those
conscripted for such work among the doomed and their cadavers
(from whose teeth gold must be carefully extracted) Szmul understands that he too is doomed, even as he hopes that in some way his
testimony will prevail.

> Somebody will one day come to the ghetto or the Lager and
> account for the near-farcical *assiduity* of the German hatred.
> And I would start by asking—why were we conscripted, why
> were we impressed, in the drive towards our own destruc-
> tion? . . . There it is, you see. The Jews can only prolong their
> lives by helping the enemy to victory—a victory that for the
> Jews means what?

Far from being a "vulture of the crematory," Szmul is a kind of
saint of Auschwitz, ascetic and selfless; if he is not an altogether
convincing character, it is surely not Martin Amis's fault that to
give a convincing voice to such a person, who very likely did, in
some way, exist at Auschwitz as at other of the thousands of Nazi
camps scattered through Europe, is a virtually impossible task.
Szmul leaves all that he has written as a witness to Auschwitz in a

Thermos flask beneath a gooseberry bush: "And by reason of that, not all of me will die."

It is the opportunistic Thomsen who survives the defeat of the German Army. Reconstituted in September 1948, at the novel's end, as a "reformed character"—a "de-Nazified" German—Thomsen has a job working with Americans on the Bundesentschadigungsgesetz, or the guidelines on reparations: "victims' justice." He notes how, in a humbled (and hypocritical) Germany, the new national anthem is "Ich Wusste Nichts Uber Es" ("I Didn't Know Anything About It"). Yet, Thomsen can't construct for himself a "self-sufficient inner life; and this was perhaps the great national failure."

> In the Kat Zet [Zone of Interest], like every perpetrator, I felt doubled (this is me but it is also not me; there is a further me); after the war, I felt halved.
>
> Under National Socialism you looked in the mirror and saw your soul. You found yourself out. . . . Who somebody really was. *That* was the zone of interest.

Martin Amis is at his most compelling as a satiric vivisectionist with a cool eye and an unwavering scalpel, and there is much to admire in this ambitious work of fiction that seems, at perhaps its most inspired moments, to be a sort of compendium of epiphanies, appalled asides, anecdotes and radically condensed history; a novel constructed as a means of "bearing witness" to countless atrocities, ironies, and absurdities, whose narrators report to us not only the crude, cruel, unspeakable horrors of, for instance, the "stacking" of corpses ("Sardinenpackung, only vertical . . . With toddlers and babies slotted in at shoulder height") but also the commercial inter-est in Nazi doctors' experiments of "designers, engineers, admin-istrators from IG Farben plants . . . daintily picking their way past the bodies of the wounded, the unconscious, and the dead." With virtually every page of the novel reporting some horror, including reactions to the awful, pervasive smells of death *en masse,* it is a stretch of the reader's imagination to credit the "love interest" of Thomsen for Hannah Doll as much more than an expedient Mac-Guffin eclipsed by its terrible surroundings.

Martin Amis's great gift has been a corrosively savage voice, often very funny, as it has been zestfully profane, obscene, and scatological as well as mordant; one thinks of Jonathan Swift's "savage indignation," matched with Swift's passionate morality, infusing Amis's most characteristic work. There are high-voltage passages in *Money, The Information, London Fields* that are (as it's said) laugh-out-loud funny. But squeezing "black humor" out of Auschwitz would be a challenge for the Marquis de Sade, and Amis is too humane finally to do more than attempt a few swipes at such humor, through the idiot cruelties of Commandant Doll, a species of Nabokovian puppet. The effect of the Holocaust isn't singular but accumulative; one time, it is perhaps (perhaps!) funny that at a poorly executed Selektion ("selection of prisoners": some to live as forced laborers, others to be gassed) the commandant has to rely upon a small group of violinists to play music masking screams of terror ("the first strains of the violins could do no more than duplicate and reinforce that helpless, quavering cry. But then the melody took hold") but when such cruelties are repeated, and repeated, even the satirist is apt to lose heart and concur with the Nazi opportunist Thomsen: "I used to be numb; now I'm raw." It's a further anomaly that isolated passages of prose in the text are rendered in German, as if all of the dialogue and introspective material of the novel isn't "in German"; in an exchange between the Dolls one speaks in English and the other in German, which is hardly likely, and in one of Szmul's reveries the Sonderkommandofuhrer thinks, "The Sonders have suffered Seelenmord—death of the soul." But why would a German-speaking individual translate his thoughts, and for whom? The point would seem to be that the author of the novel, not the narrator of the chapter, wants to highlight certain phrases for the

benefit of the reader who can't be relied upon to know German, a
mannerism distracting as a nudge in the ribs.

Indeed it seems a relief to the author, as to the reader, when
the strained fiction of "fiction" is set aside and Amis turns to his
own unmediated (and very engaging) voice in the afterword "That
Which Happened." Here Amis acknowledges the impressively many
works of history and memoir he has read in preparation for writing
The Zone of Interest and also, perhaps unsurprisingly, his fascination with the Führer of all Führers: "He has so far gone unnamed in
this book; but now I am obliged to type out the words 'Adolf Hitler.'"
Amis concurs in a general bewilderment among historians about
"understanding" Hitler: "We know a great deal about the how—
about how he did what he did; but we seem to know nothing about
the why." Given this fascination it's curious that *The Zone of Interest*
is set at so far a distance from Hitler, who has virtually no presence
in it except as a quasi-mythic figure revered and feared by more
ordinary Nazis. unflincAmis acknowledges his longtime obsession
with the phenomenon of the Holocaust:

> My own inner narrative is one of chronic stasis, followed by a
> kind of reprieve. . . . I first read Martin Gilbert's classic *The
> Holocaust: The Jewish Tragedy* in 1987, and I read it with incre-
> dulity; in 2011 I read it again, and my incredulity was intact
> and entire. . . . Between those dates I had worked my way
> through scores of books on the subject; and while I might have
> gained in knowledge, I had gained nothing at all in penetration.
> The facts, set down in a historiography of tens of thousands
> of volumes, are not in the slightest doubt; but they remain in
> some sense unbelievable, or beyond belief, and cannot quite be
> assimilated. Very cautiously I submit that part of the exception-
> alism of the Third Reich lies in its unyieldingness, the electric
> severity with which it repels our contact and our grip.

Yet it is just as plausible to argue that Hitler and his henchmen were not at all "exceptional" in a human history that has always included warfare, unspeakable cruelty, and attempted genocide; what set the Nazis apart from less efficient predecessors was their twentieth-century access to industrialized warfare and annihilation and a propaganda machine that excluded all other avenues of information for an essentially captive German population.

The Zone of Interest, like *Time's Arrow,* focuses rather upon the vicissitudes of personality and situation, and does not undertake such larger questions except fleetingly. The author's rage at Holocaust horrors is portioned into scenes, and sentences; it does not gather in a powerful swell, to overwhelm or terrify. Is it inherent in postmodernism, that such powerful emotions are not likely to be evoked no matter the subject? "To write a mighty book you must choose a mighty theme"—as Melville declares in *Moby-Dick*; but the mode of writing may preclude "mightiness" if its ground-bass is irony rather than empathy.

In the afterword Amis cites the famous passage in Primo Levi's memoir *Survival in Auschwitz* in which Levi asks a German guard, *"Warum?"* and is told by the guard, *"Hier is kein warum"*—"Here there is no why." (This remark Amis has also alluded to in *Time's Arrow*.) Perhaps that terse reply is the only adequate response to all questions of *Why?* relating to the Holocaust.

LONDON NW:
ZADIE SMITH

Our pre-eminence: we live in the age of comparison.
                    Friedrich Nietzsche (quoted in *NW*)

How to present, in language, the shimmering, ever-shifting life of a *place*? The most obvious means, the documentary film, has its limitations: the filmmaker can record hours of visual imagery, he can interview subjects, and we can overhear subjects speaking, but we cannot hear their inner voices, and we cannot see the world inside their heads. A kaleidoscope of fascinating and "authentic" images can pass before our eyes as viewers, but we can't interpret these images through the prism of consciousness, with its myriad histories, which is the soul of a *place*. We are forever viewers, voyeurs. We "haven't a clue." Only an assiduously calibrated work of art, of the ambition and artistry of James Joyce's *Ulysses,* for instance, can take us beyond the dazzling and distracting surface, into the mysterious region in which *place* and *personality* bond; that region in which those born to a *place* are irremediably defined by it, and might be said to be its offspring. In *Ulysses,* inside Leopold Bloom's ferociously buzzing head, we experience the "Hibernian Metropolis" of midday Dublin in a way no mere tourist could:

In the Heart of the Hibernian Metropolis

Before Nelson's pillar trams slowed, shunted, changed trol-
ley, started for Blackrock, Kingstown and Dalkey, Clonskea,
Rathgar and Terenure, Palmerston park and Upper Rathmines,
Sandymount Green, Rathmines, Ringsend and Sandymount
Tower, Harold's Cross. The hoarse Dublin United Tramway
Company's timekeeper bawled them off.

—Rathgar and Terenure!

—Come on, Sandymount Green!

Right and left parallel clanging ringing a double-decker and
a single-decker moved from their railheads, swerve to the down
line, glided parallel.

—Start, Palmerston park!

In its assiduously detailed evocation of the multicultural neighborhood of Willesden, in northwestern London, where in 1975
Zadie Smith was born and where she now lives for part of the
year, Zadie Smith's *NW* is a boldly Joycean appropriation, fortunately not so difficult of entry as its great model. In *NW* you will
find what is called "stream-of-consciousness" prose—(in which
the reader is privy to the meandering thoughts of a white resident
of Willesden, Leah Hanwell, who'd grown up there)—snatches
of overheard conversation (represented in reduced type)—as well
as prose-poems ("Sweet stink of the hookah, couscous, kebab, exhaust fumes of a bus deadlock . . . Polish paper, Turkish paper,
Arabic, Irish, French, Russian, Spanish, News of the World . . .
Here is the school where they stabbed the headmaster. Here is
the Islamic Center of England opposite the Queen's Arms") and
fragmentary, disjointed passages that read like notes for a novel
as well as the lengthy section "Host," consisting of 185 numbered
vignettes seemingly modeled after the "Aeolus" chapter of *Ulysses*,
which is the novel's heart, and involves its most engaging charac-

ters. There are pleats in time, rearrangements of chronology, views of characters whom we'd believed we knew from sharply different perspectives; an aphorism shifts its tone from positive to sinister across hundreds of pages—the initial, seemingly visionary "I am the sole author of the dictionary that defines me" becomes, in the cool summary of a young black girl's "decline and fall" the terse "I am the sole author"—that is, the sole author of one's decline and fall. The novel's sketchily poetic opening, which seems to presage both hope and disaster, will be clarified, to a degree, near the end of the novel; the second chapter, taking us into the thoughts of Leah Hanwell, must be understood as preceding the opening chapter by several weeks, which isn't evident at a first reading. Many of the novel's passages don't yield their meanings readily but contribute to its polyphonic density.

Like Zadie Smith's much-acclaimed predecessor *White Teeth* (2000), *NW* is an urban epic from the perspective of "endangered species," as one of Smith's characters, the son of a Caribbean-born train guard and a well-to-do Italian woman, calls himself and others who, in England, are perceived as persons of color: the objects of well-intentioned social planning that has its goal, however inadvertently, the extinction of racial identity. ("'We have a very effective diversity scheme here,' said Dr. Singh primly and turned to speak to the blonde girl on her left.") Unlike *White Teeth*, however, *NW* is not an exuberant comedy in the mode of Salman Rushdie and Martin Amis, nor does it contain the racy ebullience of *The Autograph Man* (2002) and *On Beauty* (2005); in place of farcical/sexual escapades, there are, in *NW*, joyless couplings between individuals who scarcely know one another; sudden, paralyzing epiphanies ("I just don't understand why I have this life") and darkly Nietzschean aphorisms ("What a difficult thing a gift is for a woman! She'll punish herself for it"). A beloved dog dies of a thug's random kick, precipitating its owner into depression; a man who'd once lived in NW returns to the neighborhood and is mugged and murdered over a trifle, winding up as breaking news on local TV. Where *Ulysses* ends with the famously triumphant *yes I said yes I will Yes*, *NW* ends on a clandestine call to the police— "I got something to tell you.")

Despite its postmodernist features, *NW* is essentially a *Bildungsroman* with two protagonists who become friends as four-year-olds in a council estate called Caldwell in northwestern London—the "white" (Anglo-Irish) Leah Hanwell and the "black" (Caribbean-background) Keisha Blake ("Natalie" when she leaves Willesden for university). As in Smith's fiction generally, individuals don't come undefined by their families, and so, in *NW*, there are two primary families—the Hanwells, who prosper just enough to leave the Caldwell council estate when Leah is still in school, and the Blakes, who are trapped in Caldwell, in perpetual economic distress. (The Hanwells have a working father, the Blakes have an absentee father. The Hanwells are upwardly mobile, or wish to think so; the Blakes are encumbered by Keisha's sister, who can't seem to prevent becoming pregnant and her brother who is unemployable.) In addition to Leah and Keisha/Natalie there are two Caldwell boys whom we follow into dubious manhood: the black Felix Cooper, a self-styled filmmaker/drug dealer and the white Nathan Bogle, whom both girls have a crush on in middle school ("the very definition of desire"), who has become a homeless drug-addled pimp by the novel's end. Neither male character is portrayed with anything like the minute and loving detail Smith lavishes upon the girls, whom we come to know intimately in the novel's most fully realized section ("Host"), itself a novel in miniature, following the girls from early childhood when, acting instinctively when Leah Hanwell is drowning in an outdoor pool, Keisha saves her life by grabbing "those red pigtails" and pulling her to safety. As a consequence of this "dramatic event" the girls become "best friends bonded for life . . . and everyone in Caldwell best know about it."

The novel's few transcendent moments are shared by the women, who are clearly "sisters" in the deepest sense of the word. On an excursion together with Natalie's young children, Natalie and Leah discover, in an urban roundabout, an extraordinary "little country church, a medieval country church, stranded on this half-acre"; inside the church is the shrine of "Our Lady of Willesden, the Black Madonna," whose histrionic voice is imagined as the voice of a pre-Christian, animist power:

> How have you lived your whole life in these streets and never known me? How long did you think you could avoid me? What made you think you were exempt? Don't you know that I have been here as long as people have cried out for help? Hear me: I am not like those mealy-mouthed pale Madonnas, those simpering virgins! I am older than this place. . . . Spirit of these beech woods and phone boxes, hedgerows and lampposts, freshwater springs and tube stations, ancient yews and one-stop-shops, grazing land and 3D multiplexes. Unruly England of the real life, the animal life!

At the opening of *NW,* Leah and Keisha/Natalie are in their mid-thirties. Both are married, and both are dissatisfied with their lives. Leah, who'd studied philosophy in college ("Philosophy is learning how to die") but didn't distinguish herself academically, feels undereducated, having prepared herself for "a life never intended for her." She is visited by her deceased father, whose words she can manipulate: "I love you don't worry it's nice here. . . . I can see a light." Her work is in the "public sector"—she's poorly paid for her idealism—"the only white girl on the Fund Distribution Team" in a dreary workplace in which, at the end of the workday

> women spill out of every room, into the heat, cocoa buttered, ready for a warm night on the Edgeware Road. From St. Kitts,

Trinidad, Barbados, Grenada, Jamaica, India, Pakistan . . . still open to the sexiness of summer in a manner that the women of Leah's family can never be. For them the sun is fatal.

In mockery of herself Leah doodles "I AM SO FULL OF EM-PATHY."

Leah is married to a hairdresser of French West African extraction named Michael who is "more beautiful" than she, as Keisha/Natalie is married to an exceedingly handsome "Negroid Italian" from a bourgeois background. Both women are ambivalent about virtually everything in their adult lives: their work, their mothers, their husbands, the prospect of motherhood ("Natalie Blake and Leah Hanwell were of the belief that people were willing them to reproduce. Relatives, strangers on the street, people on television.") Natalie has children with a husband whom she doesn't respect; to please her husband Leah pretends a wish for children but has a secret abortion from which she is slow to recover psychologically. Both, as girls, are involved in underage drinking; both take recreational drugs as adults. By the novel's end both women have sabotaged their marriages.

The tangled plot of *NW* begins with the intrusion, into Leah Hanwell's life, of a cunningly manipulative "girl in a headscarf" named Shar who tells her an upsetting story calculated to arouse Leah's concern; naïvely, guiltily, Leah gives the young woman thirty pounds though she's suspicious of her behavior and her relationship with a man waiting for her on the street. Subsequently, Leah catches sight of the girl in the neighborhood, and incurs the wrath of a belligerent individual—"a tall muscled threat"—who knocks down her husband and gives her dog a fatal kick to the belly. So much in Smith's narrative is inward and contemplative that these sudden eruptions into violence are all the more startling.

Of the two women Leah Hanwell is the less coherent as a character, as she is the less convincing and interesting: the author seems to have imagined her as a foil to the more vibrant Keisha/Natalie, but her "white"-girl personality lacks resonance. It's claimed for her as an adolescent that she is a "generous person, wide open to the entire world," a paragon of multicultural idealism:

> Within Brayton [a school in Willesden] she befriended every-one without distinction or boundary, but the hopeless cases did not alienate her from the popular and vice versa. . . . A little of this universal good feeling spreads to Keisha by association, though no one ever mistook Keisha's cerebral willfulness for her friend's generosity of spirit.

After the death of her dog, Leah becomes crippled by "terrible mourning," and at the novel's end her desperate husband calls Natalie, when Leah seems to have become depressed to the point of catatonia.

Perhaps it's because we come to know Leah through her meandering stream-of-consciousness thoughts that she remains indistinct and improbable, and not sharp-edged; the reader is constrained by Leah's claustrophobic life for many pages, like a viewer standing too close to one of Chuck Close's gigantic portraits comprised of pixels, and so unable to recognize a human face.

Keisha/Natalie, however, is initially seen from the outside, by an admiring Leah: "Sleek ebony statuary. Tilts her head directly to the sun. [Her husband], too. They look like a king and queen in profile on an ancient coin." Much later in *NW* we come to know Keisha/Natalie intimately, as a child of "compulsive" willfulness who is an excellent student because she can concentrate, without distractions; she is puzzled by "what she believed she knew of herself, *essentially,* and her essence as others seemed to understand it." Perhaps there is no autobiographical core to Keisha/Natalie, but her personality suggests that of the quintessential novelist who suspects that she alone is lacking an identity:

> (Sometimes, when enjoying [a friend's] capsule descriptions of the personalities of others, Natalie feared that in her own—Natalie's—absence, her own—Natalie's— personality was also being encapsulated by Pol, although she could not bring herself to truly fear this possibility because at base she could not believe that she—Natalie—could ever be spoken about in the way that she—Natalie—spoke about others and heard others spoken about. But for the sake of a thought experiment: what was Natalie Blake's personality constructed around?)

Here, too, is a convincing account of the fiction writer's predilection:

> Walking down Kilburn High Road Natalie Blake had a strong desire to slip into the lives of other people. It was hard to see how this desire could be practicably satisfied or what, if anything, it really meant. "Slip into" is an imprecise thought. Follow the Somali kid home? Sit with the old Russian lady at the bus-stop outside Pound-Land? Join the Ukrainian gangster at his table at the cake shop? Listening was not enough. Natalie Blake wanted to know people. To become intimately involved with them.

(Just how intimately, and how recklessly, Natalie herself doesn't yet know.) Keisha/Natalie is very likely the most sustained, sympathetic, and believable figure in all of Zadie Smith's fiction, encompassing as it does an astonishing variety of characters and types. Particularly as a law student, and as a young (female, black) lawyer,

Keisha/Natalie is an astute observer of the seductive atmosphere of
the university in which she is an "endangered specimen"—both unwittingly, and deliberately; we are made to feel the thrill of cultural
assimilation, as the author herself may well have felt it as a brilliant
young undergraduate English literature student at Cambridge in the
late 1990s:

> The bad wine flowed. An ancient Judge rose to give a speech. . . .
> Natalie was enthralled. The idea that her own existence might
> be linked to people living six hundred years past! No longer an
> accidental guest at the table—as she had always understood
> herself to be—but a host, with other hosts, continuing a tradi-
> tion. "And so it falls to you," said the judge.

It's difficult not to exploit one's racial identity in a culture in
which, being black, "Natalie and her husband needn't concern
themselves too much with politics. They simply *were* political facts,
in their very persons." Painful ironies abound for one of Natalie's
sensitivity: "Something about Natalie inspired patronage, as if by
helping her you helped an unseen multitude."

Later, when she has a law degree and is looking for work, Natalie
is counseled by an older, glamorous black woman lawyer, a paragon
of multicultural success, that what is interpreted as a "passion" for
justice in a white (male) lawyer will be interpreted by the presiding
judge in a courtroom as "aggressive hysteria" in a black (female)
lawyer: "The first lesson is: turn yourself down." More importantly,

> "I suppose you're interested in a human rights set of some kind.
> Police brutality? Is that your plan?" "I'm not sure," said Natalie,
> trying to sound bullish. She was very close to tears.
>
> "It wasn't mine. In my day, if you went down that route
> people tended to associate you with your clients. I took some
> advice early on: 'Avoid ghetto work.'"

Predictably, Natalie repudiates this cynical advice, joining a tiny legal firm in a squalid part of London as a paralegal; less predictably, she soon quits the firm to take higher-paying work as a commercial barrister with former classmates from law school. (Of course, Natalie takes time to do pro bono death penalty cases in the Caribbean, as befits one in her position.) Her fragile sense of identity is further strained by the responsibilities and hypocrisies of adulthood:

> Daughter drag. Sister drag. Mother drag. Wife drag. Court drag. Rich drag. Poor drag. British drag. Jamaican drag. Each required a different wardrobe. But when considering these various attitudes she struggled to think what would be the most authentic, or perhaps the least inauthentic.

By degrees, Natalie begins to see herself as inauthentic: she isn't happily married, she secretly loathes her high-paying work as a barrister, she even feels alienated from her children, who are so very different from the child she'd been in the Caldwell council estate not so many years ago:

> She was surprised to meet herself down a dark alley. It filled her with panic and rage to see her spoiled children sit upon the floor, flicking through past images, moving images, of themselves, on their father's phone, an experience of self-awareness literally unknown in the history of human existence—outside dream and miracle—until very recently.

Though claiming to loathe the Internet, Natalie is irresistibly drawn to the Internet, where she creates for herself a shadow-identity—*KeishaNW@gmail.com*—and where she discovers that "she was what everybody was looking for." Sordid, quasi-comic promiscuous encounters with couples of various genders follow in dreamlike sequences that test the reader's credulity. So carefully self-invented, Natalie begins to fall apart as if on cue. When her husband discovers her *KeishaNW* identity on her computer, Natalie's seemingly perfect marriage is wrecked.

NW ends in confusion and disintegration. In a long nightmare sequence, perhaps in emulation of the brilliantly bizarre "Nighttown" chapter of *Ulysses,* Natalie returns on foot to her childhood neighborhood, where she encounters a debased and drug-addled Nathan Bogle, for whom she'd once felt an attraction. A sexual encounter between them—however unlikely this would appear, under the circumstances—seems to dissociate Natalie from the death-bound (white) man of her childhood. Riding a bus she sees old, familiar landmarks with a transformed vision:

> The Cock Tavern. McDonalds. The old Woolworths. The betting shop. The State Empire. Willesden Lane. The cemetery. Whoever said these were fixed coordinates to which she had to be forever faithful? How could she play them false? Freedom was absolute and everywhere, constantly moving location.

In the end, Natalie and Leah are joined together in a curious sort of conspiracy, as in a regression to their girlhood friendship in the Caldwell council estate.

NW is an unexpectedly ironic companion novel to *White Teeth,* a darker and more nuanced portrait of a multiracial culture in the throes of a collective nervous breakdown. Its perimeters are forever changing, like its accents and the tenor of its neighborhoods. In *NW* the mood is, if not precisely tragic, sober and subdued; one might wish to celebrate a truly "diverse" urban neighborhood like Willesden and yet—there are muggings, murders. There is a brisk drug trade. Bonded as individuals in NW might be, the "fixed coordinates" of their lives are finally suffocating and lethal. There are no farcical interludes here, as in previous works of fiction by Zadie Smith, as there are no paper-thin cartoon characters to enact them. Maturity may lie in the brave repudiation of nostalgia; the realization that "maybe it doesn't matter that life never blossomed into something larger than itself."

JOAN DIDION:
RISK AND TRIUMPH

We are uneasy about a story until we know who is telling it.
Joan Didion, *A Book of Common Prayer*

It is rare to find a biographer so temperamentally, intellectually, and even stylistically matched with his subject as Tracy Daugherty, author of well-received biographies of Donald Barthelme and Joseph Heller, is matched with Joan Didion; but it is perhaps less of a surprise if we consider that Daugherty is himself a writer whose work shares with Joan Didion's classic essays (*Slouching Towards Bethlehem,* 1968; *The White Album,* 1979; *Where I Was From,* 2003) a brooding sense of the valedictory and the elegiac, crushing banality and heartrending loss in American life. Only another writer of fiction could so sympathize with Didion as a creative artist in a continuous struggle with "narrative limits" as well as a social realist and critic; to Daugherty, born in 1955, Didion has long been a visionary, "a powerful voice for my generation." So identifying with his subject, who has suffered personal, familial losses in recent years, as well as a general disillusionment with American politics, the biographer inevitably becomes "an elegist, writing lamentations"; Didion's memoir *Blue Nights* (2011), a meditation upon motherhood and aging as well as an elegy for Didion's daughter Quintana, who died at the age of thirty-nine in 2005, is "not just a harrowing lullaby but our generation's last love song."

Chronological in its basic structure, *The Last Love Song* is not a conventional biography so much as a life of the artist rendered in biographical mode: we pick up crucial facts, so to speak, on the run, as we might in a novel (for instance, in Didion's debut novel *Run River*, 1963) in the midst of other bits of information: "By 1934, the year of Didion's birth, the levees [on the Sacramento River] had significantly reduced flooding." We learn that Didion's first, crucial reader was her mother, Eduene, a former Sacramento librarian descended from a Presbyterian minister and his wife who followed the Donner-Reed party west but decided to split from the doomed group in Nevada in 1847. An acquaintance of the family tells Daugherty that the Didions and their extended families "were part of Sacramento's landed gentry . . . families who called themselves agriculturalists, farmers, ranchers, progressives, but they were the owners, not the ones who got their hands dirty." With a novelist's empathy Daugherty notes: "For all its visibility and influence, the family felt prosaic, muted, sad to Didion, even as a girl. Clerks and administrators: hardly the heroes of old, surviving starvation and blizzards. . . . A whiff of decadence clung to the gentry, making their folks grip fiercely the privileges they did retain."

Many passages in *The Last Love Song* read with the fluency of fiction, and the particular intimacy of Didion's fiction, as if by a sort of osmosis the subject has taken over the narrative, as a passenger in a speeding vehicle may take over the wheel. We feel that we are reading about Didion in precisely Didion's terms:

> In considering—and not quite hitting—the real story of Patty Hearst, Didion felt sure the periphery was the key. She looked for an out-of-the-way anecdote, seemingly insignificant, channeling all of California; the pioneer experience in its modern manifestations; the historical imperative; the chain of forces shaping Tania: a verbal image as immediately impactful as the spread legs, the carbine, and the cobra.

She was after this same effect in *Play It As It Lays,* a "fast" novel, a method of presentation allowing us to see Maria in a flash.

A snake book.

A poetic impulse, surpassing narrative.

Somewhere on the edge of the story.

And:

In the final analysis, Didion's attraction to conspiracy tales, particularly in the 1980s, has less to do with the intrigues themselves than with her persistent longing for narrative, *any* narrative, to alleviate the pain of confusion. "We tell ourselves stories in order to live"—and if the story is not readily apparent, we will weave one out of whatever scraps are at hand; we will use our puzzlement as a motivating factor; we will tell our way out of any trap, or goddamn seedy motel.

Introducing the highly charged topic of Joan Didion and John Gregory Dunne's adoption of their daughter Quintana Roo in 1966:

In the mid-1960s, the preferred narrative was, We chose you. Positive. Proactive. A comfort to the child. What the narrative didn't address—a howling silence no boy or girl failed to perceive—was that if we chose you, someone else chose to make you available to us.

To relinquish you.

Family law.

Though Daugherty is never less than respectful of his subject he cannot resist the biographer's urge to interpret motives seemingly unacknowledged by the subject, as in a gently condescending film voice-over:

In retrospect, in reading this reference to the severing of families ties [in Didion's essay "Slouching Towards Bethlehem"] it's easy to see that Didion in the Haight was worrying about her adopted daughter back [home], the house cased all day by strangers driving unmarked panel trucks. And as in all her subsequent work, whenever she wrote about her daughter, she was also writing about herself.

But is this true? Is this in any way provable? In biography we are tempted to claim, as in life we are tempted to claim, that the plausible may be true; what would seem to be, to be. But in life it is rarely the case that causes and effects are so clear, and the same should hold in the art of biography, which should present possibilities, theories, inferences as tentative, not flatly, stated. You have only to examine Didion's prose before her daughter came into her life to feel that Didion would very likely have written about Haight-Ashbury residents (adolescents "who were never taught and would never now learn the games that had held the society together") exactly as she did, if she'd never adopted a baby. Or rather, the predilections that urged Didion to adopt are those that resulted in her writing as she does—out of an imagination that veers toward disorder and disaster at a time in American history (in a decade of assassinations, for instance) in which such responses are hardly aberrant. And it might be said of any writer that when he/she writes about any character, the subject is actually the self.

Years later, in the sobriety of post-9/11 America, here is Didion in her "maturity":

[Her] self-correcting quality, her ability to be ruthlessly self-evaluative and change her mind when she saw she'd been wrong, trumped her contrarian streak. If she had a strong capacity for denial, she had an even stronger will to shuck her illusions once she'd exposed them. "I think of political writing as in many ways a futile act," Didion said. But "you are obligated to do things you think are futile. It's like living. Life ends in death, but you live it, you know."

———

As a professor of English and creative writing at Oregon State, Tracy Daugherty is, like his subject, steeped in New Critical theories and stratagems. Both the biographer and his subject distrust direct statement and "abhor abstractions" and both are "wary of interpreting behavior as a clue to character." Confronted with Didion's decision not to cooperate with him (though she does not seem to have wished to hamper him) the biographer decides to approach his subject's life as if its truths do not lie easily on the surface of that life but constitute a text (my term, not Daugherty's) to be decoded:

> When presented with the private correspondence, diaries, journals, or rough drafts of a writer, I remain skeptical of content, attentive instead to presentation. It is the construction of persona, even in private—the fears, curlicues, and desires in any recorded life—that offer insights.

In this approach Daugherty echoes Didion's acknowledgment of her indebtedness to the English Department at UC-Berkeley, from which she received a B.A. in 1956: "They taught a form of literary criticism which was based on analyzing texts in a very close way." And, "I still go to the text. Meaning for me is in the grammar. . . . I learned backwards and forwards close textual analysis."

For all her insight into political intrigue and the bitter ironies of American life in the late twentieth century, Didion's essential interest, Daugherty suggests, has always been language: "Its inaccuracies and illusions, the way words imply their opposites"; Didion has many times stated her hostility to fashionable and politically correct dogma, as in her defense of the "irreducible ambiguities" of fiction vis-à-vis the "narrow and cracked determinism" of the women's movement with its "aversion to adult sexual life" ("The Women's Movement," 1972):

> All one's actual apprehension of what it is like to be a woman, the irreconcilable difference of it—that sense of living one's deepest life underwater, that dark involvement with blood and birth and death—could now be declared invalid, unnecessary, one never felt it at all.

In this passage Didion anticipates the sentiment of the anthropologist-narrator who recounts, in a stylized Conradian narrative of detachment and analysis, the story of maternal loss at the core of *A Book of Common Prayer*:

[Charlotte Douglas] had tried only to rid herself of her dreams, and those dreams seemed to deal only with sexual surrender and infant death, commonplaces of the female obsessional life. We all have the same dreams.

But do we? Feminism challenges this romantic passivity, replacing Freud's idea of women's biological destiny with a "destiny" unburdened by gender, like that of men; in her passionately written screed against the very bedrock of feminism, Didion aligns herself with other notable women writers who have scorned the notion of sisterhood. If you have suffered in the "female obsessional life" and if that life has been, for you, in its most profound moments essentially an "underground" life, it will be anathema to be told that others wish to escape this gender-fate. (See Jean Stafford on Susan Brownmiller's *Against Our Will: Men, Women and Rape*, published in *Esquire* in November 1975, in which Stafford ridicules the feminist conviction that women's bodies are not fair game for the sexual predation of men; in effect, Stafford seems virtually to be defending rapists against their accusers and to decry women for, not being raped, but for daring to publicly object to it.) An abused, humiliated, emotionally exploited woman does not want to believe that her fate might have been otherwise; she will identify with her oppressors, in the hope of courting their favor, aligning herself with their power, presumed to be greater than the power of the (sister)-oppressed. In their denunciations of feminism as a threat to their definitions of self both Didion and Stafford seem to miss the point: feminism is the politics of human equality, which means economic as well as sexual equality. To deflect the issue onto a matter of language, and the "ambiguities" of language, is perhaps misguided, however esoteric.

In her fiction, which is usually more nuanced than her nonfiction, Didion presents clearly flawed female protagonists like Maria of *Play It as It Lays,* whose masochism allows her to be swinishly exploited by men, and Charlotte Douglas of *A Book of Common Prayer,* who is seduced and misused by her Berkeley English instructor, yet falls in love with him. Maddeningly, Charlotte is incapable of defining herself except by way of masculine appropriation or as a (failed) mother of a pseudo-revolutionary cliché-spouting daughter (in the mode of Patty Hearst) who sets into motion the actions ending in Charlotte's death. We know that the spoiled Marin can only disappoint: "[Marin] would never bother changing a phrase to suit herself because she perceived the meanings of words only dimly, and without interest." Of the doomed Charlotte the narrator says, with some exasperation: "I think I have never known anyone who led quite so unexamined a life."

The most intensely examined female life in Joan Didion's oeuvre appears to have been her own exhaustively and illuminatingly examined interior life; Didion's most brilliantly created fictional character is the writer's persona—"Joan Didion."

IN ITS MOST ENTERTAINING PASSAGES *The Last Love Song* is something of a joint biography of Joan Didion and John Gregory Dunne,

Didion's writer-husband of over forty years, with whom she collabo-
rated on screenplays for *The Panic in Needle Park* (1971), *Play It as
It Lays* (1972) and, their most successful film, a remake of *A Star Is
Born* with Barbra Streisand (1976). Author of the novels *True Con-
fessions, Dutch Shea, Jr., The Red White and Blue, Nothing Lost,* and
the memoirs *Vegas: A Memoir of a Dark Season* and *Harp,* Dunne
was ebulliently outspoken, the acerbic and sometimes scandalous
extravert to Didion's "neurotically inarticulate" introvert.

Here is Didion writing with disarming candor of a stay in the
Royal Hawaiian Hotel in Honolulu in the aftermath of an earth-
quake in the Aleutians: "In the absence of a natural disaster we are
left again to our own uneasy devices. We are here on this island
in the middle of the Pacific in lieu of filing for divorce." ("In the
Islands," from *The White Album*) Didion's confiding tone suggests
a private diary entry, but it is very publicly printed in *Life* to be
consumed by hundreds of thousands of readers for whom the "confessional" mode was not a commonplace in 1969. Not surprisingly,
Dunne confides in strangers with startlingly intimacy as well, in the
quasi-autobiographical *Vegas* (1974) with its memorable, Didion-like
opening: "In the midst of my nervous breakdown, I went to live in
Las Vegas, Clark County, Nevada."

Coolly Dunne observes: "Sometimes, living with [Didion] was
like 'living with [a] piranha.'"

> Sometimes, at his most depressed, [Dunne] would imagine
> writing suicide notes, but "whatever minimal impulse I had for
> suicide was negated by the craft of writing the suicide note. It
> became a technical problem." He could not stop revising.
>
> "When are you coming home?" [Didion] asked when she
> called.

A nuanced, nostalgic, and loving portrait of Dunne emerges decades later in *The Year of Magical Thinking,* but Dunne's droll, of-

ten raucous voice pervades virtually all of Didion's prose fiction and gives to certain of her male characters a distinctly comic-aggressive tone in welcome contrast to her repressed, temperamentally inarticulate female characters.

In December 2003 John Gregory Dunne died, of a heart attack, in the couple's Manhattan apartment as abruptly as Jack Lovett dies of a heart attack at the end of *Democracy*. As Inez Victor is a stunned witness to her lover's death so Joan Didion was a witness to her husband's death: in prose eerily forecasting the opening lines of *The Year of Magical Thinking,* the narrator of *Democracy* recounts Lovett's death in a swimming pool at a hotel in Jakara:

> It had been quite sudden.
>
> She had watched him swimming toward the shallow end of the pool.
>
> She had reached down to get him a towel.
>
> She had thought at that exact moment of reaching for the towel about the telephone number he had given her, and wondered who would answer if he called it.
>
> And then she had looked up.

———

"You see the shards of the novel I am no longer writing, the island, the family, the situation. I lost patience with it. I lost nerve."

Of course, Didion's narrator has not really lost nerve: she has in fact just begun "her" novel. The narrator so intimately addressing us is not Joan Didion and we should not confuse her with the author whose name is on the title page of the book, though we have been, in the teasing manner of Philip Roth, invited to confuse the two:

> Call me the author.
>
> Let the reader be introduced to Joan Didion, upon whose

character and doings much will depend of whatever interest these pages may have, as she sits at her writing table in her own room in her own house on Welbeck Street.

And, with an air of weary disdain in *The Last Thing He Wanted*:

The persona of "the writer" does not attract me. As a way of being it has its flat sides. Nor am I comfortable around the literary life: its traditional dramatic line (the romance of solitude, of interior struggle, of the lone seeker after truth) came to seem early on a trying conceit. I lost patience somewhat later with the conventions of the craft, with exposition, with transitions, with the development and revelation of "character."

Didion uses such authorial intrusions to lend credence to her fictional subjects, as she has often used herself in her nonfiction pieces to lend credence to their authenticity; in this, she is unlike her contemporaries John Barth, Robert Coover, Donald Barthelme, and others associated with postmodernist literary experimentation of the 1970s and 1980s, who call attention by such devices to the fabrication of "fictional subjects"—in fact, their inauthenticity. But Didion is a social realist and a passionate, one might say old-fashioned moralist: she is too much under the spell of the real to wish to debunk it, and she has, unlike the postmodernists, exciting and meaningful stories to tell. Her much-stated anxieties about storytelling—"We tell ourselves stories in order to live. . . . We live entirely, especially if we are writers, by the imposition of narrative line upon disparate images, by the 'ideas' with which we have learned to freeze the shifting phantasmagoria which is our actual experience" ("The White Album")—seem to spring more from aesthetic considerations, than from considerations of truth-telling; the anxieties of Didion's several fictitious narrators are characteristic of writers seeking something other than conventional forms with which to tell their stories. On the one hand, there is the material ("the island, the family, the situation"), on the other hand the way in which the material will be presented. Ezra Pound set a very high standard with his admonition "Make it new!"—a Modernist standard whose significance would not have been lost on any ambitious literary writer coming of age in the 1950s.

Whatever her doubts about the limitations of narrative fiction Didion seems to have thrown herself into journalism with much enthusiasm, optimism, and unstinting energy— a perfect conjunction of reportorial and memoirist urges. *The Last Love Song* traces in detail the provenance of Didion's nonfiction pieces, which secured a reputation for her with the publication of *Slouching Towards Bethlehem* in 1968; originally published in such diverse journals as the *Saturday Evening Post, Vogue, National Review,* and *Esquire* the essays were urged into book form by Henry Robbins, an editor at the time at Farrar, Straus and Giroux, who became a personal friend of the Dunnes. (*After Henry,* Didion's essay collection of 1992, is named for the legendary Robbins, who died of a heart attack, at fifty-one, in 1979.)

It has been Didion's association with *The New York Review of Books,* however, that seems to have stimulated what is perhaps the most productive phase of her career. Daugherty notes how "as an editor, Robert Silvers intuitively grasped her literary gifts and untapped potential." Of Didion, Silvers says:

> I just thought she was a marvelous observer of American life. . . . She is by no means predictable, by no means an easily classifiable liberal or conservative, she is interested in whether or not people are morally evasive, smug, manipulative, or cruel—those qualities of moral action are very central to all her political work.

Out of Didion's meticulously researched journalism for *NYRB* would come several of her most important books—*Salvador* (1983),

Miami (1987), *After Henry, Political Fictions* (2001), and *Where I Was From;* in all, more than forty pieces by Didion would appear in *NYRB* over a period of forty years. Among these is the corrosively brilliant "Sentimental Journeys" (1990), an investigation into the "high concept"[*We Tell Ourselves Stories*]narrative surrounding the Central Park jogger rape case of April 1989, which resulted in the convictions, on virtually no forensic evidence, of five young black men who'd been coerced into confessing to white NYPD detectives; Didion's focus is upon the sensational media coverage of the case, the play of "white" and "black" stereotypes "aimed to obscure the city's actual tensions of race and class but also . . . the civic and commercial arrangements that made those tensions irreconcilable." Running so counter to public opinion—that is, white public opinion—Didion's essay aroused much controversy for its determination to expose, with the precision of a skilled anatomist performing an autopsy, how the mainstream media presents to a credulous public "crimes . . . understood to be news to the extent that they offer . . . a story, a lesson, a high concept." (In 2002, Didion's skepticism about the case would be vindicated when the New York State Supreme Court vacated the convictions of the "Central Park Five" after a reexamination of DNA evidence and the confession of a serial rapist named Matias Reyes.)

Political Fictions, which had the misfortune to be published at the time of 9/11, is a collection of essays analyzing the ways in which the American political process has become "perilously remote from the electorate it was meant to represent." In this media-driven process even politicians of integrity are obliged to concoct "fables" about themselves. Didion's tone suggests Swiftian indignation modulated by a wry resignation:

> There was to writing about politics a certain Sisyphean aspect. . . . Even that which seemed to be ineluctably clear would again vanish from collective memory, sink traceless into the

stream of collapsing news and comment cycles that had become our national River Lethe.

THE LAST LOVE SONG is not an "authorized" biography and yet it exhibits few of the negative signs of an "unauthorized" biography: it is brimming with quoted material from Didion, both her writing and her interviews, and with a plethora of conversations with, it seems, virtually everyone who knew Didion, even at second hand. It is warmly generous, laced with the ironic humor Didion and Dunne famously cultivated. The biographical subject acquires a hologram-like density, and her voice is everywhere present.

In his consideration of Didion's personal life, Daugherty can't avoid touching upon the vicissitudes of living intimately with the sometimes volatile John Gregory Dunne and with their adopted daughter Quintana Roo, who as a young adolescent, living in California, had already begun exhibiting signs of depression and a penchant for self-medication. ("Just let me be in the ground. Just let me be in the ground and go to sleep"—Didion quotes Quintana, echoing lines from *Democracy* uttered by Inez Victor's unhappy daughter Jesse: "Let me die and get it over with. . . . Let me be in the ground and go to sleep.") Passages dealing with Quintana's difficult adolescence, her stints in rehab and her final, protracted illness within two years of John Gregory Dunne's death are the most painful passages in *The Last Love Song*. Of her daughter's collapse Didion comments in *Blue Nights* with a disconcerting frankness that manages yet to be oblique:

> She was depressed. She was anxious. Because she was depressed and because she was anxious she drank too much. This was called medicating herself. Alcohol has its well-known defects as a medication for depression but no one has suggested— ask any doctor—that it is not the most effective anti-anxiety agent yet known.

Didion's early work is associated with a particular tone, what might be called a higher narcissism ("What makes Iago evil? some people ask. I never ask."), and a predilection for establishing herself as a center of consciousness.

"It occurred to me during the summer of 1988, in California and Atlanta and New Orleans, in the course of watching first the California primary and then the Democratic and Republican national conventions, that it had not been by accident that the people with whom I had preferred to spend time in high school had, on the whole, hung out in gas stations."

But overall, the range of her writerly interests is considerable: from the chic anomie of *Play It as It Lays* to the sharp-eyed sociological reportage of *Slouching Towards Bethlehem* and *The White Album*; from small gems of self-appraisal ("On Keeping a Notebook," "On Going Home," "Goodbye to All That") to the sustained postmodernist skittishness of *A Book of Common Prayer* and *Democracy*; from the restrained contempt of "In the Realm of the Fisher King" (Reagan's White House) to the vivid sightings of "Fire Season" (Los Angeles County, 1978); from the powerful evocations of clandestine politics in Salvador and Miami to family autobiography with a title precisely chosen to emphasize the past tense, *Where I Was From*, and the more recent memoirs of loss, *The Year of Magical Thinking* and *Blue Nights*. Who but Joan Didion could frame the stark pessimism of *The Last Thing He Wanted*—with its incantatory reiteration that deal-making, gun-running (in this case, illegally supplying arms to overthrow the Sandinista government in Nicaragua in 1984) is the essential American dream—within a romantic tale of a daughter fulfilling a dying parent's wish for a "million-dollar score."

Rare among her contemporaries and, it would seem, against the grain of her own unassertive nature, Didion has forced herself to explore subjects that put her at considerable physical risk, involving

travel to the sorts of febrile revolutionary-prone Central American
countries that have figured in her fiction ("Boca Grande," for instance, of *A Book of Common Prayer,* the purposefully unnamed
island of *The Last Thing He Wanted*) and a seeming restlessness
with staying in one place for long: "If I have to die, I'd rather die up
against a wall someplace. . . . On the case, yes." ["Didion & Dunne:
The Rewards of a Literary Marriage" by Leslie Garis, *New York
Times Magazine,* February 8, 1987]

The Last Love Song:
A Biography of Joan Didion
By Tracy Daugherty

OTHER BOOKS CONSULTED IN THIS
REVIEW

Run River
By Joan Didion
Vintage, 272 pp.

Play It as It Lays
By Joan Didion
FSG Classics, 240 pp.

A Book of Common Prayer
By Joan Didion
Vintage, 272 pp.

We Tell Ourselves Stories in Order to Live:
Collected Nonfiction
By Joan Didion
Everyman's Library, 1160 pp.

The Last Thing He Wanted
By Joan Didion
Vintage Books, 227 pp.

The Year of Magical Thinking
By Joan Didion
Vintage Books, 272 pp.

Blue Nights
By Joan Didion
Vintage, 188 pp.

UNFLINCHING ABOUT WOMEN:
THE SHORT STORIES OF LUCIA BERLING

What I hope to do is, by the use of intricate detail, to make this woman so believable you can't help but feel for her.

Lucia Berlin, "Point of View"

In "Point of View," Lucia Berlin's most intricately imagined short story, a woman writer confides in us, her readers, her intentions in writing a story, which will turn out to be not quite the story she intends to tell us, or, indeed, the story we finally absorb, with a belated pang of emotion at the final line—a surreptitious erasure. We are told by Berlin's fictitious woman writer that she prefers writing in a voice that emulates "Chekhov's impartial voice" in order to imbue her (fictitious) woman character with a modicum of dignity; if the character, a "single woman in her fifties" were to tell her own story, complete with "all the compulsive, obsessive boring little details of . . . life," we would be likely to feel embarrassment, discomfort, "even bored."

However, Berlin's woman writer assures us: "But my story begins with, 'Every Saturday, after the laundromat and the grocery store, she bought the Sunday *Chronicle*'"—that is, the writer has strategically altered point of view so that it appears to be in the "third person" and not the first. Not the self's self-pity but a writerly impartiality is the ruse that will draw us into the story of a "dreary creature" for whom otherwise, she thinks, we would feel little sympathy.

Is this Lucia Berlin confiding in us, or an entirely "other" woman writer who resembles Lucia Berlin to an unnerving degree? Is this writer proud of being so clever, or is such cleverness, so advertised, an oblique form of despair, even rage at the diminished circumstances of her life? Whoever she is, she tells us, somewhat boastfully:

> Most writers use props and scenery from their own lives. For example, my Henrietta eats her meager little dinner every night on a blue place mat, using exquisite heavy Italian stainless steel cutlery. An odd detail, inconsistent, it may seem, with this woman who cuts out coupons for Brawny towels, but it engages the reader's curiosity. At least I hope it will.

Not surprisingly the writer goes on to tell us that she too eats with such "elegant cutlery"—as she once worked for the nephrologist with whom her character Henrietta is hopelessly in love; but the writer herself was "certainly not in love with him."

Planning her story, the writer recalls working for Dr. B., though she is careful to distinguish between herself and Henrietta, a figure of pathos. We are privy to the writer's self-doubt: "I'm having a hard time writing about Sunday. Getting the long hollow feeling of Sundays. No mail and faraway lawn mowers, the hopelessness."

Following (fictitious) Henrietta through her meager life, we are moved to pity her: "no matter how nasty [Dr. B] is to her Henrietta believes there is a bond between them." The nephrologist has a clubfoot, while Henrietta (like Lucia Berlin) has scoliosis, a curvature—

"A hunchback, in fact." In a brilliant and heartrending sleight of hand at the story's end author Berlin, the (unnamed) narrator, and Henrietta blur into a single poignant voice of loss:

> Henrietta turns off the light, raises the blind by her bed, just a little. The window is steamed. The car radio plays Lester Young . . . I lean against the cool windowsill and watch him. . . . In the steam of the glass I write a word. What? My name? A man's name? Henrietta? Love? Whatever it is I erase it quickly before anyone can see.

ZESTFULLY WRITTEN, SEEMINGLY ARTLESS, drawn from eight previously published collections, the forty-three stories of the posthumously published *A Manual for Cleaning Women* by Lucia Berlin (1936–2004) seek to persuade us of their authenticity by this quick, deft, unerring selection of "intricate detail" while making no claim at all for "impartiality"—that may be Chekhov's way, and perhaps it is an ideal—(masculine?) way of literature—but it is not the way of Lucia Berlin, whose voice suggests the taut vernacularisms of Raymond Carver as well as the engaging warmth and authority of Grace Paley; the serio-comic frankness of Charles Bukowski (like Berlin for much of her publishing career a mainstay of John Martin's avant-garde Black Sparrow Press of Santa Barbara, California) and a younger contemporary Denis Johnson (*Jesus' Son*). Like these, Berlin has a predilection for first-person narrations about those whom life has battered, but not defeated; like these she is led to record, in the most minute and unsparing detail, the degradations of alcohol/drug addiction; she is most comfortable at the edge of proper middle-class life, or a little below, like the highly articulate cleaning-woman protagonist of the title story whose "alcoholic husband has just died, leaving me and the four kids" and whose thefts from her employers are petty—sleeping pills, a bottle of Spice Islands sesame seeds.

Despite her gritty life Berlin's protagonists rarely complain. "I like working in Emergency—you meet men there, anyway. Real men, heroes. Firemen and jockeys." A ride from Oakland to a county jail, that might be an ignominious experience, is given an aura of beauty in the hippy-addict-protagonist's imagination: "The avenue is lined with trees and that last morning it was foggy, like an old Chinese painting."

As a teenager in the 1950s Berlin lived in an affluent household, in Santiago, Chile, where her father worked as a mining engineer and her mother became a reclusive alcoholic, eventually a suicide; here, if we are to trust the reminiscences of the unnamed narrator of "Good and Bad," who attends a Catholic school in Santiago in the early 1950s and falls under the spell of an idealistic Communist lay teacher named Miss Dawson, she first becomes aware of social injustice and its tragic consequences for the poor.

"What if I asked you to give me your Saturdays, for one month, would you do it? See a part of Santiago that you don't know." "Why do you want me?" "Because, basically, I think you are a good person. I think you could learn from it." [Miss Dawson] clasped both my hands. "Give it a try." Good person. But she had caught me earlier, with the word *revolutionary*. I did want to meet revolutionaries, because they were bad.

Despite such mixed motives Berlin's protagonist does become sympathetic with the impoverished living in a shantytown at the Santiago dump ("they were the color of the dung, their rags just like the refuse they crawled in. No one stood up, they scurried on all fours like wet rats.") and takes up her teacher's courageous but quixotic cause, until her bullying father intervenes and has the teacher fired. But Berlin's protagonists are invariably sympathetic with that class of persons now called the working poor, in these stories both Americans and Mexicans. (The collection's strongest story is "Mijito," a devastating account of a young Mexican mother adrift amid drug dealers and petty criminals in an Oakland, California, slum, whom well-intentioned Caucasians cannot save.) The author's writerly eye is unsparing, but it is not a cold eye, that casts a glimmering sort of light on even the most sordid of situations, and moves us to identify with her hapless protagonists, virtually all of them women, if not indeed variants of the same, singular woman.

A Manual for Cleaning Women is a catchy but not perhaps the most appropriate title for this collection of memoirist stories and prose pieces about a hard-drinking, hard-living, unsentimental and unself-pitying woman who is indeed a cleaning woman, but only briefly, in Oakland and Berkeley; more often, Berlin's protagonist is a teacher (in a Catholic school), a doctor's receptionist, an emergency room attendant, a hospital switchboard operator and, above all, a writer either actively engaged in writing, or preparing to write. (Even in the throes of advanced alcoholism, in the mordantly narrated "Let Me See You Smile," the woman writer manages to write; her admiring lawyer says: "Ben handed me an *Atlantic Monthly* with a story of hers in it. I . . . thought it was great.") Like Lucia Berlin this woman has lived, as young girl, in a mining settlement near Juneau, Alaska, as well as in Santiago; as a girl she had to wear a painful back brace, to correct a curvature of the spine. Her parents divorced when she and her sister were young, and her mother was an alcoholic, severely depressed and suicidal, though wickedly funny (at times), mourned belatedly after her death as a woman deeply and mysteriously unhappy with her life, seeking isolation so that she could drink uninterrupted in (as her daughter recalls in a grim inventory): "Deerlodge, Montana; Marion, Kentucky; Patagonia, Arizona; Santiago, Chile; Lima, Peru." With this mother, as a girl, Berlin's woman-protagonist has lived for a while in El Paso, Texas, in the home of her dentist-grandfather Dr. H. A. Moynihan, a thoroughly repellent figure hated by virtually everyone who knows him, who places a sign in large gold letters in a window looking out onto the street: DR. H. A. MOYNIHAN. I DON'T WORK FOR NEGROES. The abysmally awful grandfather is a memorable character—"filthy, slopping food and spitting, leaving wet cigarettes everywhere. Plaster from teeth molds covered him with white specks, like he was a painter or a statue." An alcoholic like others in his family, Dr. Moynihan is revealed in a later story as a crude sexual molester of his own granddaughters. Sleeping, he is observed with "teeth bared in a Bela Lugosi grin."

Like the author, Berlin's typical woman protagonist has had several (failed) marriages, one of them to a sculptor who left her with young children, and another with a musician ("'Marry me,' he said. 'Give me a reason to live'") who turned out to be a heroin addict; she has had numerous love affairs, some of which are very brief (in "Toda Luna, Toda Ano," the coupling is undersea: "When he left her his sperm drifted up between them like pale octopus ink.") She has had four sons with two of these husbands, boys whom she loves very much and who appear to love her despite their disapproval of her alcoholism and carelessly lived life: "Everything was somehow always okay. She was a good teacher and a good mother really. . . . If they awakened [in the night], her sons would stumble upon her madness which, then, only occasionally spilled over into morning."

Berlin's strongest stories, verging upon the surreal, are those that deal frankly with her alcoholism. Sometimes the tone is comic-grotesque, in the Bukowski mode, as in this glimpse of the physician's assistant helping the "painfully shy" Dr. B. do a cervical examination of a patient who is "obese, with difficult access":

He squatted on a stool, his eyes level with their vagina, with a light on his forehead. I handed him the (warmed) speculum and, after a few minutes, with the patient gasping and sweating, the long cotton-tipped stick. He held it, waving it like a baton, as he disappeared beneath the sheet, toward the woman. At last his hand emerged with the stick, now a dizzy metronome

aimed at my waiting slide. I still drank in those days, so my
hand, holding the slide, shook visibly as it tried to meet his. But
in a nervous up-and-down tremble. His was back and forth.
Slap, at last. This procedure took so long that he often missed
important telephone calls. . . . Once [an associate] knocked on
the door and Dr. B was so startled he dropped the stick. We
had to start all over again.

Berlin is unflinching in self-castigation, which is not to be confused with self-loathing; as she forgives others, with a readiness
that may surprise the reader at times, so she forgives herself for
her chronic bad behavior. (It is related more than once how, in a
drunken state, the Berlin protagonist forgets to secure her car on
a steep street in Oakland, causing the car to detach itself from the
curb, roll downhill with gathering momentum, and crash into a
parked vehicle.) Despite the gritty nature of her subject matter the
tone of her writing is often uplifting, even ebullient; here is a writer,
again like Bukowski, who can write about being a drunk, about
the very poetry of drunkenness, with something like a surprised
pleasure in the unexpected camaraderie of alcoholics. In "Her First
Detox" a woman wakes in a county detox ward remembering only
"handcuffs, a straitjacket." She learns that she'd wrecked her car
against a wall and been violent when apprehended, but police officers had brought her to detox "instead of to jail when they found
out she was a teacher, had four sons, no husband."

Carlotta had a good time in the detox ward. The men were
awkwardly gallant toward her. She was the only woman, she
was pretty, didn't "look like a lush. . . ." Most of the men were
street winos.

A later story, "Unmanageable," begins: "In the deep dark night
of the soul the liquor stores and bars are closed. She reached under

the mattress; the pint bottle of vodka was empty." The focus of this very short story is a simple one: how to get through the night until the liquor stores open, in Oakland at 6:00 A.M., in Berkeley not until 7:00 A.M.

> She was panting and faint by the time she got to the Uptown [liquor store] on Shattuck. It wasn't open yet. Seven black men, all old except for one young boy, stood outside on the curb. . . . On the sidewalk two men were sharing a bottle of NyQuil cough syrup. Blue death, you could buy that all night long. An old man they called Champ smiled at her. "Say, mama, you be sick? Your hair hurt?" She nodded. That's how it felt, your hair, your eyeballs, your bones.

The unnamed woman is in such distress that Champ will have to help her drink the wine she has purchased, pouring it into her mouth. Later, alone, able to drink at last, she cries "with relief that she had not died." Yet the story ends with her sons kissing her good-bye in the morning as they rush off to school.

Elsewhere Berlin writes with sympathy and without condemnation of the addictions of others, in particular heroin addiction; the husband she seems to have loved most, a musician named Max with whom she'd run away to Mexico, is discovered soon after their elopement injecting himself with heroin:

> That sounds like the end of a story, or the beginning, when really it was just part of the years that were to come. Times of technicolor happiness and times that were sordid and frightening. . . . We were happy, all of us, for a long time and then it became hard and lonely because he loved heroin much more.

In another ill-fated relationship, with a fellow alcoholic named Jesse, a composer and street musician, the protagonist (here called

Carlotta) acknowledges that "I was so poisoned with alcohol that a drink wouldn't work, didn't make me stop shaking. I was terrified, panicked." Having decided that Jesse is a failure as a musician, and Carlotta is a failure as a mother, they decide to commit suicide together, but nothing comes of this decision and the last we see of the besotted lovers they are walking off together in drenching rain, "each of them deliberately stomping in puddles, bumping gently into each other."

It is not surprising to be told by one of Berlin's narrators: "I don't like Diane Arbus"—meaning that she has a deep sympathy for the freaks and outcasts who populate her stories, and she is slow to judge even unconscionable behavior:

> I tried to hide when Grandpa was drunk because he would catch me and rock me. He was doing it once in the big rocker, holding me tight, the chair bouncing off the ground inches from the red-hot stove, his thing jabbing jabbing my behind. He was Singing "Old Tin Pan with a Hole in the Bottom." Loud. Panting and grunting. Only a few feet away Mamie [grandmother] sat reading the Bible while I screamed, "Mamie! Help me!"

The sexually abused child does nothing to prevent the grandfather from abusing her younger sister Sally: "I had watched with a mixture of feelings: fear, sex, jealousy, anger." Later, as an older child, she will say of her abuser, "Everybody hated Grandpa but Mamie, and me, I guess." In a grotesquely protracted, blood-splattered scene in "Dr. H. A. Moynihan," the granddaughter helps the old man pull out his rotted teeth so that he can fit himself with false teeth he has prepared.

> "Pull them!" he gasped. I was afraid, wondered quickly if it would be murder if I pulled them and he died. "Pull them!" He spat a thin red waterfall down his chin. I pumped the chair

way back. He was limp, did not seem to feel me twist the back top teeth sideways and out. He fainted, his lips closing like gray clamshells. I opened his mouth and shoved a paper towel into one side so that I could get the three teeth that remained.

The teeth were all out. I tried to bring the chair down with the foot pedal, but hit the wrong lever, spinning him around, spattering circles of blood on the floor.

When the teeth are finally fitted into the grandfather's mouth:

"A masterpiece, Grandpa!" I laughed too, kissed his sweaty head.

Estranged by their dysfunctional childhood and by the toxic presence of their unstable alcoholic mother, Berlin's protagonist and her sister Sally are reconciled as adults. In a number of overlapping stories, which read at times, somewhat summarily, like passages in a memoir, Berlin's protagonist joins her sister in Santiago, where Sally is stricken with terminal cancer. These stories of sisters establishing a close, intimate relationship in middle age contain the most tender of Berlin's memories, enshrined in set pieces in which the sisters reminisce. Their favorite subject, of course, is their impossible mother, who continues to haunt them years after her death.

When our father died Sally had flown from Mexico City to California. She went to Mama's house and knocked on the door. Mama looked at her through the window but she wouldn't let her in. She had disowned Sally years and years before.

"I miss Daddy," Sally called to her through the glass. "I am dying of cancer. I need you now, Mama!" Our mother just closed the venetian blinds and ignored the banging banging on her door.

And,

Even her humor was scary. Through the years her suicide notes, always written to me, were always jokes. When she slit her wrists she signed it Bloody Mary. When she overdosed she wrote that she had tried a noose but couldn't get the hang of it. Her last letter to me wasn't funny. It said that she knew I would never forgive her. That she could not forgive me for the wreck I had made of my life.

(From such casual asides we understand that, within Berlin's family, Lucia was hardly acknowledged as a writer, let alone a talented and successful writer.)

Of the many characters in Berlin's stories it is Sally who emerges as the most appealing, even saintly. It is Sally whom the narrator most mourns, among the dead who have gradually accumulated in the beautiful and stoically rendered stories of *A Manual for Cleaning Women*:

It has been seven years since you died. Of course what I'll say next is that time has flown by. I got old. All of a sudden, de repente. I walk with difficulty. I even drool. I leave the door unlocked in case I die in my sleep. . . . But there's never enough time. "Real time" like the prisoners I used to teach would say, explaining how it just seemed that they had all the time in the world. The time wasn't ever theirs. . . .

A lazy illumination, like a Mexican afternoon in your room. I could see the sun in your face.

Lucia Berlin published seventy-six stories during her lifetime, in such publications as Saul Bellow's *The Noble Savage, Atlantic*

Monthly, and *New American Writing;* most of these were collected in three volumes from Black Sparrow Press: *Homesick* (1999), *So Long* (1993), and *Where I Live Now* (1999). *A Manual for Cleaning Women* includes a little more than half these stories but in an inde-terminate order—it isn't clear that the editor's principle of organiza-tion is chronological, or thematic; indeed, if there is any principle of organization at all. In his breezy introduction Stephen Emerson remarks that Berlin's short, sketchy story "B.F. and Me" is the last story she wrote, but it is not the last story in the collection. (This is "Homing," a meandering meditation upon mortality and the passing of time: "A weird thing happened to me this week. I could see these small quick crows flying past my left eye. I'd turn but they would be gone.") As a memoirist piece "Homing" is poignant and essential, but it is not a fully realized work of short fiction that could stand alone, apart from preceding memorist pieces in *A Manual for Cleaning Women;* you would have to already know a good deal about Berlin's woman-writer character, or persona, to make emotional sense of it.

In her enthusiastic and generous foreword to this volume Lydia Davis singles out Lucia Berlin's gift for sharply observed metaphors and arresting sentences but does not seem to acknowledge, or per-haps to have noticed, that very few of Berlin's stories are what might be called "fully realized" works of fiction that might be included in anthologies beside work by Berlin's accomplished contemporaries (among them, Cynthia Ozick, Alice Adams, Alice Munro, John Cheever, Donald Barthelme, Grace Paley, John Updike, Joy Wil-liams, Raymond Carver, Tobias Wolff, Thom Jones). Brevity isn't the issue, for Carver's stories, some of them severely minimalist, are yet fully realized, requiring no context to complete them.

It is customary for short story writers to carefully arrange their stories for hardcover publication, in the way that poets arrange their poetry; it is never the case that writers toss stories together hap-hazardly, and it is unlikely that a writer would arrange his stories merely in chronological order of writing or of publication. (There are distinctive instances of story "collections" that constitute a subgenre midway between story collection and novel: Sherwood Anderson's *Winesburg, Ohio,* James Joyce's *Dubliners,* Alice Munro's *Lives of Girls and Women,* to name but three. In these, the arrangement of stories is as crucial as the arrangement of chapters in a novel.) It's to be assumed that Lucia Berlin gave some thought to the order in which her stories appeared in the Black Sparrow volumes *Homesick, So Long,* and *Where I Live Now* and that, if she had lived to oversee her *Selected Stories,* surely she would have made clear which stories were taken from which books, and there would have been, very likely, a grouping of stories that had not yet appeared in any hardcover publication. Customarily, a Selected Stories, like a Selected Poems, will either begin or end with a section consisting of new, not-yet-published work. But Stephen Emerson has indicated nothing in the table of contents—forty-three titles are simply lumped together with no identification at all, not even dates of publication. Consequently we have no way of knowing if the first story in the volume, "Angel's Laundromat," is placed in this crucial position because it was Berlin's first published story, or whether its positioning is thematically significant. (Though vividly and engagingly written, the story is far from being one of the more fully realized of Berlin's works; like "Sex Appeal," "My Jockey," "Teenage Punk," and others, it is essentially a character sketch, of a terminally alcoholic Jicarilla Apache who frequents the Laundromat frequented by the unnamed woman protagonist.) The title story "A Manual for Cleaning Women," like "Emergency Room Notebook 1977," seems to be comprised of sharp-eyed journal entries tenuously attached to a story of loss; a "young cowboy, from Nebraska" named Terry has died, but we know very little of Terry, other than the narrator's grief for him. It isn't clear why Berlin's *Selected Stories* has been titled *A Manual for Cleaning Women,* out of other possible titles.

Thanks are due to Stephen Emerson, however, who speaks in his introduction of Lucia Berlin being "as close a friend as I've ever had," and who has assembled this collection of Berlin's work for a new generation of readers. Those unfamiliar with Berlin's fiction are advised to read *A Manual for Cleaning Women* at least twice, for essentially this is a memoir of the author's life related in installments and fragments, that fit together upon a second reading, and generate a considerable emotional power. As such, *A Manual for Cleaning Women* is an achievement greater than the sum of its heterogeneous parts.

A Manual for Cleaning Women:
Selected Stories
By Lucia Berlin
Edited by Stephen Emerson

EDNA O'BRIEN:
THE LITTLE RED CHAIRS

Edna O'Brien's boldly imagined and harrowing new novel, her twenty-third work of fiction since *The Country Girls* (1960), is both an exploration of those themes of Irish provincial life from the perspective of girls and women for which she has become acclaimed and a radical departure, a work of alternate history in which the devastation of a war-torn Central European country intrudes upon the "primal innocence, lost to most places in the world" of rural Ireland. Here, in addition to O'Brien's celebrated gifts of lyricism and mimetic precision is a new, unsettling fabulist vision that suggests Kafka rather more than James Joyce, as her portrait of the psychopath "warrior poet" Vladimir Dragan suggests Nabokov in his darker, less playful mode. Should we not recognize immediately the sinister "Dr. Vladimir Dragan of Montenego" the author has placed this poignant passage as an epigraph to the novel:

> On the 6th of April 2012, to commemorate the twentieth anniversary of the start of the siege of Sarajevo by Bosnian Serb forces, 11,541 red chairs were laid out in rows along the eight hundred metres of the Sarajevo high street. One empty chair for every Sarajevan killed during the 1,425 days of the siege. Six

hundred and forty-three small chairs represented the children killed by snipers and the heavy artillery fired from the surrounding mountains.

Like a figure in a malevolent Irish fairy tale a mysterious stranger appears one day seemingly out of nowhere on a bank of a tumultuous river in western Ireland, in a "freezing backwater that passes for a town and is called Cloonoila." The stranger is himself "mesmerized" by the "manic glee" of the deafening water. (It is helpful to know that *"Cloonoila"* is Gaelic for "despoiled field.")

Soon, the curious, credulous inhabitants of Cloonoila fall one by one under the spell of Dr. Dragan, "Vuk," or "Dr. Vlad", a self-styled poet, exile, visionary, "healer and sex therapist." To one, he resembles a "Holy man with a white beard and white hair, in a long black coat"; so priestly, one might "genuflect." To another, he is a figure of hope: "Maybe he'll bring a bit of Romance into our lives." Schoolchildren think he looks "a bit funny in a long black smock with his white beard" but consider him harmless. The village schoolteacher is suspicious, suggesting that the stranger may be a kind of Rasputin, another notorious "visionary and healer," but no one chooses to listen. The young Catholic priest Father Damien is initially wary of Dr. Vlad only because the outsider represents a threat to Catholic authority, and because he has advertised himself as a "sex therapist"—"This is a Catholic country and chastity is our number one commandment." Edna O'Brien's portraits of Irish Catholic priests are rarely flattering, and Father Damien is a font of clichés and empty rhetoric: "You see, many [local residents] feel a vacuum in their lives . . . marriages losing their mojo . . . internet dating . . . nudity . . . hedonism . . . the things I have heard in confession." The presumed spiritual leader of the community is as readily taken in by Dr. Vlad as the others, confiding in him that "repentance and sorrow for sin is woven into our DNA."

In these briskly satiric exchanges Edna O'Brien can be as wit-
tily lethal as Muriel Spark eviscerating the foolish, but O'Brien's
sympathy is more fully engaged by those women—lonely, childless,
naïve—who fall more deeply under the spell of Dr. Vlad: a Catholic
nun who pays for a massage from the practitioner of "Holistic Healing in Eastern and Western Disciplines"—"[Sister Bonaventure] felt
a flash of blinding light and was transported to the ethereal"; and,
more crucially, the "town beauty" Fidelma, married to a man much
older than she, and desperate to have a child, who contrives to be
impregnated by the charlatan-therapist, but with disastrous results
for both her marriage and for herself. Their union verges upon the
surreal, it is so self-consciously "mythic":

> "Undo your necklace," he said and kissed her and they lay
> down, his body next to hers, seeking her with his hands, with
> his mouth, with his whole being, as if in the name of love,
> or what she believed to be love, he could not get enough of
> her. Her breath came in little gasps, their limbs entwined, the
> healer and she, the stranger and she, like lovers now, as in a
> story or in a myth.

Later, Fidelma will feel that the union with Dr. Vlad has brought
a "terrible curse on her village"—like a union with the devil. For
her audacity, which (the reader knows) is a consequence of naïveté,
not lust, Fidelma will be viciously punished, as in a fairy tale in
which consequences are wildly disproportionate to causes. (The
scene of Fidelma's punishment by betrayed allies of Dr. Vlad is not
for the fainthearted; O'Brien does not gloss over details.) Yet, somehow, perhaps not altogether plausibly, Fidelma regains not only her
health and strength but acquires a confidence she had previously
lacked; by the novel's end she is determined to expiate the curse of
a union with the devil by dedicating herself to the aid of desperate,

displaced persons at a shelter for the homeless in London: "I could not go home until I could come home to myself."

THE MOST BOLDLY IMAGINED element of *The Little Red Chairs* is, of course, the positing of an alternate universe in which a Balkan war criminal, the object of an international search for twelve years, turns up in a remote Irish village in the hope of establishing a new, much diminished life as a healer-therapist. In a more conventional work of fiction, and certainly in a work of genre mystery, the exact identity of Dr. Vlad would constitute the plot, and his outing would be the consequence of detection on the part of a canny protagonist among the villagers. One can well imagine a sly Nabokovian hide-and-seek with the reader in which the man's exact identity is never quite established and we are confronted with the possibility that Dr. Vlad, like the mad narrator of *Pale Fire,* may be imagining his own lurid history. Instead, in an audacious move in which every creative writing admonition is tossed blithely aside, the author simply presents seven pages of densely iterated exposition in the (again, audaciously awkward) form of a dream of Dr. Vlad in which he is chastised by an old, now dead "blood brother" and comrade in the genocidal Serbian onslaught against Bosnian Muslim and Bosnian Croatian communities in the early 1990s: "You had been christened Young Torless because of the two terribly contrasting aspects of your character, the sane, the reasonable and the other so dark, so vengeful." Later, the "Beast of Bosnia" will argue in his own defense at his trial in The Hague: "If I am crazy then patriotism itself is crazy." ("Dragan David Dabic" was a false identity for the president of the Serb Republic in Bosnia, Radovan Karadžić, apprehended in Serbia in 2008 after twelve years in hiding; known as the "Butcher of Bosnia," Karadžić was tried in The Hague by the UN war crimes tribunal for war crimes including genocide. While he was in hiding, Karadžić practiced "alternative medicine.")

But Edna O'Brien is not interested in sensationalizing her material, and *The Little Red Chairs* is not a novel of suspense, still less is it a mystery or a thriller; it is something more challenging, a work of meditation and penance. How does one come to terms with one's own complicity with evil, even if that complicity is "innocent"? Should we trust the stranger who arrives out of nowhere in our community? Should we mistrust the stranger? When is innocence self-destructive? Given the nature of the world, when is skepticism, even cynicism, justified? Much is made of innocence in fiction, as in life, but in O'Brien's unsentimental imagination the innocent suffer greatly because they are not distrustful enough; and usually these innocents are girls and young women, as in O'Brien's compelling novel *Down by the River* (1996), in which a young rural Irish girl is impregnated by her father and further humiliated by being forced to endure the public politicization of her pregnancy by pro- and anti-abortion rights spokeswomen. As one of O'Brien's female characters has said of her native Ireland: "Ours indeed was a land of shame, a land of murder and a land of strange sacrificial women."

The Little Red Chairs, much farther-reaching in its historic scope, much more terrifying in its portraiture of the unrepentant war criminal, yet shares with other works of Edna O'Brien the pervading sense of guilt that is "woven into our DNA" and a determination to be free of this guilt. Initially one of Dr. Vlad's dupes, Fidelma evolves into O'Brien's most resourceful heroine as she throws off her very identity to live amid the homeless in London, and to remake herself by painful degrees (chambermaid, dog kennel worker) into a woman strong enough to help others. In her new awareness she hears stories told by refugees in a homeless shelter: displaced persons, victims of unspeakable horrors: "It is essential to remember and nothing must be forgotten." She finds her community in a place that promises "We Help Victims Become Heroines."

In her lyric, candid memoir *Country Girl,* Edna O'Brien remarks that, wild as it must sound, she had wanted, as a girl, at
least for an impassioned while, to become a Catholic nun. Such a
vocation, in the service of others, is exactly what her courageous
heroine Fidelma undertakes, in the midst of much struggle, choosing "not to look at the prison wall of life, but to look up at the sky."

"DISPUTED TRUTH":
MIKE TYSON

God, it would be good to be a fake somebody than a real nobody.
—Mike Tyson, *New York Times,* May 21, 2002

The afterlife of a champion boxer recalls Karl Marx's remark about history repeating itself first as tragedy, then as farce. Even when the boxer manages to retire before he has been seriously injured, it is not unlikely that repeated blows to the head will have a long-term neurological effect, and the accumulative assault of arduous training and hard-won fights will precipitate the natural deterioration of aging; it is certainly likely that the boxer has witnessed, or even precipitated, very ugly incidents in the lives of other boxers. As welterweight champion Fritzie Zivic once said, "You're boxing, you're not playing the piano." The boxer has journeyed to a netherworld of visceral, violent experience of which most of us, observing from a distance, can have but the vaguest glimmer of comprehending; he has risked his life, he has injured others, as a gladiator in the service of entertaining crowds; when the auditing is done, often it is found that, after having made many millions of dollars for himself and others, the boxer is near-penniless, if not in debt to the IRS, and must declare bankruptcy—(Joe Louis, Ray Robinson, Leon Spinks, Tommy Hearns, Evander Holyfield,

Mike Tyson* among others.) Ironic then, or perhaps inevitable, that the afterlife of the champion boxer so often replicates this tragic role in farcical form: recall Joe Louis, one of the greatest heavyweights in history, ending his career with two ignominious defeats at the hands of younger boxers and a brief interlude as a professional wrestler, then impersonating himself as a "greeter" in a Las Vegas casino; recall the ghastly comedic effort of former middleweight champion Jake La-Motta (brilliantly portrayed by a bloated Robert De Niro at the beginning and at the end of Martin Scorsese's *Raging Bull*) in smoke-filled nightclubs; Max Baer, Rocky Graziano, Sugar Ray Robinson, Marvin Hagler, Héctor Camacho, among others pursued careers in films or on television, with varying degrees of success.

Arguably the greatest of heavyweight champions, unmatched in his prime for spectacular ring performances, Muhammad Ali too ended his career after a succession of humiliating and battering defeats, exploited by his de facto manager Don King, and badly in debt; in his visibly diminished state, afflicted with Parkinson's disease, and unable to speak, Ali is frequently displayed on public occasions, often in formal attire: face impassive as a mask, Ali can't respond to the chant of crowds—"Al-i! Al-i!"—though his wife and handlers claim that he can hear these chants, and enjoys the public exposure. Mike Tyson, at twenty the youngest heavyweight champion in history, and in the early, vertiginous years of his career a worthy successor to Ali, Louis, and Jack Johnson, has managed to reconstitute himself after his retirement from boxing in 2005† into

---

* In 2003, after having earned between $300 and $400 million, Mike Tyson declared bankruptcy with $23 million in debt and $17 million owed in back taxes.

† Replicating the infamous "No mas" of the boxer Tyson most admired, Roberto Duran, who quit in mid-fight when losing badly to Sugar Ray Leonard in 1980, Tyson abruptly quit before the seventh round of a fight with the undistinguished boxer Kevin McBride, and retired soon afterward.

a bizarre, postmodernist replica of the original Iron Mike, subject of a video game, cartoons, and comic books, cocaine-fueled caricature of himself in the crude *Hangover* films, star of a one-man Broadway show directed by Spike Lee, titled *Undisputed Truth,* and the HBO film adaptation of that show; and now the author, with collaborator Larry Sloman, of the memoir *Undisputed Truth.*

Though in his late teens in the 1980s he was a fervently dedicated old-style boxer under the tutelage of the legendary trainer Cus D'Amato and more temperamentally akin to the boxers of the 1950s than to his slicker contemporaries, Mike Tyson in his forties looks upon himself with the absurdist humor of a Thersites for whom loathing of self and of his audience has become an affable schtick-performance. What has his professional life been but that of the black gladiator performing before predominantly white audiences, crazed and dangerous, screaming in self-parody at press conferences:

> I'm a convicted rapist! I'm an animal! I'm the stupidest person in boxing! I gotta get outta here or I'm gonna kill somebody! I'm on this Zoloft thing, right? But I'm on that to keep from killing y'all. . . . I don't want to be taking Zoloft, but they are concerned about the fact that I'm a violent person, almost an animal. And they only want me to be an animal in the ring.

———

The aesthetics of boxing is crucially bound up with time. Where once prize fights were marathons that might involve as many as one hundred rounds of three minutes each—(the record is one hundred ten rounds in 1893, over seven hours; in 1915, in the blazing sun of Cuba, the black champion Jack Johnson fought his "White Hope" challenger Jess Willard for twenty-six rounds before Johnson collapsed)—the tempo of the ring was naturally much slower than it is today; with so much time ahead, boxers had to calculate how to use their strength, and sheer physical endurance was a high priority. The marathon fight provided time for reflection for the rapt audience, as the balance of power might shift from one boxer to the other, in the way of a protracted play; when an abrupt knockout isn't so very likely, qualities other than swarming, in-fighting aggression are valued. (Virtually unique in twentieth-century boxing is the legendary match between then-undefeated heavyweight champion George Foreman and former champion Muhammad Ali. Their fight in Zaire in 1974, in which Ali's "rope-a-dope" strategy was simply to endure against his younger, more powerful opponent, who "punched himself out" on the older boxer's body after seven brutal rounds.) Fights scheduled to be marathons that ended quickly might be interpreted as mismatches, thus frauds; one of the most disappointing title fights in boxing history lasted only ninety-six seconds, in 1896, when boxing was outlawed in the United States and the heavyweight title fight was held on a sandbar in the Rio Grande River, four hundred miles from El Paso. And the most notorious heavyweight fight of the twentieth century, Jack Dempsey-Luis Ángel Firpo, 1923, is also one of the shortest, ending with a victory for Dempsey in the second round after a succession of spectacular knockdowns of both fighters and Dempsey's fall through the ring ropes onto a sports writer's typewriter; it is clear to us today that Dempsey lost the fight, the beneficiary of the referee's "long count" (an extra four seconds) that allowed Dempsey to recover after he'd been pushed back into the ring by reporters.

A classic long fight divides into acts, or scenes, as in a play; it is virtually impossible to envision the entire fight but only to "see" it as a sequence of dramatic scenes, or possibly only its final scene, or round. Or the final seconds of the final round. The greatest of long twentieth-century fights—(a category that would include the Ali-Frazier trilogy of 1971, 1974, and 1975 as well as Leonard-Hearns, 1981 and 1989)—unfold as oscillating actions: now one boxer has dominance, and now the other; the outcome is unpredictable, and, if the fight goes the distance, can be disputable (as in the case of Leonard-Hearns II).

By contrast, a fight in which one boxer is knocked out quickly is a very different aesthetic experience. There is no time for reflection or contemplation on the part of the audience, as there is no time for the boxers to "box" in a traditional manner; in such historic short fights as Hagler-Hearns, 1983, which ends after eight astonishing minutes in a knockout victory for Hagler, there is nonstop, escalating action as the aggressor moves inexorably forward with the finesse of an ax chopping at his opponent. (Of great short fights, Hagler-Hearns is likely to be the most memorized by boxing fans.) The fight that ends with a knockout is preferable to the fight that ends in a decision, since decisions involve judges' opinions, and opinions can be mistaken, as referees' rulings can be mistaken, though usually indisputable. When a boxer is counted "out" it isn't that he has been "knocked out"—that is, knocked unconscious—but rather that he has been counted "out of time"—he has failed to recover sufficiently to continue the fight within a space of ten seconds. Since the lethal boxing matches of the 1980s—(Mancini-Kim, 1982; McGuigan-"Young Ali," 1983)—referees stop fights far more readily than they once did; Hagler-Hearns was stopped in the third round, when the referee determined that Hearns was too badly beaten to continue.

Already as a young, ascendant boxer in his mid-teens Mike Tyson was drawing attention for the rapid-fire, nonstop aggression of his ring style even in amateur boxing matches in which points are scored by hits, as in fencing, without respect to the power of punches. He'd been trained by Cus D'Amato (a revered if controversial and contentious trainer whose previous world champions were Floyd Patterson and José Torres) to fight like a professional—"The whole amateur boxing establishment hated me. . . . And if they didn't like me, they despised Cus." Typically, Tyson terrified his opponents by his very size and manner. At the Olympics trials in 1983 the Tyson legend was beginning: "On the first day, I achieved a forty-two-second KO. On the second day I punched out the front teeth of my opponent and left him out cold for ten minutes. Then on the third day, the reigning tournament champ withdrew from the fight. . . . The next day we went to Colorado Springs for the U.S. National Championship. When I got there, four of the six other fighters dropped out of the competition. Both of my victories were first-round KOs." To see Tyson's early fights, both amateur and professional, is to see young boxers stalked, cornered, and swiftly beaten into submission by a younger boxer who pursues them across the ring with the savagery and determination of Jack Dempsey, whose nonstop, combative, and punitive ring style Tyson imitated under D'Amato's guidance; to see these fights in quick succession, the shared incredulity of the boxers who have found themselves in the ring with the relatively short, short-armed Tyson, their disbelief and astonishment at the sheer force of their opponent as he swarms upon them, is to witness a kind of Theater of the Absurd, which is perhaps the most helpful key to understanding boxing. By the time he turned professional in 1985, Tyson was modeling himself more conspicuously after Dempsey by adopting the iconic boxer's black trunks and black ring shoes worn without socks; he would enter the arena without a robe, unsmiling, truculent and deadly-looking, to the terror of his opponents. Here was Iron Mike, D'Amato's "antisocial" creation—"I even began to fantasize that if I actually killed someone inside the ring, it would certainly intimidate everyone."

At nineteen, Tyson began to establish his media image as an avatar of the murderous Dempsey in an interview following his demolition of Jesse Ferguson: "I wanted to hit him on the nose one more time, so that the bone of his nose would go up into his brain." With twelve first-round knockouts in his early career, some within seconds, no boxer has ever ascended more rapidly and more spectacularly through the heavyweight ranks than Tyson; with the genius for publicity of his managers Jimmy Jacobs and Bill Cayton, longtime associates of Cus D'Amato, and investors in Iron Mike's future, no boxer has ever been more heralded and more excitingly anticipated as a title contender. Unfortunately, D'Amato was to die in November 1985, aged seventy-seven.

Grieving for D'Amato, but determined to fulfill the trainer's prophecy that he would become the youngest heavyweight title-holder in history—(the record holder was Floyd Patterson, D'Amato's previous champion, twenty-two at the time of his first title)—Tyson executed one of his stylish, rapid-fire dramatic victories against thirty-three-year-old title-holder Trevor Berbick on the night of November 22, 1986, at the age of twenty, before a wildly cheering crowd in Las Vegas. Stopped by the referee after two minutes and thirty-five seconds into the second round, moving swiftly to its conclusion like a malevolent ballet, the Tyson-Berbick fight is one not likely to be forgotten by anyone who has seen it, as its predominant image is an older man hammered into submission by a younger man, falling hard, managing to get to his feet and then falling hard again, helpless onto the canvas. Even Berbick's trainer Angelo Dundee had to concede that "this kid" created the pressure of the fight to which his boxer could not react: "He throws combinations I never saw before. When have you seen a guy throw a right hand to the kidney, come up the middle with an uppercut, then throw a left hook. He throws punches . . . like a trigger." Though Tyson had entered sports history that night, as Cus D'Amato had planned for him, he would one day claim to a psychotherapist:

> The scariest day of my life was when I won the championship belt and Cus wasn't there. I had all this money and I didn't have a clue how to comport myself. And then the vultures and the leeches came out.

The strongest and most moving chapters of *Undisputed Truth* are those that deal with Tyson's background. Made familiar to many readers through countless retellings since his ascendency to fame in 1986, burnished with retrospective insight of a kind the young Tyson couldn't have had as a boy, these recollections of his childhood in Brooklyn with his biological family and his boyhood in Catskill, New York, with his "white" family—(Cus D'Amato and D'Amato's longtime companion Camille Ewald, with whom he lived intermittently until D'Amato's death in 1985)—are touched with nostalgia and a bittersweet sort of regret. It isn't so surprising to learn that Tyson's sporadic career as a criminal began when he was less than ten years old—"I was running with a Rutland Road crew called The Cats. . . . We didn't normally deal with guns, but . . . we stole a bunch of shit: some pistols, a .375 Magnum, and a long M1 rifle with a bayonet attached from World War I. You never knew what you'd find when you broke into people's houses"—as it is to learn that Tyson's criminal and drug activities continued through his teens, when he was living upstate and being trained by D'Amato. (How much D'Amato knew of his young protégé's ghetto life apart from Catskill isn't clear. But the dubious pattern is established early on that Mike Tyson is "special" and when he gets into fights at his Catskill school, Cus D'Amato persuades school authorities that "allowances had to be made for him," as D'Amato is loath to chastise Tyson for his coercive behavior with girls.)

Born in Fort Greene, Brooklyn, in 1966, Tyson would one day say that he didn't know much about his family background. His mother, a prison matron at the Women's House of Detention in Manhattan at the time of his birth, had been born in Virginia; for unclear reasons, possibly related to alcoholism and drugs, Lorna Mae Tyson soon lost her prison job, was evicted from her apartment, and moved to Brownsville, a rougher neighborhood: "Each time we moved, the conditions got worse—from being poor to being serious poor to being fucked-up poor." Tyson's mother's friends were now mainly prostitutes and her lovers inclined to violence—though Tyson recounts how his mother once poured boiling water over one of her male friends: "This is the kind of life I grew up in. People in love cracking their heads and bleeding like dogs. They love each other but they're stabbing each other. Holy shit, I was scared to death of my family." Tyson had been told that his biological father, who played no role in his life, was a pimp—but also a deacon in a church.

Difficult to believe that Mike Tyson, who would weigh two hundred pounds by the age of thirteen, was once "a pudgy kid, very shy, almost effeminate shy, and I spoke with a lisp. The kids used to call me 'Little Fairy Boy.'" At the age of seven he is introduced to petty theft by an older boy, taught to pick locks and rob houses; his first arrest for credit card theft is at the age of ten; at eleven he begins street fighting. More frequently than he is beaten on the street, he is beaten by his mother: "That was some traumatizing shit." That Tyson's recitation of his impoverished childhood has become somewhat rote doesn't lessen its poignancy: "I was a little kid looking for love and acceptance and the streets were where I found it."

Continuously in trouble with the police, Tyson is remanded to Spofford Juvenile Detention Center and treated with the psychotropic Thorazine, the first of countless psychotropic medications to which he would be prescribed through the decades. By his account Tyson would appear to have been emotionally disturbed, prone to violence and impulsive behavior, but he feels at home in Spofford, where many of his friends are also incarcerated. One day, Muhammad Ali comes to speak to the boys and makes a powerful impression on Tyson: "Right then I decided I wanted to be great."

Incorrigible at age thirteen, Tyson is finally sent upstate to the Tryon School for Boys near Catskill, where in a boxing program for incarcerated boys he is introduced to Cus D'Amato. As in a benevolent fairy tale, this is the encounter that changes the lives of both the juvenile delinquent and the elderly boxing trainer who has despaired of ever finding again another prodigy like Floyd Patterson.

As Tyson says, "I was this Thorazined-out nigga who was diagnosed as retarded and this old white guy gets ahold of me and gives me an ego." It is boxing lore that after D'Amato's first encounter with Tyson in his Catskill gym in March 1980 he called his friend and associate Jimmy Jacobs in Manhattan to tell him: "I've just seen the next heavyweight champion of the world."

In this way begins the metamorphosis of a clumsy, overweight adolescent who "always thought I was shit" into one of the most disciplined and accomplished athletes of the twentieth century. Much has been written of D'Amato's impassioned devotion to training young boxers and particularly of his training of Mike Tyson for virtually five years nonstop in his Catskill gym, a training that is as much, or more, psychological as it is physical. D'Amato teaches Tyson that boxing is a great tradition, that the boxer is a warrior: "My job is to peel off layers and layers of damages that are inhibiting your true ability to grow and fulfill your potential." D'Amato is the Zen master whose teachings are to be internalized: "There is no difference between a hero and a coward in what they feel. It's what they *do* that makes them different." Tyson becomes the apprentice willing to exhaust himself in the effort to obey his master:

"Cus wanted the meanest fighter that God ever created, someone who scared the life out of people before they even entered the ring. He trained me to be totally ferocious, in the ring and out."

And: "We fought to hurt people; we didn't fight just to win." (In the assimilation of the individual into the quasi-mystic discipline of training, there is no "I"—there is only "we.")

Time not spent at the gym is spent talking avidly about boxing and watching fight films and tapes:

When I started studying the lives of the great old boxers, I saw a lot of similarity to what Cus was preaching. They were all mean motherfuckers. Dempsey, Mickey Walker, even Joe Louis was mean, even though Louis was an introvert. I trained

myself to be wicked. . . . Deep down, I knew I had to be like
that because if I failed, Cus would get rid of me and I would
starve to death.

Tyson's portrait of the eccentric, controversial, slightly paranoid
and easily infuriated D'Amato is intimate and affectionate without
being sentimental; Tyson perceives that D'Amato is exacting revenge
for real or imagined slights against himself by way of his ferocious
young boxer, but never judges him harshly.

I was madly in love with Cus. He was the first white guy who
not only didn't judge me but who wanted to beat the shit out
of someone if they said anything disrespectful about me. . . . If
he told me to kill someone, I would have killed them. . . . I was
happy to be Cus's soldier; it gave me a purpose in life.

More coolly, Tyson observes of himself and D'Amato: "You give a
weak man some strength and he becomes addicted."

Though the death of Cus D'Amato would be devastating to Tyson, the young boxer would continue on his succession of winning
bouts for several years afterward with such opponents as James
"Bonecrusher" Smith (1987)—so terrified of Tyson, Smith grabbed
the young champion and clinched for dear life to lose each of twelve
rounds in arguably the only boring fight of Tyson's career; Pinklon
Thomas (1987)—knocked out in six rounds; Tony Tucker (1987);
Tyrell Biggs (1987)—whom Tyson said he could have knocked out
in the first round of their title fight at Atlantic City but chose to
knock out slowly "so that he would remember it for a long time.
I wanted to hurt him real bad"; Larry Holmes (1988)—a former
world champion who'd once defeated an aging Muhammad Ali, and
who had never before been knocked out in seventy-five professional
fights; Tony Tubbs (1988)—in two rounds; Michael Spinks (1988)—
in ninety-one seconds, the defeat of the former light-heavyweight

champion who had never before been knocked down; Frank Bruno (1989)—in five rounds; Carl Williams (1989)—in one round. In retrospect, Tyson-Spinks would be considered the most spectacular fight of Tyson's career, along with Tyson-Berbick. It is possible that Tyson's dazzling career would have begun to self-destruct eventually, given the evidence in *Undisputed Truth* of the young boxer's self-doubt as early as 1987 ("The truth is . . . I was sick of fighting in the ring. The stress of being the world's champ and having to prove myself over and over just got to me. I had been doing that shit since I was thirteen") and his self-destructive behavior between fights. But with the unexpected death in 1988 of Tyson's manager Jimmy Jacobs, who had been Cus D'Amato's longtime friend and associate, and a part of his "white family," Tyson was devastated anew, and left with no close advisers whom he could trust. "With Jim gone the vultures were circling for the fresh meat: me."

By this time Tyson has married TV actress Robin Givens, having been told that Givens is pregnant; in one of the two worst mistakes of his young life, Tyson gives his new wife, to whom he would remain married a scant year, his power of attorney. (Shortly after their marriage Givens has a "miscarriage.") Tyson's other disastrous mistake is to sign contracts with the controversial boxing promoter Don King, a former convicted felon who'd served time in an Ohio prison for manslaughter ("'I got three bodies, two on record,' Don bragged") and whose exploitive treatment of Muhammad Ali, among other fighters, should have been known to Tyson.

For boxing purists, Tyson's ignominious loss of the heavyweight title in 1990 to the 42–1 underdog James "Buster" Douglas marks the end of the Tyson era—that is, the end of the boxer whom Cus D'Amato had so carefully crafted as a fighter with extraordinary defensive skills as well as an extraordinary offense. No one who has seen this fight, one of the great upsets in boxing history, is likely to forget the sight of Tyson knocked to the canvas by Douglas in the tenth round, groping desperately for his mouthpiece to fit back into his mouth—a futile gesture. But for the lackluster performance of the titleholder, there would be something Shakespearean in such a fall. Tyson would say negligently of this fight that he hadn't taken it seriously, had scarcely trained and was thirty pounds overweight, had been "partying" virtually nonstop (in Tokyo, where the fight took place)—but the fact would seem to be simply that the reign of Iron Mike Tyson was over. The posthumous glory of Cus D'Amato was over. However Tyson would continue as a boxer with an erratic public career and a yet more erratic private life as a celebrity exploited by others as by himself, it would be a champion's afterlife he would inhabit.

———

The title *Undisputed Truth* is a play on the familiar boxing phrase "undisputed champion"—as in "Mike Tyson, undisputed heavyweight champion of the world" delivered in a ring announcer's booming voice and much-heard during the late 1980s and early 1990s. A more appropriate title for this lively hodgepodge of a memoir would be *Disputed Truth,* for much in these recollections of Tyson's tumultuous life, begun as a one-man Las Vegas act at the MGM casino, subsequently brought to Broadway in 2012, and now shaped into narrative form by a professional writer best known as the collaborator of the "shock comic" Howard Stern, is aimed to shock, titillate, amuse. and entertain, since much is wildly surreal and unverifiable. (Like the claim that "I'm such a monster. I turned the Romanian Mafia onto coke" and that Tyson was a guest in a Sardinia Billionaires Club "where a bottle of champagne cost something like $100,000.") Mostly, *Undisputed Truth* is a celebrity memoir of indefatigable name-dropping and endless accounts of "partying"; there is a photograph of Tyson with Maya Angelou, who came to visit him in Indiana when he was imprisoned for rape; we learn that Tyson converted to Islam in prison ("That was my first encounter with true love and forgiveness") but as soon as he was freed, he returns to his old, debauched life, plunging immediately into debt:

> I had to have an East Coast mansion . . . so I went out and bought the largest house in the state of Connecticut. It was over fifty thousand square feet and had thirteen kitchens and nineteen bedrooms. . . . Thirty wooded acres, an indoor and outdoor pool, a lighthouse, a racquetball court, and an actual nightclub. . . . In the six years I owned it, you could count the number of times I was actually there on two hands.

This palatial property is but one of four luxurious mansions Tyson purchases in the same manic season along with exotic wild animals (lion, white tiger cubs) and expensive automobiles—"Vipers, Spyders, Ferraris, and Lamborghinis" in addition to more commonplace Mercedes-Benz and Rolls-Royces. We hear of Tyson's thirtieth birthday party at his Connecticut estate with a guest list boasting Oprah, Donald Trump, Jay Z, and "street pimps and their hos." In line with Tyson's newfound Muslim faith, he stations outside the house "forty big Fruit of Islam bodyguards."

Apart from generating income for Tyson, the principal intention of *Undisputed Truth* would seem to be settling scores with individuals whom Tyson dislikes, notably his first wife Robin Givens and her omnipresent mother Ruth—("Robin and Ruthless were really deplorable people. There was nothing they wouldn't do for money, nothing. They would fuck a rat. They had no boundaries—money was like paper blood to them. They were evil people.")—and the infamous Don King, whom Tyson sued for having defrauded him of many millions of dollars—("this other piece of shit, Don King. Don is a wretched, slimy reptilian motherfucker. He was supposed to be my black brother, but he was just a bad man. . . . He was a real greedy man. I thought that I could handle somebody like King, but he out-

smarted me. I was totally out of my league with that guy.")* Nor is
Tyson above using *Undisputed Truth* to revisit his Indiana rape trial
of 1992 and speak scathingly another time of the eighteen-year-old
Miss Black America contestant Desiree Washington whom he was
convicted of raping—("I told her to wear some loose clothing and
I was surprised when she got into the car, she was wearing a loose
bustier and her short pajama bottoms. She looked ready for action.")
Tyson's strategy in the memoir is to acknowledge bad behavior on
his part—("I'm a real dirty fighter. . . . I think I really wanted people
to talk about how dirty and vicious I was")—as a way of validating
his vicious treatment of others. It's a technique not unlike smearing
a modicum of mud on yourself before tossing mud at others.

To the extent that Tyson has a predominant tone in *Undisputed
Truth* it's that of a Vegas stand-up comic, alternately self-loathing
and self-aggrandizing, sometimes funny, sometimes merely crude:

> Without sounding too egotistical, the whole Tyson thing was
> too big for Jimmy [Jacobs] and Bill [Cayton]; it was probably
> even too big for Cus. They never saw anyone like me. Nobody
> in the whole history of boxing had ever made as much money
> in such a short period of time as I did. . . . I was like some re-
> ally hot, pretty bitch who everybody wanted to fuck, you know
> what I mean?

Defending his friend Michael Jackson against charges of pedophilia:

---

* "[An attorney] asked me about the Spinks fight payment and I told him
I couldn't recall if I had been paid. When Puccio showed him that I had
been paid my twelve million dollars, I couldn't recall what I did with the
money. I didn't even have my own accountant at the time; I was just using
Don's. I didn't have anyone to tell me how to protect myself. All my friends
were dependent on me. I had the biggest loser friends in the history of
loser friends."

It was weird, everyone was saying that he was molesting kids then, but when I went there he had some little kids there who were like thug kids. These were no little punk kids, these guys would have whooped his ass if he tried any shit.

Alternately flush with money, which he spends with the giddy abandon of a nouveau rich black athlete stereotype, and alternately near-bankrupt:

I was so poor that a guy who'd stolen my credit card went on-line to complain that I was so broke he couldn't even buy a dinner on my credit card.

Admirers of Tyson's early boxing career will be stunned if not mystified to learn that even when Tyson was undefeated as a heavy-weight champion—*even when Tyson was training with Cus D'Amato as a teenager in the 1980s*—he often drank heavily, like his mother, and took drugs, favoring cocaine: "I started buying and sniffing coke when I was eleven but I'd been drinking alcohol since I was a baby. I came from a long line of drunks." It is generally believed that Tyson's downward spiral began at the time of the Buster Douglas debacle, but this memoir makes clear, as Tyson admits countless times, that he'd been a "cokehead" more or less continuously. At one point his co-caine addiction is so extreme, he seems to have infected his wife Kiki, whose probation officer detects cocaine in her system, a consequence of Tyson having kissed her before she went for her drug test:

[Kiki] had me there. I was a licker when it came to my blow. And I'm not talking about licking no little bit of residue off that folded sliver of paper that the coke might be in. I'm talk-ing about a jar of coke. I stuck my tongue down that jar and I hit pure cocaine. So much that you don't even feel your tongue anymore.

I was high on cocaine. Let me tell you something about me. When I was getting high and it was nighttime or early in the morning, I was not a good person to meet. I was just nasty, looking for trouble, almost Jekyll and Hyde shit.

There's a comical account of Tyson in a fit of road rage violently attacking a driver whose car has accidentally rear-ended his own:

Someone had called the police and they pulled us over a few miles from the scene. I was high as a kite and I started complaining about chest pains and then I told them that I was a victim of racial profiling.

After Tyson's conviction on charges of assault he is sentenced to two years in prison in Maryland ("with one year suspended"); though he has fewer celebrity visitors than he'd had in the Ohio prison, his most attention-getting visitor is John F. Kennedy Jr., who bizarrely assures Tyson that "the only reason you're in here is you're black." Tyson encourages John Jr. to "run for political office," an idea that is evidently new and startling to John Jr. Tyson elaborates to the Kennedy heir:

No, nigga, you've got to do this shit. . . . That's what you were born to do. People's dreams are riding on you, man. That's a heavy burden but you shouldn't have had that mother and father you did.

With admirable prescience Tyson tells John Jr. that he's "fucking crazy" to be flying his private plane. Though Tyson has been stressing his humility in prison he can't help but brag, "Shortly after John-John was there, boom, I got out of jail."

As if in rebuke of such self-aggrandizement, every few pages there is a perfunctory sort of self-chastisement, like a tic: "I might not have been a scumbag but I was an arrogant prick."

And, "I was a slave addicted to the chaos of celebrity."

And, on the occasion of acquiring the Maori tribal tattoo that now covers nearly half his face: "I hated my face and I literally wanted to deface myself."

Upon the occasion of accepting an Honorary Doctorate in Humane Letters from Central State University in Wilberforce, Ohio, in 1989, Tyson in cap and gown says to the commencement audience:

"I don't know what kind of doctor I am, but watching all these beautiful sisters here, I'm debating whether I should be a gynecologist."

(Don King was also awarded an "honorary doctorate" at this historic commencement.)

The funniest jokes in *Undisputed Truth* trade upon racial stereotypes. Tyson speaks of being taken up by a Jewish billionaire named Jeff Greene who'd made a "billion dollars playing the real estate market" while "I was a Muslim boxer who'd spent almost a billion dollars on bitches and cars and legal fees." Greene invites Tyson to dinner during Rosh Hashanah—"Shit I even got to read from the book during the Passover seder." This is Tyson's introduction to what he calls "Jewish jubilance." In "white honky heaven" Tyson is relaxing with his "new Jewish friends and suddenly this rude, obnoxious Saudi Muslim comes up to us"—so rude, the Saudi Muslim alludes to Tyson's rape charge. Tyson thinks indignantly:

What kind of guy does something like that? What arrogance. Suppose my new friends here didn't know I was in prison for rape? Suppose they asked, "What were you in prison for, Mike? Did you embezzle money? Insider trading?"

Funnier yet, a joke that must have drawn peals of appreciative laughter in Vegas:

I was on another rich Jewish guy's yacht and I watched him checking out this other Jewish guy whose boat was moored nearby. They were looking at each other, like black people do, you know how we look at each other? And then one guy said, "Harvard seventy-nine?" "Yes, didn't you study macroeconomics?"So I'm on this boat and I see this black guy. He's the bodyguard for a very well-known international arms dealer. And I'm looking at him and looking at him and I just can't place him. He came over to me.

"Spofford seventy-eight?" he asked.

"Shit, nigga, we met in lockdown," I remembered.

A hilarious interview with *USA Today*:

I'll never be happy. I believe I'll die alone. I would want it that way. I've been a loner all my life with my secrets and my pain. I'm really lost, but I'm trying to find myself. I'm really a sad, pathetic case. My whole life has been a waste—I've been a failure. I just want to escape. . . . I think I want to be a missionary. . . . I love Jesus and I believe in Jesus too—and I'm a Muslim. I've got an imam, I got a rabbi, I got a priest, I got a reverend—I got 'em all. But I don't want to be holier than thou. I want to help everybody and still get some pussy.

One of the more lurid incidents in the afterlife of Tyson's career is the ear-biting fracas of Holyfield-Tyson 1997. Provoked by his opponent's head-butting, which opened gashes in his forehead (and which referee Mills Lane unaccountably ruled "an accident"), Tyson lost control and bit one of Holyfield's ears—and then, as the fight was resumed, when Holyfield butted Tyson's forehead again, Tyson bit Holyfield's other ear. "I just wanted to kill him. Anybody could see that the head butts were so overt. I was furious, I was an undisciplined soldier and I lost my composure." The referee stopped the fight, with Holyfield declared the winner. Though Tyson's behavior was roundly condemned as poor sportsmanship, an examination of the video shows clearly that the referee behaved with unwarranted leniency toward Holyfield and prejudice against Tyson. (Ironically, in a Golden Gloves tournament, Holyfield himself had once bitten an opponent.)

Undisputed Truth ends with Tyson in a somber, even elegiac mood, reflecting upon his Muslim faith and the "old-time fighters" like Harry Greb, Mickey Walker, Benny Leonard, John L. Sullivan. His mood is nostalgic, remorseful—"Now I'm totally compassionate. . . . I've really come to a place of forgiveness." But *"sometimes I just fantasize about blowing somebody's brains out so I can go to prison for the rest of my life."* Tyson acknowledges that he has returned to AA and that his sobriety is a precarious matter, like his marriage. After the jocular excesses of *Undisputed Truth* it is ironic to end on so subdued and tentative a note: "One day at a time."

Undisputed Truth
By Mike Tyson with Larry Sloman

THE FIGHTER:
A FILM BY DAVID O. RUSSELL

The Fighter might more accurately have been titled *The Fighter and His Family*: it's a brilliantly orchestrated ensemble piece at the paradoxically near-still center of which is the boxer Micky Ward (Mark Wahlberg), whose once-promising career, like his grim hometown Lowell, Massachusetts, is on what appears to be an inevitable downward spiral. Based upon the life and career of former junior welterweight champion Micky Ward, most famous for his three brutally hard-fought bouts with Arturo Gatti in 2002 to 2003, *The Fighter* is a group portrait of working-class Irish-Americans in a blighted post-industrial urban landscape: the brawling, clannish, emotionally combustible Ward-Eklund family for whom Micky is their great hope and from whom, if he wants to survive, let alone prevail as a boxer of ambition, Micky must separate himself.

In a sequence of sharply realized scenes, not unlike the rounds of a boxing match, *The Fighter* pits the matriarch Alice (Melissa Leo) and her favored son, ex-boxer Dicky (Christian Bale), the half-brother of Micky, against Micky Ward and his girlfriend Charlene (Amy Adams): the film traces a highly contentious, often darkly funny tug-of-war for Micky's soul, which is to say Micky's career. The viewer is made to experience, like Micky, the almost literally suffocating and coercive "love" of a family for its own; the heroic, if desperate, effort an essentially nonrebellious son like Micky must make simply to be allowed to be an adult—though he's at least thirty years old, divorced, with a young daughter from whom he's separated, and, in his own words, "Not getting any younger." (In professional boxing, most boxers are burnt out by thirty and in risk of serious injury.) Dramatizing the historic Micky Ward's life, but only to a degree, *The Fighter* follows the archetypal pattern of the generic boxing film—see *Cinderella Man* (2005) as a recent example, as well as the cruder, more slickly produced *Rocky* films—in its modestly uplifting ending.

These are not great boxers of the quality of the young Mike Tyson or the legendary Muhammad Ali, Sugar Ray Robinson, or Joe Louis but journeyman fighters who've managed through sheer dogged effort to win just a little more than they've lost. Though touted as a "warrior," Micky Ward isn't even, by nature, aggressive; he's far from the "raging bull" counterpuncher Jake LaMotta, of Scorsese's film. He is so desperate in his ring stratagems that even his victories have an air of the haphazard and the tentative. (By default, while losing a crucial fight with the British boxer Shea Neary in 2002, Micky is forced to fall back upon the strategy that brought Ali victory against George Foreman in 1974 in Zaire: the notorious "rope-a-dope" ploy in which the weaker boxer allows the stronger to literally punch himself out on the weaker boxer's body through round after devastating round until, as in an astonishing fairy-tale reversal of fortune, the "weaker" boxer knocks out the "stronger." It's a strategy that gave the thirty-two-year-old Ali an unexpected, historic victory against his twenty-five-year-old opponent, but certainly contributed to Ali's physical deterioration, including the "Parkinsonian" condition with which he has been afflicted now for decades. The effect of such a beating on the less physically exceptional Micky Ward may lie sometime in the future—*The Fighter* doesn't come near suggesting the physical consequences of Micky Ward's fighting style. We never see a doctor examining poor Micky though, in fact, following even his victory against Arturo Gatti in 2002, he'd had to be hospitalized, as he was following the punishing rematch-fights with Gatti, which he lost.) It's a relief to the viewer to learn at the film's end that Micky has retired from boxing—not a moment too soon.

In his portrayal of the talented but unexceptional athlete who makes of himself through dogged, diligent training a "champion"— (if only junior welterweight)—Mark Wahlberg is quietly compelling, the film's anchor as he is the film's core; his is a steady, stolid performance, subtly nuanced in the way of the early, young Al Pacino—a kind of "acting" indistinguishable from "real life." By contrast—and the contrast is considerable—Christian Bale as Dicky Eklund, Micky's half-brother and trainer, gives a tour de force of a performance, not unlike the manic LaMotta brother Joey, played by Joe Pesci in his first film role, in *Raging Bull*. Dicky Eklund is a former boxer himself, whose single moment of glory is his having "knocked down" Sugar Ray Leonard in a match Leonard won, years before; he's Micky's trainer, when he manages to show up at the gym, clearly intelligent, shrewd, self-destructive and unreliable—a crack addict, yet charismatic—with the gaunt cheeks and sunken eyes of the doomed. It's a measure of Christian Bale's brilliant performance that the viewer can't look anywhere else when "Dicky" is on-screen, even if our feeling for him verges upon revulsion: there's a perverse heroism about Dicky, deluded into believing that an HBO film (*"Crack Addiction in America"*) in which he's a subject of clinical pathos, is somehow a film about *him*. Another vibrantly kinetic performance is Amy Adams as Charlene, Mickey's tough, tenderly protective bartender girlfriend, who, it's revealed, has a college degree and had been a champion high jumper: Charlene scarcely hesitates before flinging herself into the Ward-Eklund fray, taking on not only Micky's harridan-mother and manipulative half-brother but Micky's seven harpie-sisters, irresistibly awful on the screen, yet strangely touching, clearly their mother's offspring and frightening in the aggregate as figures in a Hogarthian allegory.

And there is Melissa Leo in the role of her career as the nightmare mother-manager Alice, determined to exploit her boxer-son as she's sublimely indifferent to the terrible danger she places him in by matching him with opponents who outweigh him by as much as twenty pounds—the demonic mother who sincerely believes that she's doing the right thing, her witchy face contorted with disbelief that anyone should doubt her good intentions. Bouffant-haired, improbably slim after having borne nine children (!), Melissa Leo's Alice reminded me of James Joyce's description of Ireland—"The sow that devours her own children."

DESPITE ITS STELLAR ACTING PERFORMANCES, *The Fighter* is a curious film—mysteriously incomplete in essential ways, over-determined and repetitive in more predictable ways. So sharply reminiscent of Martin Scorsese's *Raging Bull* that one might expect to see Scorsese's name among the credits, *The Fighter* is, like *Raging Bull,* a portrayal of boxing as the public, professional, and singularly ugly face of what might be called the primal pathology of the human condition—the compulsion to fight, to subject oneself to injury and humiliation, matched with the hardly less perverse compulsion to witness such extremes of human endurance in a catastrophic public place. (Both *The Fighter* and *Raging Bull* depict ringside observers reminiscent of those quasi-bestial figures in George Bellows's early, highly unromantic boxing paintings *Both Members of This Club* and *Stag at Sharkey's.*)

Unlike *Raging Bull*, which suggests, in the nightmare-surreal scenes in which the dogged, flailing "bull" middleweight Jake La-Motta is defeated by the superior boxing skills of Sugar Ray Robinson, that there is a transcendent, bitter beauty to this grim sport, *The Fighter* never suggests that boxing is a sport that allows superior athletes to perform brilliantly and memorably; Micky Ward and his opponents are not athletes of distinction but brawlers in the mode of LaMotta, Rocky Graziano, and Rocky Marciano, working-class heroes of the 1950s, fighting for money, all offense and little defense, as if the crude, coarse savage desire of the crowd were manifest in the ring, never mind how even the winning boxer might be seriously, irrevocably injured—such matches are not boxing, with its myriad skills and particular, cherished histories, but mere fighting. (It's traditional for boxers, especially young boxers in training, to study films of great boxing matches under the tutelage of their trainers, and in this study, they acquire a reverence for past champions, as well as exemplary models to follow: yet we don't have a glimpse of Micky Ward in such a context, as if, for him and his entourage, boxing had no history and was essentially a brainless endeavor. There is not even an excited awareness of the reigning welterweight/light-middleweight champion and crowd-pleaser of the era—the spectacular Oscar De La Hoya. The only glimpse we have of a superior boxer, the wily and ingenious Sugar Ray Leonard, is refracted through the coke-blurred memory of Dicky Eklund, whose delusion is that, for a split second at least, he was the equal of one of the great middleweight boxers of the second half of the twentieth century; what pathos then, when Dicky meets Leonard at a boxing match and tries to engage conversation with him, as the celebrity-boxer just barely politely tries to discourage him, before turning and walking away even as, undeterred, Dicky calls happily after him.)

The most puzzling omission in *The Fighter* is the trilogy of fights with Arturo Gatti in 2002 to 2003 that made both Ward and Gatti famous—at least, in the netherworld of contemporary boxing, in which both men are enshrined in the way, not exactly condescending but qualified, that LaMotta and Graziano are enshrined in boxing history: boxers who fought heedlessly, desperately, with little defensive skills and much "heart," to please voracious and unforgiving boxing audiences with a taste for blood. The Gatti-Ward trilogy of fights far better displays Micky Ward's boxing skills and his indomitable spirit than the abbreviated bouts of *The Fighter,* for in Gatti, an Italian-born Canadian with a fierce and seemingly unstoppable ring personality, Ward met his just slightly more talented doppelgänger. (Gatti allegedly said, "I always wondered what would happen if I met my twin—now I have.")* Ending *The Fighter* before the great brawling fights with Gatti is equivalent to ending *King Lear* before the blinding of Gloucester and the murder of Cordelia: one might do it, and still have a viable work of art, but—why?

SINCE ITS RELEASE IN 1980, when it received "mixed" critical reviews, *Raging Bull* has attained the status of a genuine American classic, not merely a cult film. Admirers of the Scorsese film may see in *The Fighter* a work of directorial homage that compares respectably with its distinguished predecessor. As *Raging Bull* begins with the middle-aged, overweight ex-middleweight champion doing his painfully unfunny nightclub comedy routine, then flashes back to 1941 when LaMotta was a young, undisciplined, and audacious fighter, so *The Fighter* begins with film footage of Dicky Eklund being interviewed for an HBO documentary—only later do we learn the nature of the documentary, having been led to believe, at

---

* Arturo Gatti (1972–2009) was the contemporary boxer who most resembled Micky Ward in ring style, talent, and ambition. As prone to injuries as Ward, Gatti had a slightly more successful career, winning championships in three weight divisions (super featherweight, lightweight, and junior welterweight), always at considerable physical cost. Near the end of his career, Gatti acquired Micky Ward as his trainer, but he did so poorly in a comeback in 2007, he retired abruptly. Gatti was a "warrior" whose post-fight photographs frequently depicted a badly bruised, battered face, both eyes swollen near-shut; his hands were often injured, requiring surgery. His mysterious death in Brazil in 2009, ruled "suicide" by Brazilian authorities, was allegedly caused by strangulation with the strap of his wife's handbag and is being investigated, by Canadian forensics specialists, as a possible homicide.

the outset, that it's a documentary about the "comeback" of Dicky Eklund, Micky's half-brother. (These crude-rhyming nicknames are quintessentially working-class Irish, suggesting the playful camaraderie of a pub society in which men remain adolescent and "unattached" through their lives, so long as they don't return to their homes where wives and mothers exert authority.) As *Raging Bull* ends with LaMotta as a retired boxer, a figure of pathos whose marriage with a beautiful much-younger woman (played by a first-time actress named Cathy Moriarty) has ended in divorce, and whose life has careened downward since, so *The Fighter* ends with a return to the Ward-Eklund half-brothers and, in a cinematic sleight of hand that arouses a stirring of pity and terror, a brief film clip of the "real" Micky and Dicky of 2010—the former looking like a slightly older and thicker-bodied Mark Wahlberg and the latter looking much older than the mercurial Christian Bale, his Irish-boy's face now ravaged and pale as a corpse's. One would have liked to see the entire Ward-Eklund clan—the ferocious mother Alice and her seven ferociously loyal daughters—and not least Micky Ward's real-life wife, Charlene.

Like Clint Eastwood's *Million Dollar Baby* (2004), a similar amalgam of gritty pathos, unabashed sentiment, and very good boxing footage that earned accolades for its principal actors Eastwood and Hilary Swank, *The Fighter* is, if not a champion film for all time, a very good, poignant and commendable film of its era—post-industrial working-class urban America, bereft of history as it is bereft of jobs, strong unions, pride in one's work. Lowell, Massachusetts, is the ideal setting for this modest fairy tale of an underdog who finally comes out on top—if but temporarily, and with what cost to him, no one quite knows or seems to care. Boxing may be cruel and pitiless to its most ardent practitioners but bountiful to its gifted chroniclers.

THE MYSTERY OF MUHAMMAD ALI

"I was determined to be one nigger that the white man didn't get."
—Muhammad Ali, 1970

For the boxing historian, the greatness of Muhammad Ali is beyond question and it has little to do with the young boxer's brash self-promotion ("This is the legend of Cassius Clay/The most beautiful boxer in the world today") or his subsequent fame/notoriety as a convert to the Nation of Islam who repudiated his Christian religion in April 1967 and refused in to be inducted into the U.S. Army to fight in the Vietnam War. Nor has it to do with Ali's post-boxing career as a public figure of enormous charity, compassion, and integrity.

Ali is a great champion because he brought to boxing an idiosyncratic early style that was astonishing to witness, as the spectacular ring style of the first black American heavyweight champion Jack Johnson (1908–1915) was astonishing in Johnson's time. It is difficult to describe the ring presence of the young Ali—"Float like a butterfly, sting like a bee" doesn't capture the viper-quickness and deadliness of Ali's technique, nor does it suggest the quickening of the audience's collective pulse at the very sight of the tall, strongly-built Ali in the ring virtually dancing around his tall, strongly-built but much slower-moving opponents.

(An exemplary fight of Ali's early career is the brilliantly executed, dramatically compressed two-and-a-half-round title match with Cleveland Williams, 1966.)

The young Olympic medal winner (1960) defied boxing experts from the start, as if it were Ali's destiny to do things in his unique and exasperating way: holding his gloves defiantly low, as if courting disaster; leaning away from jabs with an air of disdain, instead of slipping them as one is trained; flicking out a jab so light and casual as to seem negligent, cavalier; feinting, clowning, shrugging head and shoulders distractingly; performing a "shuffling" motion to upset opponents and entertain the audience.

Here was a heavyweight who stood at 6' 3" and weighed more than 210 pounds but moved with the dazzling ring style of a Sugar Ray Robinson (middleweight), even a Willie Pep (featherweight). His fights were incandescent dramas because they titillated crowds with the possibility of catastrophe for the mouthy Ali—if his opponent could catch him. (As Cassius Clay he'd once met the campy pro wrestler Gorgeous George, who'd impressed upon the young boxer the fact that people will buy tickets to see someone lose as well as to see someone win.)

At his most playful Ali was a trickster—though not a black, taunting trickster in the style of Jack Johnson (who not only beat his white opponents but ridiculed and humiliated them in the ring, and provoked outrage among whites by publicly flaunting his relationships with white women.) The objects of Ali's insults were fellow black boxers: he scorned the formidable Sonny Liston as "an ugly, slow bear" and boasted of himself as "pretty"; he jeered at Floyd Patterson in a way that might be considered not-so-subtly racist: "I'm going to put him flat on his back/So that he will start acting black." Even as a mature boxer, fighting the worthy (and dangerous) opponent Joe Frazier, Ali dared to taunt Frazier in similarly race-tinged ways: "Joe Frazier is a gorilla/and he's gonna fall in Manila"—"Joe Frazier's the only n___ in the world ain't got rhythm." It was Ali's maddening and diabolical strategy to make his opponents into some semblance of "white men's Negroes" in order to isolate them from the black community and enhance himself.

Cassius Clay, born in 1942, was the grandson of a slave; in the United States of his boyhood and young manhood, the role of the black athlete, particularly the black boxer, was a forced self-effacement and "modesty."

White male anxieties were, evidently, greatly roiled by the spectacle of the strong black man, and had to be assuaged. The greater the black boxer (Joe Louis, Archie Moore, Ezzard Charles) the more urgent that he assume a public role of caution and restraint. Kindly white men who advised their black charges to be a "credit to their race" were not speaking ironically.

And yet, the young Cassius Clay/ Muhammad Ali refused to play this emasculating role. He would not be the "white man's Negro"— he would not be anything of the white man's at all. Converting to the Nation of Islam at the age of 22, immediately after winning the heavyweight championship from Sonny Liston, he denounced his "slave name" (Cassius Marcellus Clay, which was also his father's name) and the Christian religion; in refusing to serve in the U.S. Army he made his political reasons clear: "I ain't got no quarrel with them Vietcong." An enormous backlash followed: where the young boxer had been cheered, now he was booed. Denunciations rained upon his head. Such revered publications as the *New York Times* refused to identify Ali by his Muslim name, and continued to print the "slave name" Cassius Clay for years. Threatened with imprisonment for his refusal to comply with the U.S. draft, Ali stood his ground; he was fined $10,000 and his boxing license revoked so that he could not continue his professional career, in the very prime of that career. In a gesture of sheer pettiness the state department took away his passport so that he couldn't fight outside the United States. When finally the Supreme Court ruled in his favor, and Ali was reinstated as a professional boxer two and a half years later, he had lost much of his youthful agility. Yet he'd never yielded, he'd never given in.

The heart of the champion is this: one never repudiates one's deepest values, one never *gives in.*

Though Ali had risen to dizzying heights of fame in the 1960s it was in the 1970s that his greatness was established. Who could have imagined that, being reinstated as a boxer after a lengthy suspension, Ali would expand the dimensions of the sport yet again; that, past his prime, his legs slowed, his breath shorter, out of an ingenuity borne of desperation he would reinvent himself as an athlete on whose unyielding body younger boxers might punch themselves out. He could no longer "float like a butterfly," but he could lie back against the ropes, like a living heavy bag, and allow an opponent like the hapless George Foreman to exhaust himself in the effort of trying to knock him out. What is the infamous Rope-a-Dope stratagem of 1974 but a brilliantly pragmatic stoicism in which the end (winning) justifies the means (irreversible damage to body, brain). The spectator is appalled to realize that a single blow of Foreman's delivered to a non-boxer might well be fatal; how many dozens of these blows Ali absorbed, as in a fairy tale in which the drama is one of reversed expectations. In this way, with terrible cost to come in terms of Ali's health, he won back the heavyweight title at the age of 32, defeating the 25-year-old Foreman.

Great as Ali–Foreman is, it can't compare to the trilogy of fights between Ali and Frazier in 1971, 1974, 1975; Frazier won the first on points, Ali the second and third on points and a TKO. These are monumental fights, displays of human stamina, courage, and "heart" virtually unparalleled in the history of boxing. In the first of these, Ali experienced the worst battering of his life, yet he did not give up; in the second and third, Ali won against an exhausted Frazier, at what cost to his health we can only guess—"The closest thing to dying," Ali said of the ordeal. Yet, incredibly, unconscionably, Ali was exploited by managers and promoters who should have protected him; his doomed career continued until 1981 with a devastating final loss, to the much-younger Trevor Berbick. Ali then retired, belatedly, after 61 fights, with 56 wins.

The mystery of Muhammad Ali may point to something basic in the human psyche: the deeper, more spiritual, more courageous and transcendental self that emerges, in some, out of a more superficial personality in times of crisis. What does it mean to say that a fighter has "heart"? By "heart" we don't mean technical skill, nor even unusual strength and stamina and ambition; by "heart" we mean something like spiritual character. A normal person would never struggle to his feet to continue a fight in which he has been terribly hurt; the great champion is one who not only struggles to his feet, but is more dangerous than previously. Though boxing arises out of fighting, and fighting would seem to be universal in our species, yet boxing is contrary to nature, and defies comprehension in terms of Darwinian evolutionary theory. It is not natural to perform with such extraordinary courage, but rather more it is natural to surrender, to retreat, in order to survive. Indeed, the young Cassius Clay came close to quitting in his first fight with Sonny Liston, but was dissuaded by his trainer; if he had quit, we would not be mourning him now, and perhaps by now his name would have faded. The mature Ali persevered in fights in which he might well have lost, and frequently did lose. Out of such stoicism and a sense of destiny, a legend is borne; the cost exacted is one's health.

The mystery of Muhammad Ali is this spiritual greatness, that seemed to have emerged out of a far more ordinary, even callow personality. With the passage of time, the rebel who'd been reviled by many Americans would be transformed into an American hero, especially in the light of a general disenchantment with the Vietnam War. The young man who'd been denounced as a traitor was transformed into the iconic figure of our time, a compassionate figure who seems to transcend race. A warm, sepia light irradiates the past, glossing out crude or jarring details. Ali had long ago transcended his own origins and his own, specific identity. As he'd once said: "Boxing was nothing. It wasn't important at all. Boxing was just a means to introduce me to the world" (1983).

Who can say that there are no second acts, let alone third or fourth acts, in American lives?

IV

REAL LIFE

A VISIT TO SAN QUENTIN

We came to San Quentin on a chill sunny morning in April 2011.

The visitor to San Quentin is surprised that, from a little distance, the prison buildings are very distinctive. The main building is likely to be warmly glowing in sunshine and more resembles a historic architectural landmark, or a resort hotel, than one of the most notorious prisons in North America. Beyond the prison compound, to the south, are hills as denuded of trees as the rolling, dreamlike hills in a Grant Wood painting; to the north, blue-sparkling San Francisco Bay and beyond it the glittering high-rise buildings of the fabled city of San Francisco several miles away.

San Quentin Point is one of the most valuable real estate properties in the United States, and so it's ironic that the prison, first built in 1852, the oldest prison in California, takes up 275 acres of this waterside property. Almost you would think that some of the inmates must have spectacular views from their cell windows—except you will learn that San Quentin's cells, arranged in densely populated "cell blocks" in the interior of buildings, like rabbit warrens, don't have windows.

On the morning we drove to San Quentin from Berkeley, the sky was vivid-blue and the air in continual gusts. The hills beyond the prison were vivid-green from an unusually wet and protracted Northern California winter.

Is that the *prison?*—a first-time visitor is likely to exclaim.

But this is from a distance.

I had visited a maximum-security prison once before, in Trenton, New Jersey, in the 1980s. It had not been a pleasant experience nor one I had ever anticipated repeating, and yet, on this day, I was scheduled to be taken on a guided tour through San Quentin with approximately fifteen other individuals of whom the great majority were young women graduate students and their female professor from a criminology course at a university in San Francisco.

Waiting in line for the guided-tour leader to arrive, the young women—(you would have to call them girls in their behavior, appearance, mannerisms)—talked loudly and vivaciously together, as if oblivious of their surroundings, and eager for an entertaining adventure; once the tour began, they were to fall silent; and when the tour led us into the very interior of the prison, where the fact of what a prison *is* becomes viscerally evident, they were very silent, abashed, and intimidated. That is always the way with the guided tour into a maximum-security prison: you are not being taken on a mere tour but "taught a lesson." And you are not quite the person emerging whom you'd believed yourself to be, entering.

In the parking lot, in the trunk of our car, we'd had to leave behind all electronic devices, as well as our wallets, from which we'd taken our ID's. In San Quentin you are forbidden to bring many things designated as "contraband" and you are forbidden to wear certain colors—(primarily blue, the prisoners' color). Even men must not wear "open" shoes, i.e., sandals. Your arms must be covered, and clothing "appropriate."

Despite the warning beforehand, one of our group, an older man, was discovered to be wearing sandals and had to acquire proper footwear from one of the guards before he was allowed into the facility.

Our tour guide was late. From remarks told to us, the man's "lateness" was a matter of his own discretion: he was not often "on time." There was the sense, communicated to us subtly by guards, that civilians were not particularly welcome in the facility; it was a "favor" to the public, that guided tours were arranged from time to time. And so we were made to wait in the sunny, gusty air outside the first checkpoint, which was both a vehicular and a pedestrian checkpoint manned by a number of guards.

In the imagination a prison is a remote and lonely place but in reality, a prison is a place of business: a busy place. Delivery vehicles constantly arrived to move through the checkpoint. Corrections officers and other employees arrived. When at last our tour leader arrived, a lieutenant corrections officer, we were led singly through the pedestrian checkpoint and along a hilly pavement in the direction of the prison, some distance away; to our left, beautiful San Francisco Bay reflecting the sun; to our right, the rolling hills of a pastoral landscape. The visitor is tempted to think *This is a magical place. This is not an ugly place.*

Now through the second checkpoint, where we signed into a log and where, when we left, we had to sign out: otherwise, the prison would go into "lockdown"—the assumption being that a visitor was unaccounted-for inside the facility.

Our wrists were stamped with invisible ink. Grimly we were told that if we forgot and washed our hands, and washed away the ink, we would precipitate another "lockdown"—the assumption being that there was a visitor unaccounted-for inside the facility.

Corrections officers were passing through the checkpoint, as we prepared to go through. It was prison protocol to allow them to go first. The guards were both female and male—the females as sturdy-bodied as the males, sexless in their dun-colored uniforms. They did not greet us, smile at us, acknowledge us at all.

The lieutenant led us into a spacious sun-filled courtyard. Here were extensive flowerbeds, planted by prisoners. There was not a prisoner in sight.

"The flag always flies at half-mast here."

We stared at a memorial stone as the lieutenant spoke of CO's who'd "died in the line of duty" at San Quentin, a double column of names dating back to the nineteenth century. The lieutenant recounted for us how as a young CO he'd been on duty during the "most violent ten minutes" in the prison's history: in 1969 a Black Panther defense attorney had smuggled a firearm into the prison to give to his client, who hid it inside his clothing until, as he was being escorted back to his cell block, he suddenly began shooting, killing several CO's and fellow prisoners before tower guards shot him dead.

We were aware now of tower guards. We were aware of high stone walls strung with razor wire like a deranged sort of tinsel. We were told that if a siren sounded, if the commandment *All down! All down!* was broadcast, we were to throw ourselves down to the ground without question. If we remained standing, we would be in danger of being shot down by guards in the towers. They would be training their rifles on us, invisibly.

Did we understand?

My old unease, which had begun at the first checkpoint, quickened now. For always you think, too late—*I have made a mistake coming here. Why did I come to this terrible place!*

The answers are idealist: to learn. To learn more about the world. To be less sheltered. To be less naïve. To *know.*

Americans imprison—and execute—so many more individuals in proportion to our population than any other country in the world except China, one is compelled to *know.*

The lieutenant was saying that a CO's family doesn't know if he or she will be returning home from the prison. Inside, anything can happen, and it was likely to happen suddenly and unexpectedly and irrevocably.

"Irrevocably" was not the lieutenant's exact word. But this was his meaning.

He led us across the square and into the prison chapel, which was non-denominational. At the front of the room, which had seats for perhaps 150 people, was, not a crucifix, but a large cross in the shape of a T.

At a pulpit stood an inmate in prison attire, to address the tour group. He was in his thirties perhaps, with Hispanic features. Like one who has given a presentation many times before he told us with disarming frankness of his life: how he'd belonged to a gang, how he'd killed his own sister in a moment of panicked confusion, how he'd been sentenced to thirty-years-to-life—meaning that he was a "lifer," who might be granted parole sometime, if he didn't jeopardize his chances inside the prison.

The inmate wore blue: blue shirt, blue sweatpants, loose clothing. Down the sides of the trouser legs were letters in vivid white:

P
R
I
S
O
N
E
R

The inmate prayed, he said. Every day of his life he prayed for his sister, his mother, his family, himself. His manner was eager, earnest. He was due to meet with the parole board that very afternoon, he said. (He'd been turned down for parole at least once; inmates are typically turned down many times before being granted parole, if ever.) You could see that this was a San Quentin inmate who had accrued the approval of the prison authority and would not ever risk losing it: once a gang member, now he was one of *theirs*.

One of *ours*. Someone like *ourselves*.

Obviously he'd been "rehabilitated" in prison. And this was the goal of the enlightened prison—of course.

Abruptly then the session ended. The inmate was escorted from the pulpit by guards, and the tour group was led out of the chapel by the lieutenant.

Now we were being led into the interior of the prison—the "real" prison. We were led from the picturesque courtyard along a hilly paved walk, in a chilly wind. Around a corner, and into the "Yard."

That is, we stepped onto the edge of the "Yard." Here was a vast windswept space, part pavement and part scrubby grassland. We stared. Hundreds—could it really be *hundreds*?—of inmates in the Yard under the supervision of what appeared to be, to the casual eye, a dismayingly few guards.

Of course, there were the guard towers: the armed guards.

The prison population was somewhere beyond 5,000 inmates though the "design capacity" was for 3,082. Clearly just a fraction of these inmates were in the Yard at this time but their numbers seemed daunting.

We were led relentlessly forward, skirting the edge of the Yard. We were surprised to see a number of older inmates, several with long white beards, like comic representations of elderly men; they walked with canes, on the dirt track, while younger inmates jogged past them or, elsewhere in the Yard, tossed basketballs at netless rims, lifted weights and did exercises, or stood together talking, pacing about. You had the impression of rippling, seething, pulsing energy and restlessness, and you had the impression that the nearer of the inmates were watching us covertly, intensely. Everyone in the guided tour was very quiet now. The young women visitors were quiet now. The fact of the prison and what it contained was beginning to become real to us not merely an idea. For there were no fences between the inmates and us, only just open space.

The lieutenant advised us not to look at the inmates. Not to stare.

"No 'eye contact.' No 'fraternizing' with inmates."

The lieutenant explained how the prison population was divided into gangs, primarily; and these gangs—African-Americans, Hispanics, Mexicans (Northern California, Southern California), "whites"—with now, in recent decades, "Chinese"—(Asian) had territorial possession of particular parts of the Yard that were off-limits to non-gang-members. There were desirable areas of the Yard dominated by Hispanics and "whites"—(Aryan Brotherhood)—and less desirable areas, near the urinals, where African-Americans gathered. (Why? Because Californian African-Americans are so divided into warring gangs, they can't make up their differences in prison.)

We were shocked to see, not many yards away, open urinals in a row, against a wall. We were warned—*If anybody is using a urinal, don't look.*

It was a protocol of the Yard: *Don't look, don't stare. A man using one of the open-air urinals was invisible, and to cause him to feel visible is to invite trouble.*

The lieutenant led us past the single-story wooden structure that held classrooms. He led us into a dining hall—a vast, double dining hall—with rows of tables—empty at this time of day. You could not imagine this enormous dining hall filled with men—the noise, the restlessness; the food-smells, the smells of men's bodies. The lieutenant spoke of the murals on the walls, which had been painted by an inmate named Alfredo Santos in the 1950s: striking, bizarre, a collage of renderings of newspaper photos and more ordinary individuals including a heroin addict (Santos himself). This art called to mind the slickly illustrative work of Thomas Hart Benton but also the matter-of-fact distortions of Hieronymus Bosch.

The lieutenant meant to entertain us by summoning a food worker, to provide us with food-samples from the kitchen—"Any volunteers?"

Two members of the tour volunteered: a man and one of the young criminology students, who took bites of what resembled chicken nuggets, burritos, French fries, something that resembled cornmeal, and bravely pronounced them "Good"—"Pretty good."

The lieutenant told of the feat of "feeding" thousands of men three times a day. There was something disconcerting in the word "*feeding*": you had a vision of a cattle or a hog trough into which "feed" was dumped.

The lieutenant spoke proudly of the fact that the prison was mostly inmate-staffed—"Otherwise, there couldn't be a prison."

The original San Quentin had been built by prisoners, in fact. It had housed only sixty-eight inmates. Prior to that, California's first prison had been a 268-ton wooden ship anchored in San Francisco Bay and equipped to hold thirty prisoners.

But the prison facility was now badly overcrowded, like all prison facilities in the economically stressed state of California. Where there is overcrowding, three men to a cell, men quartered in places meant for other purposes, like a gym, there is likely to be more trouble.

The lieutenant told of uprisings in the dining hall, sudden riots, gang killings. At any meal there is the possibility of violence, with so many men crammed into so relatively small a space. The lieutenant showed us a cache of homemade weapons: a toothbrush sharpened to a deadly point, a razor blade attached to a papier-mâché handle, a metal hook fashioned out of paper clips, a spike, a nail, a pencil. . . . In the Yard, buried in the ground in certain places, were similar weapons, which gangs controlled; as soon as guards discovered the weapons and confiscated them, more weapons appeared and were buried in the ground.

Ingenious! The wish to harm others is a stimulant to the most amazing creativity and patience.

Wasn't it likely, most of the contraband to be fashioned into weapons was smuggled into San Quentin by guards—CO's? For there was a drug trade here, and there were forbidden cell phones— how otherwise could such things be smuggled into the facility except by CO's?

(The California corrections officers union is one of the strongest unions in the state. Much stronger, and its members much better paid, than the members of the teachers' union. The prison authority could not risk antagonizing such a powerful union.)

At no point in the tour did I think it would be prudent to ask questions about smuggled contraband. No one else asked, either.

During our visit in the dining hall, sirens erupted. Bells clanged. For a terrible few seconds it seemed to us that the prison was after all going to go into "lockdown"—(whatever precisely that meant: we had a vague, ominous sense of its meaning); but, fortunately, the sirens turned out to be a false alarm.

Maybe it was a suicide attempt, the lieutenant said. Adding laconically, or a suicide.

Next, the lieutenant led us to another grim building; and another time, we went through a checkpoint. The invisible ink on our wrists was examined by frowning guards in ultraviolet light.

I was trying to imagine a plausible scenario in which an individual who had not been officially admitted to San Quentin as a visitor was now discovered in the very interior of the prison, somehow having managed to attach him- or herself to a tour group, who would be identified as an impostor or an intruder through this scrutiny, but I could not imagine this scenario.

He was taking us to Cell Block C, the lieutenant said. Into the very bowels of the prison he might have said.

Until now, the visit to San Quentin had been bearable. It had not provoked anxiety or even much unease, I think. If there was unease, I had resolved not to think about it, at least not yet. I had come here to be educated and illuminated and not entertained. And the others in our group must have felt more or less the same. For nothing threatening had happened to us, except the temporary alarms in the dining room, which had turned out to be false alarms. Our only firsthand experience of an inmate had been the speaker in the chapel, who had seemed to want to please us, like an earnest student. In the Yard, we'd seen men at a distance—it had seemed, a safe distance.

But now in Cell Block C there was a very different atmosphere. The air was tense as the air before an electrical storm. A powerful smell of men's bodies. There was a high din as of the thrum of a hive—if you brought your ear close to the hive, you would be shocked at the myriad angry-sounding vibrations, that never sleep. We would see now the typical inmates of San Quentin, in their own habitat.

These were "new recruits" in Cell Block C. Their gang identifications had not yet been determined. They were younger than the typical San Quentin inmate, and more "restless." This was the population that was most susceptible to suicides, the lieutenant said, as well as "other kinds of violence."

The lieutenant introduced us to cell block guards, who barely nodded at us. We were of no interest to them and if they felt anything for us, it was likely to be contempt. What the criminology students were thinking by this time, I could only guess. I knew, from my experience at the Trenton prison, that any close confrontation with prison inmates, though there are bars between you and them, is not going to be a pleasant one and still less is it a pleasant experience for women.

As the lieutenant was telling us about the history of the cell blocks—and of their present-day overcrowding—a movement overhead attracted my attention and I looked up to see, on a catwalk about five feet above the lieutenant's head, a uniformed guard with a rifle resting in the crook of his arm. The guard did not so much as glance down at me. He was indifferent to the guided tour as to the recited words of the tour guide. The barrel of his rifle did not seem quite aimed at anyone in the cell block, but it was clearly in readiness of being aimed. On a wall nearby was the ominous sign NO WARNING SHOTS.

Three inmates had been taken from their cells and were standing in the narrow passageway, not far from us. We could not help but stare—as they stared at us, in turn—for these were prison inmates of a kind you would find in a Hollywood action film. Two Hispanics, and a "white" man—husky, muscled, beefy, deep-chested, with thick necks. The white man had a shaved head and was covered in tattoos of a lurid sort: Nazi swastikas primarily. I had never seen anyone with a scalp tattooed in Nazi tattoos. The man had had to be a member of the notorious Aryan Brotherhood, a prison gang. Yet this man had been taken from his cell, and he stood quietly in the aisle among guards as if in an easy sort of fraternization; apparently he was no threat to the guards or to us. For as it turned out, he and the other two inmates had been paroled—or had served their full sentences—and would be now escorted out of the prison.

I thought *But who would hire a man covered in Nazi tattoos?*

The answer could only be *Another man covered in Nazi tattoos.*

The lieutenant now said, as I'd been hoping he would not, that it was time for a "walk around the block."

In Trenton, something of the same phraseology had been used. But the inmates we'd seen had not been confined to a cell block, but to a large grim windowless space like an animal pen. They'd been loose, milling and pacing about, restless, edgy, staring in our direction as we'd looked down at them from a raised platform, at a height of about five feet.

The situation is different here, I thought. Yet I felt a stab of panic, for perhaps the situation would come to the same thing. It had been a nightmare I'd more or less managed to forget, or had pushed out of my mind. I told myself, *It won't be the same thing again. I am prepared this time.*

I was safer here in the cell block because of the abundance of other, younger women in the group. To the inmates, some of whom had already glimpsed them, the criminology students must have looked like high school girls. Their presence in this grim place was a kind of outrage, a provocation; it would arouse excitement, frustration, incredulity, wrath. Adroitly I'd maneuvered myself to the front of the line, just behind the lieutenant. I would walk just behind him "around the block"—I would not make the mistake of holding back and coming late in the line. For, at the start of the walk, the inmates whose cells we passed wouldn't quite grasp the situation, as we walked quickly by; but, by the time the fourth or fifth visitor passed a cell, all the prisoners would have been alerted to the tour by shouts and whistles. There would be a nightmare, but it would be a contained nightmare and it would not be mine this time.

The lieutenant warned: "Walk fast—move along. Don't stare into the cells. Don't get too close to the cells. Walk as far to the left as you can. If they can reach you, if they grab you, you might be seriously hurt. And the prison might go into lockdown."

Several of the criminology students were asking if they could stay behind. If they could just wait, and rejoin the group after the walk-around-the-block. Their voices were plaintive and pleading, but the lieutenant explained that this was not possible.

"The tour takes us through Cell Block C. We are all going to 'walk around the block' together."

Quietly enough the walk began along a walkway that spanned the full length of the first tier of cells. I was close behind the lieutenant and I was not going to look into the cells, for I did not want to make "eye contact" with an inmate whose desire at that moment might be to reach grunting through the bars and grab me and not let go until guards swarmed to his cell. I did not have that sort of curiosity—I was determined to walk fast, and to keep in motion. And so, as I passed the cells, one after another after another, the men inside had but a blurred awareness of me, as, at the periphery of my vision, they were but a blurred presence to me, though I glimpsed enough to be aware of the cramped living conditions: bunk beds so close to the wall, inmates would have to pass sideways between the bunks and the walls; and a cell size of about nine by twelve feet. I was very nervous, and I was perspiring; and I could hear, behind us, the uplifted voices of men, shouts, whistles, whooping noises of elation, derision. I would have liked to press my hands over my ears. I did not glance back, at the terrified young women, forced to walk this gauntlet as close as possible to the wall, away from the prison bars. I knew what they were feeling, as I'd had to run a gauntlet of a kind, in Trenton.

But I'd been alone in my misery, in Trenton. For there, by chance, I'd been the single female in the guided tour, a much smaller group than that at San Quentin, only about five or six people. The Trenton prison had not seemed so "secure" as San Quentin, and the tour guide not so experienced; but that might have been a misconception.

In a haze of discomfort, I followed the lieutenant in the "walk-around-the-block." I did not inflame any inmate by passing too near his cell, or looking overtly into it; but I was aware of the rippling, rising excitement in my wake, as the young women were forced to march past the cells, one by one by one. The slumberous hive was being roused, shaken; the buzzing hum rose to crude shouts, whistles, whoops. *But I am spared, this time.*

When we left the cell block, to return to the outside air, the tour group was abashed, shaken. What relief to get outside, to *breathe!* Especially the young women had been made to realize how little their *femininity* was valued, in such a place; to be *pretty* here, to suggest *sexual empowerment* here, was to invite the most primitive and pitiless violence, as in an atavistic revenge of the male against the female. Civilization protects the female against the male, essentially: this is a hard, crude truth to ponder if you hope to transcend the rigid gender-limits of sexism.

The meaning of the walk-around-the-block is to make a woman understand this simple biological fact, that may be mistaken as a feminist proposition.

The meaning of the walk-around-the-block is to make both men and women understand: you must be protected from your fellow man by high walls, bars, razor wire, and high-powered rifles manned by guards in the service of the State. And if you don't think so, you are very naïve, or a fool.

This is not the sunlit rationalist world of the Enlightenment, still less an evolving America envisioned by liberal intellectuals. It is very far from the affable mysticism of California's New Age. In San Quentin we recognize the starkly familiar dead end of Thomas Hobbes's *Leviathan* (1651) in which life is defined as "nasty, brutish, and short"—unless it is a highly controlled, defined, and subjugated life not unlike a maximum-security prison.

———

We were exhausted by the cell block gauntlet and we were eager for the (interminable) tour to end, but there was a final destination awaiting.

Not Death Row: "We don't take visitors to Death Row."

Our guide led us past a tall fortress-like building—the "Condemned Unit"—which housed over seven hundred men awaiting execution. (Condemned women, of whom there are far fewer, are housed at the Central California Women's Facility in Chowchilla.) With a sort of grim boastfulness the lieutenant spoke to us of the famous inmates who'd been executed at San Quentin: Caryl Chessman, William Bonin (the "Freeway Killer"), Clarence Ray Allen (at seventy-six, the "oldest person ever executed in California, in 2006) among many others. And there were those awaiting execution: pregnant-wife-killer Scott Peterson, serial killer-sadist Charles Ng, Richard Ramirez, the "Night Stalker" of the 1980s. In a perverse way the San Quentin authority appeared to be proud of its list of executed and condemned prisoners and proud of its distinction as the sole Death Row for men in the state of California.

When I asked the lieutenant which part of San Quentin he most liked to work in, without hesitation he said Death Row.

This was a surprise to me. I asked why and he said that the Death Row inmate was "more settled."

Death Row inmates had "come to accept" that they were going to die and some of them had acquired "wisdom."

Of course, some of these inmates were hoping for reprieves. Many were involved with Legal Defense lawyers and anti-capital punishment volunteers working to get their death sentences commuted. But the ones the lieutenant had liked to work with, he said, were the older men, who were "settled" in their minds.

The lieutenant had not spoken at such length to anyone else on the tour, or so warmly, as he was speaking now to me.

The lieutenant led us now to a nondescript building that housed the execution chamber. With a flourish of an old-fashioned key he unlocked the door that led directly into the chamber; it was noted that we did not have to pass through another checkpoint. ("No prisoners enter here except if they are going to be executed. And then, they do not return.") No one in our group was very enthusiastic about entering the execution chamber, but there was no escape: you could see that this was a ritual of the San Quentin tour, not to be avoided.

"When the death warrant is signed, the clock starts ticking for the condemned man. When it's time, the Death Team comes for him and brings him here."

There was a particular horror to these matter-of-fact words, that had surely been uttered many times in this somber place.

The room was not large, windowless and dimly lighted. There was a feeling here of *underground*. Plain straight-back wooden chairs arranged in a semicircle in an incongruously ordinary space except that, at the front of the room, was a bathysphere.

A bathysphere! Painted robin's-egg blue.

The lieutenant explained to his surprised charges that the San Quentin authority had purchased a "deep-sea diving bell" from a marine carnival some years ago, in an era when execution was by cyanide gas. The diving bell was airproof, and efficient.

Slowly we shuffled inside. There was a sour, sad odor here. The young women had lost all remnants of their initial vivacity, and the men in the group were looking grimly stoic. Like an MC on a TV reality show the lieutenant was hoping to seat some of us in "witness's chairs" at the front of the room—"C'mon! These are great seats." The hardback chairs provided an intimate look through the slotted Plexiglas windows of the diving bell into the interior at what appeared to be a hospital gurney, outfitted with straps.

"In the days when there was gas, it was practical to execute two at a time. Now, with lethal injection, they don't do that. And when we had an electric chair, they had just the one chair, not two."

"Two men executed at once?"

"Yes, sir. When there was gas."

But now, the lieutenant explained, gas had been declared *cruel and unusual punishment*. So there was just lethal injection—"People think it's some easy way to die. But it ain't."

A few of the young women students were sitting, weakly. But not at the front of the room; no one wanted to sit in these chairs, which brought witnesses within mere inches of the diving-bell windows. (The chairs were so bizarrely close, a witness's knees would be pressed against the exterior of the diving bell. Unless you shut your eyes, you would be staring at a dying man's contorted face from a distance of about twelve inches.) Most of us shrank from sitting down at all, as if to remain standing might be to accelerate the visit, and escape.

The plain wooden chairs so arranged suggested amateur theatrics—very amateur, as in a middle school. The (somewhat dingy) robin's-egg blue diving bell suggested sport, recreation, carny fun. But inside the bell, the death-apparatus with its sinister black straps suggested a makeshift operating room, as in a cheap horror film.

I thought of, but did not mention, Franz Kafka's "In the Penal Colony," one of the great prophetic surrealist tales of the twentieth century, by a writer who might very likely have perished in a Nazi death camp if he had not died prematurely of tuberculosis in 1924.

The lieutenant was indicating those front-row chairs reserved for "family members of the victim." Beside these were chairs for the warden and other prison officials and law enforcement officers who'd apprehended the inmate; in the second row were chairs for other professionals and interested parties; in the back row, chairs for the "press."

Someone asked if executions were televised or recorded. The lieutenant shook his head with a frown, as if this were a foolish question—"No, sir."

I was wondering how the family of the victim could bear to sit so close to the diving bell, to peer through the narrow windows at the writhings of a dying man only inches away. Was this a way of assuaging grief, horror? Was this a way of providing "closure"? I thought rather it must be another element of nightmare, a stark and irremediable image to set beside other, horrific images of loss and degradation. *Eye for an eye, tooth for a tooth.* Was that a gratifying sort of folk-justice?

Yet it certainly seemed to be an honored custom that the family of a murderer's victim was invited to the execution. The somber way in which the lieutenant spoke of the "family of the victim" and the special seats reserved for them suggested the importance of such witnessing—this was a gift, perhaps the only gift law enforcement could provide, to the families of victims.

Perhaps in older, less civilized societies the murderer's heart or severed head was also given to the victim's family, to do with it what they would.

But then I thought, it isn't given to us to understand, who have not suffered such losses. The appetite for blood, for revenge, for a settling of "injustice," that so fueled ancient Greek tragedies as well as the great revenge tragedies of the Renaissance, amid which Shakespeare's *Hamlet* is the surpassing model.

Yet I don't think I would want to "witness" such a horrific sight. Probably, I could not forgive—(I certainly could not forgive in place of someone who'd been murdered)—and I could not forget; but I would not want to witness another's death, even for the sake of revenge.

The lieutenant was telling us that no one had been executed at San Quentin since 2006—"There's some court case pending." But, he said, in a neutral voice that nonetheless suggested optimism, that was going to change soon—"In another year or two, executions will be resumed."

In the meantime, the "backlog" of the condemned was increasing in the Condemned Unit.

"Now ladies, gentlemen—how would *you* choose to die?"

It was a jaunty friendly question posed to us by the tour guide. Of course, it was a ritual question: you could assume that the lieutenant had asked it many times before.

"Gas, or lethal injection? Or—electrocution, hanging, firing squad? All were approved methods at one time."

At first no one spoke. It was a disconcerting question, and there seemed no good answer.

More fancifully the lieutenant said: "Or maybe—hit by a truck? Jump off Golden Gate Bridge?"

There were hesitant answers. Reluctant murmurs of "lethal injection."

The criminology students and their female professor concurred: "lethal injection."

The newest way of execution must always seem the most humane, I supposed. At one time, hanging. Or firing squad. Then, electrocution. Then gas. And now, with its suggestion of hospital care gone just slightly wrong—"lethal injection."

I said, I would start with one way of being executed and if I didn't like it, I'd switch to another.

It was an awkward sort of joke. It was the sort of joke a bright, brash ninth grade boy might make, to startle and impress his teacher. Why I said this, when I was feeling in no way like joking, I have no idea.

Except I resented the tour guide quizzing us in this way. I resented the tour guide punishing us for our civilians status.

No one laughed at my joke. The lieutenant frowned at me. "But you have to choose," he said. "Gas, electrocution, lethal injection, hanging—"

I could not seem to reply. My awkward joke had been a surprise to me. Did I hope to alleviate the mood?—the mood of an *execution chamber*? Did I wish to appear naïve, that I might not be revealed as agitated, angry, indignant?

One of the men in the group said that he would refuse to choose—he would not participate in his own death. Triumphantly the lieutenant objected, if you don't choose, the warden will choose for you, but the man persisted: he would not participate in his own death.

This was a good answer, I thought. But a depressing answer.

For really there is no good answer to the lieutenant's question.

It is said that, if you are resolutely against capital punishment, you should not educate yourself in the sorts of crimes for which the "condemned" are executed. "An eye for an eye, a tooth for a tooth"—

originally, this was a liberal principle, to discourage disproportionate punishments, and punishments against relatives of the alleged
criminal. It was not considered harsh but rather a reasonable and
equitable punishment.

By this time I'd begun to feel very strange. I had been staring at
the gurney for too long.

My sense of myself was shrinking like a light made dim,
dimmer—about to be extinguished. In a panic I thought, *Not here!*
I can't faint here.

Somehow I made my way outside, into fresh air. Or maybe the
tour was ending now. I was careful not to trip and fall, lose my
balance and fall, for I did not want to attract attention, and I did
not want to be "weak." It was my impression that the women in
the group did not want to appear "weak." We had managed to get
through the tour, and we were all still standing, though exhausted,
and light-headed. A prison facility will suck the oxygen from your
brain: you are left dazed and depleted and depressed, and the depression will not lighten but in fact increase for several days as you
think back over the experience; then, the depression will begin to
fade, as even the worst memories will fade.

The execution chamber was the last stop at San Quentin. The
lieutenant led us around a maze of buildings to the inner checkpoint
(where we were as carefully monitored as we'd been on our way in;
and where our signatures in the logbook were checked against our
previous signatures) and through the courtyard where the American
flag flew at perpetual half-mast and so to the first, outer checkpoint
(where we were again as carefully monitored as we'd been on our
way in) and to freedom outside the gates. We dispersed, we were
eager to be free of one another, hurrying in the parking lot to our
vehicles, wind whipping our hair.

I felt the surge of relief and joy I'd felt in Trenton, exiting the
much smaller prison there after what had seemed several hours of

misery but had been only a little more than a single hour. *Never again!*

On San Francisco Bay sunlight glittered in dazzling ripples in slate-blue water. In the distance was the great city like a vision or a mirage you might hallucinate from within the walls of San Quentin, improbably beautiful.

Acknowledgments

These essays and reviews have appeared previously in a number of publications, often in different forms, and with different titles. To all the following, acknowledgments and thanks are due.

I am particularly grateful to Robert Silvers, for whom the time-worn epithet "legendary" would seem to have been coined, of the *New York Review of Books,* who invited me to write on most of these subjects and whose encouragement has been inestimable.

"Is the Uninspired Life Worth Living?" was delivered, in a shorter form, as the Robert Silvers Lecture at the New York Public Library, December 2014, and subsequently appeared in *New York Review of Books.*

"This I Believe: Five Motives for Writing" appeared in *Kenyon Review.*

"The Writing Room" appeared in the *Wall Street Journal.*

"J. M. Coetzee: *The Childhood of Jesus,*" "*My Life in Middlemarch,*" and "Edna O'Brien: *The Little Red Chairs*" appeared in the *New York Times Book Review.*

"*My Faraway One: Selected Letters of Georgia O'Keeffe and Alfred Stieglitz*" appeared in *Times Literary Supplement.*

"*Two American Prose Masters: Ellison, Updike*" appeared in a work edited by Andre Dubus III.

"A Visit with Doris Lessing" appeared in *Southern Review.*

"Storyteller of the 'Shattered Personality': Patrick McGrath" is the introduction to *Collected Stories of Patrick McGrath* (Centipede Press).

"*Charles Dickens: A Life* by Claire Tomalin," "The King of Weird: H. P. Lovecraft," "The Detective as Visionary: Derek Raymond," Catastrophe into Art': Julian Barnes," When the Legend Becomes Fact: Larry McMurtry," "Paper Losses: Lorrie Moore," "Emotions of Man and Animals: Karen Joy Fowler," "Wiindigoo Justice: Louise Erdrich," "*In Other Worlds*: Margaret Atwood," "*Why Be Happy When You Could Be Normal?*: *Jeanette* Winterson," Diminished Things: Anne Tyler," "The Inventions of Jerome Charyn," "London NW: Zadie Smith," "Joan Didion: Risk & Triumph," "Unflinching about Women: Lucia Berlin," "Disputed Truth: Mike Tyson," "*The Fighter*: A Film by David O. Russell" appeared in *New York Review of Books*.

"Smiling Woman: Margaret Drabble" and "After Auschwitz: Martin Amis" appeared in the *New Yorker*.

"A Visit to San Quentin" appeared in *Better Than Fiction: True Travel Tales* (Lonely Planet).

"The Mystery of Muhammad Ali" appeared in the *New York Times*.